HEINEMANN HISTORY

THE WORLD
SINCE
1914

JOE SCOTT

HEINEMANN
EDUCATIONAL

Heinemann Educational,
a division of Heinemann Educational Books Ltd,
Halley Court, Jordan Hill, Oxford OX2 8EJ

OXFORD LONDON EDINBURGH
MELBOURNE SYDNEY AUCKLAND
IBADAN NAIROBI GABORONE HARARE
KINGSTON PORTSMOUTH NH (USA)
SINGAPORE MADRID

First published 1989

British Library Cataloguing in Publication Data
Scott, Joe
    The world since 1914
    1. World, 1900–
    I. Title
909.82

ISBN 0-435-31032-1

Designed and produced by
The Pen & Ink Book Company Ltd, Huntingdon

Printed and bound in Spain by Mateu Cromo

Acknowledgements

The author and publisher would like to thank the following for
permission to reproduce photographs on the pages indicated:

J. Allan Cash Photo Library: pp. 159 (middle), 161 (top right) and
168; The Associated Press: pp. 46, 92, 112 (top), and 157 (lower);
The British Library: pp. 29 and 126 (top); Bundesarchiv Koblenz:
pp. 52 (lower), 64 and 156 (lower); Larry Burrows/Life Magazine 9
September 1966 © Time Inc. Colorific: p. 144 (bottom right); Camera
Press: pp. 23, 79, 91, 101, 104, 105 (left), 106, 110, 128 (right), 133
(right), 134, 157 (inset) and 184 (lower right), 163, 166 and 187 (top
left), 172, 174 (lower) and 183 (top left); Camera Press/D. Angeli: p.
174 (top) Centre for the study of Cartoon and Caricature: pp. 54,
55, 60, 75 (lower) and 84; Jonathan Clowes Ltd, London, on behalf
of Gordon Thomas and Max Morgan-Witts for permission to
reprint the photograph on p. 43; The Communist Party Picture
Library: pp. 100 (top) and 115 (right); The *Daily Express*: p. 91;
Kaven Edestan/Reflex: p. 176; The collections of Henry Ford
Museum and Greenfield Village: p. 43; Les Gibbard: pp. 143 (top
right) and 187 (lower); Goldwater/Network: p. 159 (top left);
Greenpeace: p. 169 and 186 (top left); Hanna-Barbara Productions,
Inc © 1988: p. 10; The Robert Harding Picture Library: p. 151
(lower), 153 and 186 (lower right), 159 (top right) and 177; Jeremy
Hartley/Oxfam: p. 170; The Hulton Picture Company: pp. 8, 17
(top), 25 (right), 34 (lower), 62 (lower), 74 (top), 98 and 185 (middle
right), 100 (lower) and 158; Hutchison Picture Library: pp. 17
(lower), 107, 122 and 185 (top), and 152 (top); The Illustrated
London News Picture Library: p.124; Imperial War Museum: pp. 6,
20 and 184 (lower left), 25 (bottom left), 56, 71, 77, 82 and 89;
International Planned Parenthood Federation: p. 164; The
Keystone Collection: pp. 48 (top and lower right), 50, 99, 128 (left),
135, 136 (left) and 150 (top); The David King Collection: pp. 39 (top

and bottom right) and 68; Library of Congress: p. 47; Magnum
Photos: pp. 105 (right), 139 (lower and top right) and 185 (middle
left); The Mansell Collection: p. 97 (top); Nissan: p. 152 (middle);
Novosti Press Agency: pp. 72 and 167; Popperfoto: pp. 30 (top), 44,
57, 78 and 186 (middle right), 97 (lower), 111, 112 (lower), 119
(middle and lower), 126 (lower), 139 (top left), 142 (left and
middle), 144 (bottom left), 152 (lower), 154 (top), 156 (top) and 184
(top), 157 (top), 159 (lower) and 179; Punch Publications: pp. 30
(lower), 96 and 146; Rex Features: p. 181 (top right); Brent and Jane
Sadler: p. 13 (top); Ronald Searle: p. 102 (top); The Society for
Anglo-Chinese Understanding: p. 121 (right); Frank Spooner: pp.
143 (lower), 144, 145, 151 (top right), 177, 180 and 181 (top left) and
186 (middle left); Society for Cultural Relations with Russia: pp. 31
(lower); Süddeutscher Verlag: pp. 11, 22, 51, 74 (lower), 75 (top),
136 (right) and 173; The *Sunday Times*: p. 183 (right); *The Times*: p.
178; Topham Picture Library: pp. 62 (top), 93, 109, 123 and 186
(lower left), 125, 140, 144 (top), 148, 150 (lower), 154 (lower) and
185 (lower), 155, 183 (lower and middle); Ullstein Bilderdeinst: pp.
25 (top left), 48 (lower left), 52 (top) and 73; UBP/Bettman
Newsphotos: p. 108 (right) and 186 (top right); Werner Braun:
p.133 (left); Wellcome Institute for the History of Medicine: p. 12.

We have been unable to contact the copyright holders of the
photographs and cartoons which appear on pages 30, 34 (top), 39
(top and bottom left), 48 (middle right), 87, 95, 102 (lower) and 161
(lower) and would be grateful for any information which would
enable us to do so.

Cover photograph by J. Allan Cash.

CONTENTS

1.1 | CAUSATION

CAUSATION

One day a boy came home from school. He tried to creep up to his bedroom without his father noticing that he had come in, but this didn't work. His father noticed him and called him into the kitchen. 'John,' his father said, 'I can see why you are creeping upstairs like that. What has happened to your trousers?'

John's father had seen that his trousers were covered in mud. There was a pause, and then John explained what had happened. In the three boxes below you can see three possible answers John might have given. Read them carefully and then consider the questions which follow. One further thing is that John is an unusual boy in that he always tells the truth!

London, 1916.

Explanation one

'Mud, as I am sure you know, Dad, is a rather sticky mixture of water and dirt. My trousers are made from fairly coarse cloth which is a very good base for mud to stick on. Also, I am considerably taller than I am wide, which means that under certain conditions I am unstable and likely to fall. What happened is that I was crossing some mud, which is rather slippery, and thus I was more likely to fall. I fell, and the adhesive qualities of the mud meant that some of it stuck to my trousers.'

Explanation two

'I was going through a field and I slipped and fell into a puddle.'

Explanation three

'I had to stay late at school because I had not done my homework. Because I was late, I thought I would take the short cut over the field. There were some big kids on the field who said they were going to beat me up unless I gave them all my money. I started to run away, and some of them chased after me. They were still chasing after me when I tried to jump over a muddy patch but I slipped and fell right in it. They all just laughed at me.'

Adapted from J.H. Hexter 'The History Primer', 1971.

EXERCISE

1 Can all three of these explanations cover the same incident and still be true?

2 If you were the boy's father, which explanation would you think was the best?

3 Which of these explanations do you think is the most scientific?

4 All three explanations cover something which happened in the past. Which do you think is the best piece of history?

CAUSATION

QUESTIONS

1 What event does this photograph show?

2 What do you think caused the event?

3 a What are the advantages of photographs as explanations of the causes of events?

  b What are the disadvantages of photographs as explanations of the causes of events?

CONCLUSION

Some of the following sentences about how historians think about **causes** are sensible, and others are not. Make up a paragraph about causation by copying the sentences you think are sensible into your excercise book. Keep the sentences you use in the order they are here.

When historians try to explain the causes of events they have a very difficult job.

When historians use the word 'cause' they do not mean quite the same thing as scientists.

The best explanation of causes in history is the most simple. You only ever need one cause to explain one event.

Historians usually find that the best explanations of causes have more than one cause in them.

Because the actions of people usually have some part in a historian's explanation of causes, good explanations will have motives in them. (Motives are people's reasons for doing things.)

People are the only things that matter in explaining the causes of events.

People don't matter at all when you try to explain the causes of events; only the conditions at the time matter.

Historians find that the best explanations show how people's motives and actions are affected by the conditions at the time.

1.2 **EVIDENCE**

EVIDENCE

Historians have to work out what they think happened in the past from their **sources** – things which have survived from the past. These sources, however, are not always easy to use. Before the historian can use them as **evidence** to answer a particular question about the past, sources must be tested. Usually historians want to know three things. First the source's **provenance** – how and why it was created, and how it has come down to us. Second its **reliability** – whether the source, or some part of it, is accurate or not. Third its **utility** – how useful it will be. The answers to these questions are usually linked, as you will see from the sources here which are about working-class people in the early part of this century.

SOURCE **B**

SOURCE **A**

Mr Y is a builder's handyman, whose wages average 25 shillings a week. He allows, as a rule, 22 shillings and 6 pence to his wife, out of which she gives him back 3 shillings for his dinners when at work. There are six children under thirteen. The rent for the two rooms is 6 shillings and 6 pence, and burial insurance is 1 shilling.

Sunday – Breakfast: 1 loaf, jam and tea. A bloater for him. Dinner: Half shoulder of mutton, greens, potatoes, and suet pudding for all. Tea: Bread, butter, and tea.

Monday – Breakfast: Bread, dripping and tea. Cold meat from Sunday for him. Dinner for mother and children: cold meat and potatoes over from Sunday. Tea: bread, jam, and tea.

Tuesday – Breakfast: Bread, dripping and tea for all. Dinner for mother and children: Hashed meat (over from Monday) and potatoes. Tea: Bread, radishes, and tea.

Wednesday – Breakfast: Bread, dripping and tea. Dinner for mother and children: Dumplings in yesterday's gravy. Tea: Bread, jam, and tea for all.

Thursday – Breakfast: Bread, dripping and tea. Dinner for mother and children: Rice and treacle. Tea: Bread, jam, and tea.

Friday – Breakfast: Bread, jam, and tea. Dinner for mother and children: Barley broth and potatoes. Tea: Bread, dripping, and tea.

Saturday – Breakfast: Bread, dripping, and tea. Dinner for mother and children: ¾ lb sausages and potatoes. Tea: Bread, jam, and tea.

This is one of Mrs Y's weekly budgets:

	s	d
Rent	6	6
Insurance	1	0
Gas	0	6
½ cwt coal	0	8½
Wood	0	2
Soap, soda, blue, starch	0	5
Boracic powder	0	1
Baby's soap	0	2
	9	6½
Husband's dinners	3	0
14 loaves	3	4½
1 lb dripping	0	6
12 ozs. butter	0	9
8 ozs. tea	0	8
Meat	2	3
6 lbs potatoes	0	3
Vegetables	0	6
½ quartern flour	0	3
Bloaters	0	3
Suet	0	2
3 lbs. sugar	0	6
	12	11½

Maud Pember Reeves, 'Round About a Pound a Week', 1913.

A working-class family in London, photographed just before the First World War.

ACTIVITY 1

Read Source A. This source might suggest working-class families were very poor in the early years of this century. However, historians could not just accept this straight away.

Provenance and reliability

1 Is there anything mentioned in the source which makes you think it cannot be true, or that it is likely to be true?

2 You have been told little about the source's provenance. Below are two possible provenances for it. In each case say whether this makes you think the source might be reliable or not.
   a This was part of a report by government health inspectors.
   b This was part of a book produced by a group of middle-class women campaigning to improve the conditions of poorer working-class families in London.

Utility

A historian might still decide a source could be useful even if it was not reliable. For instance you might have decided in **2b** that the report might be exaggerated. However this might still be useful evidence about what middle-class women thought was shocking poverty.

3 For each of the suggested provenances in question **2**:
   a write an example of how a historian might find Source A useful.
   b write an example of how a historian might *not* find Source A useful.

ACTIVITY 2

Photographs are difficult sources for historians to use.

1 Is the family in Source B the same as the family in Source A? Give reasons for your answer.

2 Does this photograph prove that many families in London were desperately poor? Give reasons for your answer.

3 How can you be sure:
   a this photograph was taken in London?
   b this is a photograph of normal people in their home and not actors posing so that the photographer could make a point?

CONCLUSION

Copy the following sentences into your notebooks, using the material on this page to write a sentence or two of your own to explain each one.

1 It is important for historians to know the provenance of their sources.

2 There are many reasons why all or part of a source might not be reliable.

3 Historians can only decide about the reliability of a source when they know what they want to find out.

4 Historians may sometimes find sources useful even if they don't think they are reliable.

1.3 EMPATHY

EMPATHY

SOURCE A

'Grod had nurtured the burning ember anxiously while they travelled. Maintenance of the fire could only be entrusted to a male of high status. If the coal died out it would be a sure sign that their protective spirits had deserted them. While Grod carefully placed the burning charcoal on a bed of dry tinder and blew it into flame, the women turned to other tasks. With techniques passed down for generations they quickly skinned the game. A few moments after the fire was blazing well, meat skewered with sharp green sticks set over forked branches was roasting.

With the same sharp stone knives they used to skin and cut the meat, the women scraped and sliced roots and tubers. Tightly woven waterproof baskets and wooden bowls were filled with water, and then hot stones were added. When cooled the stones were put back into the fire and new ones were put in the water until it boiled.'

Jean M. Auel, 'The Clan of the Cave Bear', 1980.

SOURCE B

Fred Flintstone, from the television cartoon about a Stone Age family.

ACTIVITY 1

Make a list of at least ten differences between Sources A and B.
Make a table like the one below. For each of the qualities listed, give both Source A and Source B a score out of 10 where 10/10 would be the best score possible and 1/10 the worst.

Source A   Source B

How realistic is the source?
How funny is the source?
Does the source tell you about people's ideas?
Are the people made out to be like us?
Is the source likely to be based on a study of evidence?
Is the source really history?

In the activity you have just completed you have been looking at two different versions of what the past might have been like. Both of these are fiction, and history is very different from fiction. In *The Flintstones*, part of the joke is that the people in the television cartoon have the same possessions as people in the United States today. They also seem to have the same **ideas** and **attitudes**.

If we are to write good history, then we have to make sure that we understand not only what people in the past **did** but also what they **thought** about things. History is about not only **what** happened but also **why** it happened. To understand this properly we have to remember the ideas that people had at the time, because this helps us understand why they did things. Historians sometimes call this **empathy**, trying to look at events in the past from the point of view of the people who were there at the time.

SOURCE **C**

A crowd in Berlin, 3 August 1914.

CONCLUSION

1 Source C shows young men waving their hats and cheering. To understand why they are doing this, you need more information. Listed below is some information that might help. Copy into your book the sentences which seem to help. Keep them as a separate list.
   - Germany declared war on Russia on 1 August 1914 and on France on 3 August 1914.
   - Straw boaters were amongst the most fashionable hats for young men in 1914.
   - Most people in 1914 thought war was glorious.
   - Young men in particular thought war would give them a chance to show their patriotism and their bravery.
   - Between 1860 and 1870 Germany had been united by a series of short wars in which the Danes, the Austrians and then the French were convincingly beaten.

2 Underline in your book those sentences which help you understand the photograph *and which tell you about how people thought and felt.*

3 Do you think a historian needs to try to use empathy when explaining events in the past?

4 Do you think there is a difference between empathy and imagination? Explain your answer.

1.4 CHANGE

CHANGE

So much of history is concerned with change that historians sometimes try to study change itself, as well as what is changing. They distinguish between a **change**, where something new happens, and a **development**, where something that existed before has been modified. They are careful to notice that change and development are not necessarily the same as **progress** (where things get better) and may sometimes be **regress** (where things get worse). They also look for the examples of **continuity**, the things which don't change over long periods of time. They are also concerned with the **rate of change**, noticing that in some periods changes happen very fast, and in others very slowly. Finally they are interested in the factors which influence change, things like religion, war, government policy, chance, brilliant individuals, the level of education, technology and jealousy etc.

The first activity looks at **smallpox**, a killer disease which the World Health Organization said had been stamped out in 1980. In 1798 Edward Jenner, a country doctor from Berkeley, Gloucestershire, suggested a way of stopping people from catching the disease. He noticed that milkmaids, who usually caught cowpox (a much milder illness) from cows didn't get smallpox. He tried deliberately infecting a child with cowpox, and then later deliberately infecting the same child with smallpox. The child didn't catch smallpox because the cowpox had given him an immunity. Jenner called the process **vaccination** and published his results, claiming that this treatment could end smallpox.

SOURCE A

'Smallpox killed some people every year in seventeenth-century London. However, it was worse in some years than others. In 1659 smallpox killed 1,523 people, while in 1660 it killed 354.'

Lucinda MacCray Beier, 'Sufferers and Healers', 1987.

SOURCE C

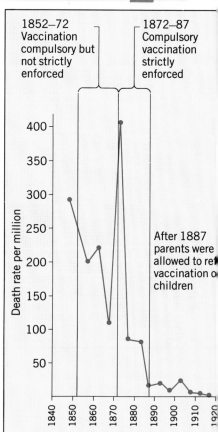

1852–72 Vaccination compulsory but not strictly enforced

1872–87 Compulsory vaccination strictly enforced

After 1887 parents were allowed to ref vaccination o children

Death rate per million

Deaths from smallpox in England and Wales, 1848–1920.

SOURCE B

Cartoon by Gilray published by the Anti-Vaccine Society, 1802.

ACTIVITY 1

1 What examples of continuity are there in the story of smallpox?

2 Was Jenner's treatment a *change* or a *development*?

3 What does Source B suggest about the reaction to Jenner's idea?

4 Would you describe the pace of change in stamping out smallpox as fast or slow? Explain your answer.

5 In 1750 smallpox was one of the most common and most deadly diseases in Britain. Today it doesn't exist. What factors do these sources suggest helped bring about this change? Give reasons for your answer.

SOURCE D

'Tally Ho', a house near Swindon, c1880.

ACTIVITY 2

Study Sources D and E.

1 What examples of change can you see between the two photographs?

2 What examples of continuity can you see between the two photographs?

3 Which do you think has been the more significant, the change or the continuity? Give reasons for your answer.

4 Do you think the differences between Source E and Source D should be described as *progress* and *regress*? Give reasons for your answer.

5 What factors do you think influenced the changes between the two photographs? Explain your answer.

SOURCE E

'Tally Ho', 1989.

2.1 EIGHTY YEARS OF CHANGE

CHANGE

Your great-grandparents' world, the world of 1914, was very different from our world today. This book is about how and why their world changed into ours.

The fastest speed at which your great-grandparents probably travelled was about 70 mph, on a steam train. Today an airliner travels at about 800 mph. If your great-grandparents were ill, their doctor (if they could afford one) had no penicillin or other drugs to kill germs inside the body. Your doctor today has many. Someone born in Britain in 1914 could expect, on average, to live to be 52. Today average life expectancy is 73.

Changes in technology, 1914 to the 1980s.

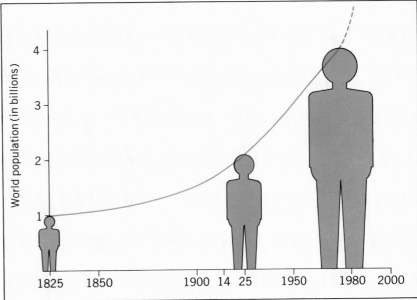

Changes in world population since 1825.

The global village

In 1914 Britain was already a nation of towns and factories. So were a small number of other countries. But nearly everybody in the rest of the world lived in villages and grew their own food. Today far more of the world's people live and work in towns or cities and depend for their food on farmers in other regions. In 1914 London, with about 7 million people, was the world's biggest city; today Tokyo with 25 million is the biggest, and there are a dozen others bigger than London.

In a village most people know each other, but this is impossible in a city. Since 1914 worldwide trade and travel have become much easier. Radio and television have also been developed, so people on one side of the world can see and hear about events on the other side. This is like the old village in which people could easily see and hear about events on the other side of the street. The world has become a bit like a village and is often called the **global village**.

This book is partly about the developments in **technology** that have changed people's lives in the last eighty years and made the global village possible. But much of the book is about **governments** and **wars**. The changes in technology have made governments more powerful and wars much more dreadful than before 1914. This makes it more important than ever for the people of the global village to understand each other and to understand and control what their governments are doing. The people of a village understood each other because they knew what everybody had done last week or last year, and had a good idea of the reason why they had done it. If the people of the global village are to understand each other in the same way, they need to know what people on the other side of the world did last year, or fifty years ago, and why they did it. They need to know some **world history**.

CHANGE

2.1

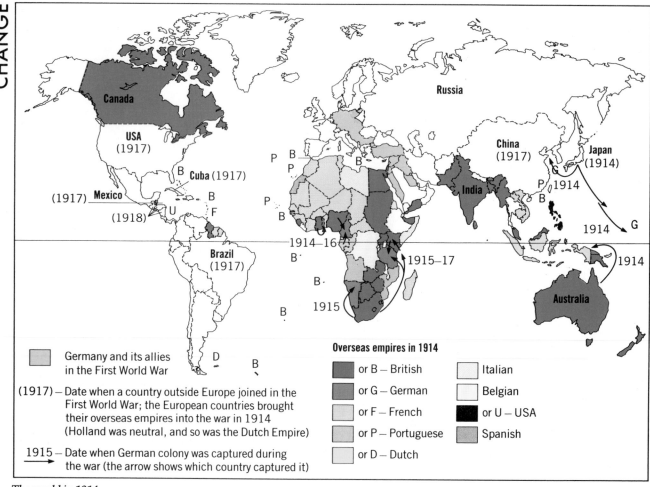

The world in 1914.

Germany and its allies in the First World War

(1917) – Date when a country outside Europe joined in the First World War; the European countries brought their overseas empires into the war in 1914 (Holland was neutral, and so was the Dutch Empire)

1915 → Date when German colony was captured during the war (the arrow shows which country captured it)

Overseas empires in 1914

or B – British
or G – German
or F – French
or P – Portuguese
or D – Dutch

Italian
Belgian
or U – USA
Spanish

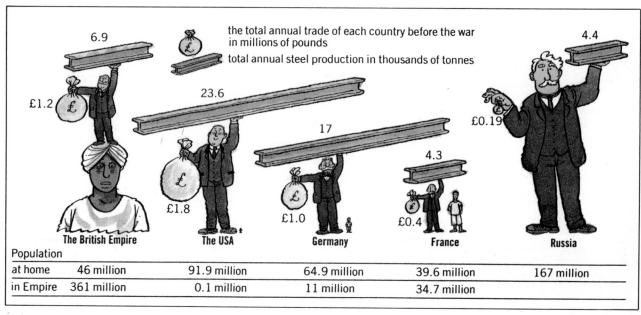

the total annual trade of each country before the war in millions of pounds

total annual steel production in thousands of tonnes

	The British Empire	The USA	Germany	France	Russia
Steel	6.9	23.6	17	4.3	4.4
Trade	£1.2	£1.8	£1.0	£0.4	£0.19

Population					
at home	46 million	91.9 million	64.9 million	39.6 million	167 million
in Empire	361 million	0.1 million	11 million	34.7 million	

The world's leaders in trade and industry in 1914.

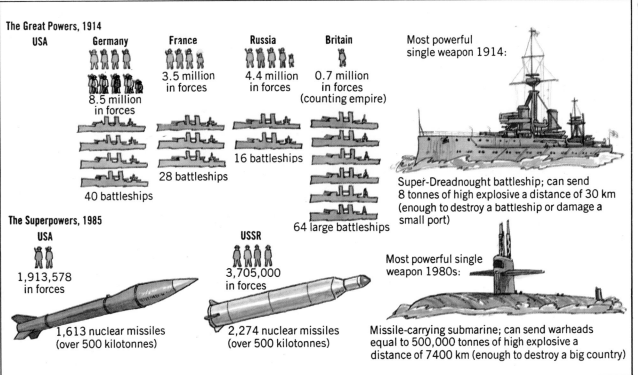

The Great Powers, 1914

USA | Germany | France | Russia | Britain

Germany: 8.5 million in forces

France: 3.5 million in forces

Russia: 4.4 million in forces

Britain: 0.7 million in forces (counting empire)

40 battleships

28 battleships

16 battleships

64 large battleships

Most powerful single weapon 1914:

Super-Dreadnought battleship; can send 8 tonnes of high explosive a distance of 30 km (enough to destroy a battleship or damage a small port)

The Superpowers, 1985

USA: 1,913,578 in forces

USSR: 3,705,000 in forces

1,613 nuclear missiles (over 500 kilotonnes)

2,274 nuclear missiles (over 500 kilotonnes)

Most powerful single weapon 1980s:

Missile-carrying submarine; can send warheads equal to 500,000 tonnes of high explosive a distance of 7400 km (enough to destroy a big country)

Changes in power, 1914–85.

Indian famine victims, about 1900.

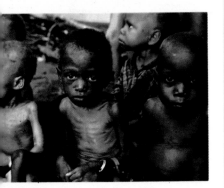

Ethiopian famine victims, 1985.

EXERCISE

1 Make a list of the changes in the years since 1914 which are illustrated in this unit.

2 Make a list of the things which have stayed the same.

3 Look at the graph of world population.
 a Roughly how many times has world population increased since 1914?
 b If the increase went on at the same rate, when would the world's population be 8 billion?

4 Look at the diagram showing 'Changes in power'. What important changes in power does it show? Which of these is most important?

5 Which of all the changes illustrated in this unit do you think most important? Explain your reasons.

6 Look at the map of the world in 1914. (Don't worry about the dates and arrows. You will find these useful when you come to read about the First World War.) What is the main difference between this map and one showing the main countries of the world today?

7 Look at the diagram showing 'The world's leaders in trade and industry in 1914'. If you made a similar list of the 'top five' today, which countries would still be there? Which new ones might be added?

8 Use the information in this unit to suggest reasons why these changes in the ranking of the world's leading nations may have happened.

3.1 WHY THE FIRST WORLD WAR BROKE OUT IN 1914

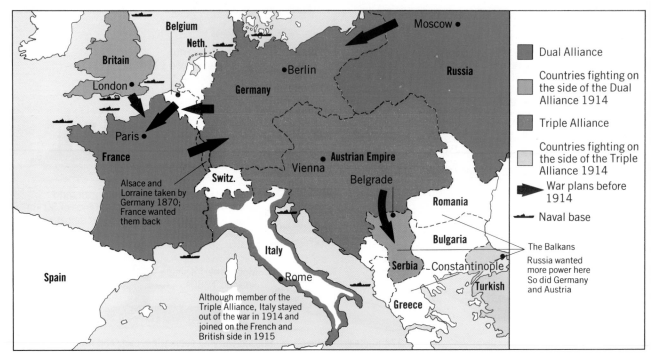

Europe in 1914.

In 1914 Europe was armed to the teeth. This was the age of railways, when millions of men and guns could be moved suddenly to strike a deadly blow. So everything had to be prepared in advance: men, horses, railway timetables, even bootlaces. Everybody knew that a war could be won or lost in the first battle, so if one country got ready like this, others had to follow suit.

As well as armies and navies, a country making war needed **allies**. After an attack had begun it would be too late to look for friends. Since the 1890s there had been two important alliances in Europe. On one side was the **Triple Alliance** of Germany, Austria and Italy, on the other the **Dual Alliance** of France and Russia. Each alliance made detailed war plans. For instance, the French and Russians agreed that, if Germany attacked France in the west, the Russians would strike Germany in the east. So if one country decided to get in the first blow quickly, the news would be flashed to all the others, and the soldiers of five countries would charge into action.

Europe was on a knife-edge. Any little push will tip you off a knife-edge. In 1914 each of the European powers had its own reasons for pushing.

The European powers

In 1870 Germany had defeated **France** and seized the French provinces of Alsace and Lorraine. Ever since then the French had talked of a war of revenge to get back the territory.

The Russian government had serious problems at home. Tsar Nicholas II badly needed a success to make him more popular. Perhaps he could achieve this by increasing Russia's power in the Balkans in south-east Europe. **Russia** had wanted this for

SOURCE A

'I no longer have any doubt that England, Russia and France have agreed among themselves to wage a war of annihilation against us. The encirclement of Germany has become an accomplished fact.

Kaiser Wilhelm of Germany, 31 July 1914.

centuries. Unfortunately for Nicholas, the Germans and the Austrians now had the same idea.

The Germans were very proud of their increasing power and wealth. Their army had helped to make **Germany** strong, and it was very popular. In 1890 they began to build up a navy too. Like Britain they traded all over the world and had a growing empire (see map on page 16). Germany was a **world power** and, like Britain, it needed a navy to defend its power.

Like Russia, **Austria** had serious problems at home. The Austrian Empire included eleven different nationalities, who mostly wanted to belong to separate nations of their own. For instance, many of the 2 million Serbs in the Austrian Empire wanted instead to be citizens of Serbia, an independent country to the south.

In the **Balkans**, **Serbia** had gained its independence from the Turkish Empire after a long struggle. Many Serbs hoped that they could go on to bring the Serb parts of the Austrian Empire into Serbia. What made the matter very serious in 1914 was that Russia was Serbia's main friend and ally.

Events of June, July and August 1914

On 28 June 1914 a Serb nationalist shot and killed **Archduke Franz Ferdinand** and his wife Sophie. Franz Ferdinand was the son of the Austrian Emperor, and the Austrians saw the murder as good excuse to attack and weaken Serbia. But they knew that Russia would probably help Serbia, so before attacking they checked with the Germans. Germany agreed to back Austria, and Austria attacked Serbia on 28 July.

Why did **Kaiser Wilhelm**, the German Emperor, and his generals agree to this? They knew that Russia might join in, bringing France in too. But they also knew that the French and Russian armies were not quite ready for war, while their own were in the peak of condition. It was a chance too good to miss.

The German war plan, known as the **Schlieffen Plan**, was to knock France out with a sudden attack through Belgium, and then to move their armies east to smash the Russians. So on 2 August they marched into Belgium.

What about Britain?

Britain had not joined either alliance but since the 1890s it had watched the growth of the German navy with great alarm. Britain depended on overseas trade for its wealth and for much of its food; the Germans might soon be in a position to cut this off. If they were to get control of ports in Belgium such as Antwerp, the danger would be greater still. So the British began to make friends with the French and the Russians. They made secret plans for their armies and navies to work together if war broke out.

These secret plans made it very likely that Britain would join in the war, but the German attack through Belgium ended any doubts. In 1839 Britain had promised to help protect Belgium if anyone attacked it. So on 4 August Britain declared war on Germany.

SOURCE B

'I had a visit at breakfast from the German Ambassador, who begged me not to side with France. I told him we had no desire to intervene and that it rested largely with Germany to make intervention impossible if she would (1) not invade Belgium and (2) not send her fleet into the channel to attack France.'

H. H. Asquith, British Prime Minister, 2 August 1914.

QUESTIONS

1 In the First World War there were three main pairs of enemies:
   - France v. Germany,
   - Austria v. Russia,
   - Britain v. Germany.
   a Explain the reasons for each of these.
   b Why did these three problems lead not to three little wars but to one big one?

2 Sources A and B were written just before war began.
   a What did Germany fear? Was this fear justified?
   b What did Britain fear? Was this fear justified?

3 Neither Britain, Germany nor any of the other countries that took part in the war actually wanted a war lasting four years and killing millions of people. Does this mean that what people want makes little difference in history?

3.2 HOW THE FIRST WORLD WAR WAS FOUGHT

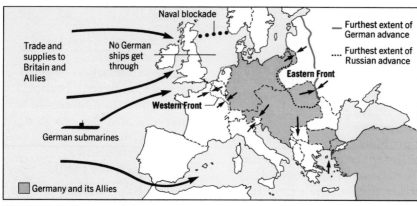

War fronts in Europe and the war at sea.

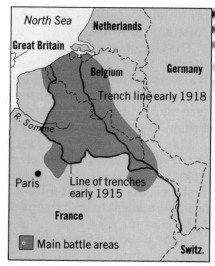

The western front, 1914–18.

1914

In 1914 the carefully prepared war plans failed. **Austria** failed to knock out Serbia; the **Russians** failed in their attack on Germany; and, most important of all, the **Germans** failed to overthrow France. After the German armies unsuccessfully tried to capture Paris, they drew back to the line shown on the map and dug themselves defensive trenches. The Allies – **Britain** and **France** – did the same, so that by 1915 a double line of trenches 650 km long stretched from the Swiss frontier to the sea.

Germany's best chance to win was in 1914. Germany was much better organized for war than its enemies, but they had far more men and resources. As long as the British navy kept command of the sea, Britain could stop Germany getting supplies. At the same time Britain could draw on the supplies of the whole world. So Britain and its allies were likely to win a long war.

British Mark I tank, 1916. Tanks came into use towards the end of the war.

SOURCE A

1915

The year **1915** was one of stalemate. There were some successes for the Germans and their allies in the east, but these did not change the shape of the war. Both sides could see that they needed new armies, with more men and more guns, if they were to break through the lines of trenches. In 1915 they were busy building up these new armies.

1916

Major offensives were launched in **1916**. Russia, Germany, France and Britain each struck a mighty blow that they hoped would win the war. All of them failed. The British attack was near the river Somme. In the **Battle of the Somme** 60,000 British soldiers were killed or wounded on the first day in July, and there were about a million casualties from both sides by the time the battle ended in November. The attack gained nothing worth having. By the end of 1916 some people began to think that victory was impossible.

1917

In **1917** the Germans decided on a bold move to cut off supplies to Britain and force it to make peace. Up to now German

Artillery 1916. High explosive shells could blow up a trench. Shrapnel shells sprayed jagged metal at a group of soldiers. An artillery barrage could drive you mad if it didn't wound or kill you.

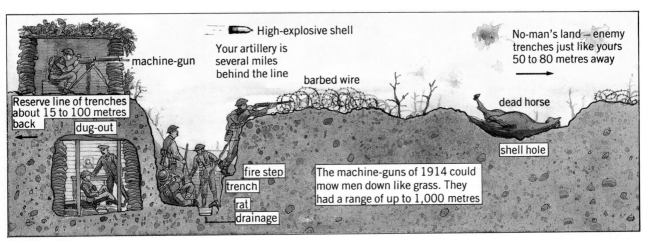

machine-gun

High-explosive shell

Your artillery is several miles behind the line

barbed wire

No-man's land — enemy trenches just like yours 50 to 80 metres away

dead horse

Reserve line of trenches about 15 to 100 metres back

dug-out

shell hole

fire step

trench

rat

drainage

The machine-guns of 1914 could mow men down like grass. They had a range of up to 1,000 metres

Trench warfare.

Trench warfare – how a battle was fought

Before a battle your guns shelled the enemy trenches with high explosives for some hours or even days. You hoped that this would break their barbed wire and kill their machine-gunners.

At dawn you attacked. When the order was given, you climbed over the top out of your trench, ran across no man's land and attacked the enemy with your bayonet. If enemy machine-guns were still in action you were a sitting target as you ran across or tried to pick your way through the wire. If you captured the trench you could be fairly certain that the enemy would counter-attack as soon as possible.

---

submarines had been careful not to sink United States ships, because they knew that if they did this the USA would probably declare war. Now they had 133 submarines ready and believed they could force Britain to make peace before the USA could act. So in February German submarines began to sink any ships they could see, including US ones. In April the USA declared war. The German plan nearly worked – in April 1917 Britain lost nearly a million tons of shipping. But in the same month the British began to introduce new methods of protecting their ships and attacking the U-boats. They also got some help from the small US navy. So Britain was able to go on fighting.

1918

Germany now saw another chance of victory. In 1917 there had been a revolution in Russia, and the Russians dropped out of the war. This meant that the Germans could move a million men from the eastern front to the west. Now, in **1918**, they had a chance to break through the Allied line before many US troops arrived. They tried desperately to do this, but by July their offensive had failed. The Allies then made a counter-attack, and the German line began to crack. **General Hindenburg**, the German commander-in-chief, could see that he was beaten. On 11 November the **armistice** was signed. The war was over.

QUESTIONS

1 The Germans seem to have had several chances of winning the First World War, but they still lost. Is this because:
   a They made mistakes?
   b They had bad luck?
   c The allies had better resources? (Look at pages 14–7.)
   d The Allies had control of the sea?
   Choose one or more of these and explain your reasons.

2 Nearly all the fighting of this war was in Europe. Why, then, do we call it a 'world' war? (Look at the map on page 16.)

3 David Lloyd George, Prime Minister of Britain in 1916, had to decide how much to spend on each of the following:
   a training more soldiers.
   b building more merchant ships.
   c building more warships.
   d getting farmers to grow more food in Britain.
   e making more guns and ammunition.
   To which of the above items of spending do you think he should have given top priority? Explain why.

3.3 CHANGING IDEAS ABOUT WAR

CHANGE

War can seem heroic and glamorous. Before 1914, when people in Europe thought about war they often thought of the glory and the excitement. Young men of the richer classes in every country were keen to be officers, and many felt that war was a noble experience, showing a nation at its best. Of course, people knew that war caused bloodshed and waste, but before 1914 it was mainly the soldiers and sailors themselves who suffered. Life at home usually went on as before, but with the extra excitement of news from the battlefield.

As you can see from the sources in this unit, not everybody thought like this even in 1914. By 1918, not many did. Most people now saw war as horrible and brutal. But there were some who still thought in the old way.

SOURCE A

SOURCE B

'We have been too comfortable. Now we can see the great everlasting things that matter to a nation, like great mountain peaks we had forgotten – Honour, Duty, Patriotism and the great pinnacle of Sacrifice, pointing like a rugged finger to heaven.'

David Lloyd George, British Chancellor of the Exchequer, September 1914.

SOURCE C

'For me, as for every other German, the most memorable period of my life now began (in August 1914). I am not ashamed to acknowledge today that I was carried away with the enthusiasm of the moment and that I sank down on my knees and thanked heaven out of the fullness of my heart for the favour of having been permitted to live in such a time.'

Adolf Hitler, 'Mein Kampf' ('My Struggle'), 1924. During the First World War, Hitler was a soldier in the German army on the western front.

SOURCE D

'As I write these words a dreadful war-cloud seems about to burst and deluge the people of Europe with fire, slaughter and ruin. This then is the world as men have made it, life as men have ordered it. A man-made civilization, hideous and cruel enough in time of peace, is to be destroyed.'

Christabel Pankhurst, a leader of the campaign for votes for women. From the magazine, 'The Suffragette', 7 August 1914.

SOURCE E

'The battlefield is fearful. One is overcome by a peculiar sour, heavy and penetrating smell of corpses. Men that were killed last October lie half in swamp and half in the beet-fields. The legs of an Englishman stick out into a trench, the corpse being built into the parapet: a soldier hangs his rifle on them.'

Letter from Rudolf Binding, a German soldier, dated 27 April 1915.

SOURCE F

'On 1 June 1917 one regiment with a fine fighting record was ordered to the front after a brief rest period. Chanting the "Internationale" the men marched in angry protest to the local town hall. The brigade commander, who tried to stop them, was attacked and his badges ripped off. Then the ringleaders freed prisoners from a detention camp and the troops ran wild, overturning lorries and smashing windows. By next evening a 2,000-strong mob was on the march, waving red flags and calling for peace and revolution.'

John Williams, 'The French Army Mutinies', 1968. In 1917–18 there were mutinies in many of the armies on both sides. In Russia the mutinies helped to cause the revolution.

EXERCISE

1 Which sources show:
   a some people thought war was a noble experience?
   b some people thought war was a horrible experience?

2 How could the same war seem so different?

3 Which source shows people changing their minds about war?

4 Which source shows that some people did not change their minds?

5 More people changed their attitude to war during the First World War than during earlier wars in history. What reasons can you suggest for this?

▲ *Young men cheering the outbreak of war, Berlin, 1914.*

SOURCE **G**

Wounded British soldier at the Somme, 1916.

3.4 THE RIGHT TO VOTE, 1914–20

Did the First World War change people's ideas about the **right to vote**?

Before the war

In 1914 the ordinary people in most parts of Europe had little say in how they were governed. A king or an emperor ruled with the help of leading nobles, generals and politicians. Usually there was a **parliament** which met regularly, and in some countries such as Britain it had real power over the government. But even in Britain no women and only three out of every five men had a vote. Many soldiers in the army had no vote.

In Germany, where all men could vote, the parliament (**Reichstag** in German) had little power. The Kaiser's government could carry on even if the Reichstag voted against it. For instance, in July 1917 the Reichstag voted for peace, but the Kaiser continued with the war.

In Russia things were even worse. Only a few wealthy men could vote, and even then the **Duma** (parliament) had no real power over the Tsar.

War for democracy

As people saw the horror of war many began to feel that the emperors and generals had led Europe and the world into a brutal mess. Ordinary people were the ones who suffered most. In March 1917 the people of Russia overthrew their Tsar and announced that Russia was now a **democracy**. Soon afterwards the USA joined in the war against Germany. In the USA all men had had the right to vote since 1870, and Americans were proud of the claim that their country was run by its people. After 1917 many people, led by US President Wilson, claimed that the war was now a war for democracy – to bring power to the people in all countries.

Post-war change

By 1920 the Austrian, Russian and German emperors had abdicated (resigned). In all three countries every adult now had a vote, including women. Several new countries were set up, such as Czechoslovakia and Yugoslavia, where every man and woman had a vote. In most of these countries the parliament had real power over the government. For the Soviet system of democracy in post-revolution Russia, see page 32. In Britain all men and some women had the vote (all women in 1928). In the USA all women were given the vote in 1920.

By 1920 there were twenty-eight countries in which all women had the vote. In 1914 there had only been four.

SOURCE A

'The muddiest, dirtiest common soldier from the slums or the factories or the fields was a hero before whom great ladies were eager to kneel in devotion and love, to cut away his bloodstained clothes, to dress his wounds. In the trenches or in the ruins under shell-fire young officers wrote home about their men: "They're too splendid for words! I am proud to command such a topping crowd. They make me ashamed of the things I used to think about the working man. There is nothing too good for them!"'

Sir Philip Gibbs, 'Ten Years After', 1926. Gibbs was a war correspondent on the western front.

SOURCE B

'The world must be made safe for democracy. It is a fearful thing to lead this great peaceful people into the most terrible and disastrous of all wars. But we shall fight for democracy, for the right of those who submit to authority to have a voice in their own governments.'

US President Wilson, message to Congress, 1917.

SOURCE C

'"Good morning, good morning," the general said,
When we met him last week on our way to the line.
Now the soldiers he smiled at are most of them dead,
And we're cursing his staff for incompetent swine.
"He's a cheery old card," grunted Harry to Jack
As they slogged up to Arras with rifle and pack.
But he did for them both with his plan of attack.'

Siegfried Sassoon, 1918. Sassoon was an infantry officer on the western front.

SOURCE D

Russia, 1917: soldiers' wives demand votes for women.

SOURCE E

Woman engineering worker, 1917.

SOURCE F

'The company has promised
all the men who are fighting
that their jobs shall be kept
open, and we would not
have it otherwise. But it's
going to be a big problem.
You see, we have all got a
contagious restless feeling.'

Wartime bus conductress, 1917.

SOURCE G

Wartime bus conductress, 1917.

QUESTIONS

1 What changes in voting systems took place between 1914 and 1920?

2 What evidence is there that these changes had already begun before the war?

3 How might each of the sources be used to explain how the war influenced these changes?

3.5 THE PEACE SETTLEMENT IN EUROPE, 1919–23

High hopes in 1919

The First World War was a nightmare for the people of Europe. It killed more than 16 million of them and injured several times as many. It laid waste great areas of northern France, and sank thousands of ships, mainly British. By 1918 most people in most countries were saying 'never again'.

The person who said this most clearly was United States **President Wilson**. When the USA entered the war in 1917 Wilson drew up a list of war aims which became known as the **Fourteen Points**. People heard about them all over Europe, even in Germany. Wilson's idea was for a peace based on justice to both sides, which both sides would accept and keep. He made two main suggestions:

First, **self-determination**: this meant that disputes over frontiers should be settled according to the wishes of the people who lived in the disputed area. This fitted in well with the idea of democracy. Wilson argued that people should not be pushed around, like pawns on a chess-board; they should have a full say in their own government, including deciding which country to belong to.

Second, the **League of Nations**: all peace-loving nations would together form an organization to prevent wars. They would agree to settle disputes by peaceful discussion. Once this had been established, nations could stop making military alliances and begin to disarm instead. It sounded wonderful to the war-weary world of 1917–18. The war might become a 'war to end war'. Perhaps all those millions had not died in vain.

When President Wilson arrived in Europe in 1919 he was welcomed like a hero.

The post-war treaties

During the years 1919–23 the various countries that had fought in the war signed a series of **treaties**. The main one, the treaty with Germany, was signed at Versailles, near Paris, in June 1919. The peace settlement as a whole is often called the **Versailles Settlement**.

Since so many countries had taken part in the war, people came from all over the world to take part in the peace discussions. But the main decisions were taken by three men, the **'big three'**: **President Wilson** of the USA, **David Lloyd George**, Prime Minister of Britain, and **Georges Clemenceau**, Prime Minister of France. As you can see from the diagram, the 'big three' had different attitudes. So did the people in their three countries. The war had taught many Europeans to hate and fear the Germans. The USA, on the other hand, had suffered little from the war, and many Americans were of German origin.

In November 1918 the fighting stopped in western Europe, but not in the east. Instead, as the old German, Austrian, Russian and Turkish empires collapsed, new struggles began. The people of these areas did not wait for the 'big three' to tell them what to do. Instead they set up new governments for themselves, and this led to much fighting about disputed areas. There were eight **new**

I want peace based on justice and self-determination. Now the Kaiser has gone, Germany will be peaceful again, and the League of Nations will keep the world peaceful. Be nice to Germany!

WILSON

CLEMENCEAU

Germany is to blame. It attacked in 1870 and 1914 – never again! Take away it's army. Make it pay for all the damage in France. Vive la France!

LLOYD–GEOR

Yes, Germany is to blame – let's take it's navy and empire, and make it pay fo the ships it sank – But afte that we should give it a chance.

Europe? Where is it?

Squeeze Germa 'till the pips squeak!

What most people at home though

The 'big three' – Wilson, Clemenceau and Lloyd George.

Germany also:
To have only a very small army and navy
Never to have conscription
Never to join with Austria
Give up all colonies
Give up all merchant ships
Pay reparations of £6.6 billion to Allies

Danzig became a free city

Rhineland — Germany not allowed to keep troops in this region

GERMANY

Saar — German manufacturing region, under League of Nations control

Austria never to unite with Germany even if the people wanted to

Lost by Bulgaria to Greece

☐ Lost by Germany 1919
■ Germany
☐ Austro-Hungarian Empire 1914
☐ Russian Empire, 1914

The peace settlement in Europe.

QUESTIONS

1 a Make a list of the main terms of the treaties affecting Germany.
  b Choose one of these terms that you consider was reasonable. Explain your choice.
  c Choose one of these that you consider was unreasonable. Explain your choice.

2 a Make a list of the new countries that did not appear on the 1914 map but did after 1919.
  b Against a country formerly mostly part of the Austrian Empire, write 'A'. Against one formerly mostly Russian, mark 'R'.
  c Many of these new countries included people of several different nationalities. What argument might be made against including them together in one country? What future problem might this cause?

3 The Treaty of Versailles blamed only Germany for starting the war (by an unprovoked attack on its neighbours). Read pages 18–19 again. Do you agree that only Germany was to blame?

4 Choose one part of the peace settlement that people in 1920 might have thought likely to cause trouble in the future. Explain your choice.

countries (see map), mostly very keen on self-determination for themselves but not so keen to allow it to their neighbours. The new **Poland**, for instance, included millions of Russians, Lithuanians and Germans. The new **Czechoslovakia** included Germans, Poles and Hungarians, as well as Czechs, Slovaks and others.

The Allies could not control these events in eastern Europe, especially after they had sent home most of their soliders. So the treaties generally accepted the new countries' frontiers. In one or two cases, however, the new League of Nations successfully organized a vote of the people to decide on the exact frontier line.

One problem made worse

You can see that some of the arrangements made by the treaties were likely to cause problems in the future. They caused one problem immediately. Instead of helping to get trade started and to send people back to work, the treaties made trade more difficult. One way they did this was by breaking eastern Europe up into so many small countries. Another was by making Germany pay **reparations** to the Allies. The new German government had no money to pay with, and the attempt to force it to pay led to the collapse of the German currency and to widespread unemployment and poverty in the 1920s. See page 50 for the trouble that was to follow.

3.6 THE PEACE SETTLEMENT OUTSIDE EUROPE

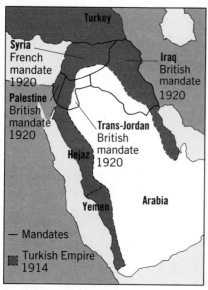

How the Turkish Empire was divided.

How Germany's overseas Empire was divided.

The mandates

During the First World War, Allied armies captured all the German colonies. The Turks were on the German side, and by 1918 the British had also captured much of their empire in the Middle East. What was to happen to these lands? Before the USA came into the war, the other Allies had secretly agreed to share many of them out among themselves. But what about the idea of a peace based on justice? One of Wilson's Fourteen Points had been that colonies should be ruled in the interests of the people who lived there. If it was wrong to push European people around like pawns on a chess-board, could it be right to do the same to non-Europeans?

The problem was solved by making all the captured colonies into **mandates** under the League of Nations. This meant that each was to be given to one of the Allies to rule in the interests of the local people. Many colonies went to the country that would have got them under the secret agreements, or whose armies controlled them in 1919. Some mandate countries were given independence fairly soon; but others, such as Namibia (then German South-West Africa), have still not got it today. The League was supposed to supervise the mandates, but this was never very effective, and some countries simply treated these territories as new possessions.

The League of Nations

Many people criticized the peace treaties as unfair or unwise, saying that they were bound to cause trouble in the future. But in spite of all their faults the treaties did set up a new organization, the **League of Nations**, which might prevent these future troubles turning into war. Could the League have succeeded? Look at the description of its organization in the box, and read about what the USA thought, before you decide whether it stood a chance.

'I can predict with absolute certainty that within another generation there will be another world war if the nations of the world do not concert methods to prevent it.'

US President Wilson, 1919.

Wilson: 'Would Australia flout the opinion of the civilized world by annexing her territory? Would she let it be said that she took part of the German Empire as the spoils of war?'

William Hughes, Prime Minister of Australia: 'That's about it, Mr President.'

End of a discussion at the Versailles Peace Conference, 1919.

The United States turns its back

The First World War showed the USA to be a great power. By 1918 it was the richest country in the world, and all the Allies owed it millions of dollars. It had shown that it could build up a large army and navy and play a decisive part in a war more than 3,000 miles from home. This was something new for Americans. Before this they had kept out of wars in Europe and Asia and had been glad to do so. When Wilson was re-elected President in 1916 one of the claims his party made was: 'He kept us out of the war.' He had then taken his country into the war and was now asking it to play a leading part in the League of Nations. This included promising to take action, perhaps even military action, against a nation which broke the peace.

Many US citizens agreed with Wilson that the time had come for the USA to act as a world leader, but others disagreed strongly. They were known as **isolationists**. Their idea was that the USA should carry on with the business of getting rich, and should not get mixed up in European or world politics more than it could help.

Before the USA can sign a treaty, two-thirds of the US Senate have to agree. In 1919 the isolationists in the Senate were able to throw out the **Treaty of Versailles**. Wilson planned to tour the USA making speeches to get people on his side and force the Senate to accept the treaty. He was a great speaker and might have succeeded, but in September 1919 he collapsed with a stroke. His opponents won the next election for President, and the new President Harding announced in 1921: 'We seek no part in directing the destinies of the world.' So the USA never joined the League. Only after another world war did the USA formally accept the fact that it was a world power.

SOURCE **C**

The Tiger: "Curious! I seem to hear a child weeping!"

Cartoon, 1919. The men shown are, from left to right, Lloyd George, Orlando the Italian leader, Clemenceau and Wilson. Children who were babies in 1919 would be the soldiers of 1940.

How the League of Nations worked

Members: at first only the Allies were members, plus some countries like Switzerland which had been neutral in the war. But it was hoped that all nations in the world would join in the end.

The **Council of Ten** met monthly to discuss problems. Britain, France, Italy and Japan were permanent members. Other countries took turns to attend.

The **League Assembly** met at least once a year. Each member nation, however small, had one vote there.

If a League member was attacked, the following was agreed:
First, if any member nation (apart from the attacker) voted in the Council or the Assembly against any action, nothing could be done at all.
Second, the League could tell other members not to trade with the attacker. This was called applying **sanctions**. Third, if this failed, the League could tell members to send troops to help the victim.

Other work: the League supervised the mandates, and set up worldwide organizations to improve health and working conditions in all countries and to stop slavery.

4.1 REVOLUTION IN RUSSIA

March 1917: the fall of the Tsar

The people of **Russia** had been discontented with their lives and their rulers since long before the war. The peasants hated the landlords and were often deeply in debt. Industrial workers lived in squalid slums and worked long hours for low wages. Even the middle classes were discontented. What they wanted was a share of power in running their country.

Tsar Nicholas II believed that it was God's will that he should rule Russia and share his power with no one. In 1905 he had been forced to agree to a parliament, the **Duma**, but it had little power. When it criticized Nicholas, he dismissed it and carried on as before. How was this possible? One key reason was a strong traditional respect for the royal family. Another was the power of the police and the army. People who opposed the government were arrested. If there were mass protests the troops were ordered to open fire. In January 1905 they fired on marchers asking for reforms and killed several hundred people.

It was the war that destroyed this system. The peasants fell deeper into debt; the workers found prices rising twice as fast as wages; the railway transport system began to break down; and there were serious food shortages. The Tsar and his government were unable to solve any of these problems. They were also incapable of running the war. Russian armies were defeated, and the soldiers lost respect for their officers and generals.

In early 1917 the flood of discontent broke out in food riots, marches and strikes in Petrograd (now Leningrad). As usual the troops were called in to restore order. But things were not 'as usual' in 1917. The Russian soldiers could no longer be relied on by the Tsar. At the battlefront they had seen their comrades killed and wounded by the thousand. They were now being ordered to fire on people like themselves, with whose grievances they sympathized. So they refused to fire. Many of them joined in the protests.

There was nothing left for the Tsar to do. When a small group of MPs from the Duma suggested that he should abdicate, he meekly agreed. The MPs announced that they were forming a **Provisional Government** to run the country for the time being until elections could be held. The **March Revolution** was over.

November 1917: Lenin seizes power

In July 1917 **Alexander Kerensky** became leader of the Provisional Government. But his was not the only group that claimed to be the rightful government of Russia in 1917. Groups of people in villages, towns, factories and army regiments began to form committees – **'soviets'** in Russian. Then they called a meeting in Petrograd of representatives of the soviets from all over Russia. At this **Congress of Soviets** they claimed to have as much right to speak for the Russian people as Kerensky and the Provisional Government.

One of those who thought this was **V. I. Lenin**. He was the leader of a small party of socialists known as the **Bolsheviks**. He had spent much of his life in exile, studying Karl Marx's books

SOURCE **A**

Nicholas II and the Tsarina in 1890. An official photograph.

SOURCE **B**

Cartoon from 'Punch', February 1905.

SOURCE C

A Red Guard in the throne-room of the Tsar's Winter Palace, November 1917. The title of this painting, the work of a Soviet artist in 1935, is 'The Inevitable'.

and planning for the revolution in which the working class would take control. Lenin saw that the chaos in Russia in 1917 gave him a chance. He told the Bolsheviks to try to act as leaders of the people wherever they were – in the army, the factory or the street. In this way a small and well-disciplined party might lead millions. The system of soviets suited Lenin's plan. If the Bolsheviks could take the lead in enough local soviets, they had a chance to seize control of the whole system.

To win most Russians over to his side Lenin promised two things. The first of these was **peace**. Kerensky wanted to go on fighting, but Lenin had opposed the war ever since 1914. Now his advice to the soldiers at the front was to stop fighting and go home. 'Vote with your feet!' he said. This was just what the tired and beaten Russian soldiers were keenest to do. The second thing the Russians wanted was **land**. Many of them were peasants who had to pay high rents. Lenin's advice was that they should take over the landlord's land themselves. 'All land to the peasants' was a popular slogan.

By November 1917 the Bolsheviks had been very successful. They controlled the Petrograd soviet, and Lenin saw that they were now strong enough to take over the government from Kerensky. They had formed a **'Red Guard'** of 20,000 soldiers and workers. On 6 November the Bolsheviks sent the Red Guard to arrest the ministers of the provisional government, and on the 7th the Congress of Soviets announced that the Soviets were now the government of Russia.

SOURCE D

Red Guards keeping warm, Petrograd, 1917.

QUESTIONS

1 How did the following help to bring about the success of the Bolsheviks?
 a The way they organized their party.
 b The system of soviets.
 c The war.

2 a Why do you think the Tsar had the photograph, Source A, published?
 b What was the aim of the cartoonist in Source B?
 c What do you think the artist meant Source C to show?
 d What was the aim of the photographer of Source D?

3 How useful are Sources A, B, C and D as historical evidence?

4.2 SOCIALISM AND COMMUNISM

Socialism was a new set of political ideas that grew up in the nineteenth century. Socialists believed that everybody ought to have an equal chance in life but that the new factories and machines of the Industrial Revolution were making life better for the rich and worse for the poor. This dreadful unfairness, they argued, could be put right only by changing the **ownership of property**. There were many different ideas about how this should be done. The person who worked these ideas out most clearly was **Karl Marx**, a German writer who lived in England in the years 1850–83.

The class struggle

Marx started by looking at the factories, the land, the railways, the mines and everything else that was needed to produce food, clothes and other goods and services. He pointed out that these **means of production** were mostly owned by rich people – **capitalists**, who lived on the profit they made. But the **workers** owned nothing: they made no profit, and lived on the wages they earned. It was in the interests of the capitalists for profits to be high and wages low. For the workers it was the exact opposite: the higher the wages, the better they could live. So between the **working class** and the **capitalist class** there was a **class struggle**.

Communism and the revolution

Marx argued that there was always one **ruling class** in a country. In nineteenth-century Britain the capitalists controlled the government and used the police and the army to keep the workers under control. But the growth of industry was bound to bring workers together and make them discontented. So sooner or later they would rise against the ruling class, overthrow it and take control of society themselves. This would be **the revolution**.

Marx wrote that the revolution was as certain to happen as day was to follow night, although he did not claim to foresee exactly when. He expected that the ruling class would not give in without violent resistance. After the revolution there would be only one class – the working class – left. At first it would have to take a firm grip on the government to stop the old ruling class making a comeback or **counter-revolution**. But after a time everybody would settle down happily in a **classless society**. Marx described this final future condition as **communism**. Socialism was the way there.

Disagreements between socialists

'Workers of the world unite!' was the call of Marx and his followers. Marx expected that, once the revolution had taken place in one country, the capitalists in other countries would try to suppress it. So **world revolution** was needed. He thought the workers in all countries would be bound to see the need to work together in the end and overthrow capitalism everywhere.

In Russia, Lenin's party, the Bolsheviks, agreed with Marx. When they seized control they believed they were starting the revolution he had prophesied. They expected revolutions in

The class struggle in Marx's view.

Time chart of Marx's revolution.

Germany and other countries to follow, leading to world revolution. But they were wrong about this. The attempted revolutions in Germany and elsewhere were all crushed. One reason for this was that most socialists in Germany and other countries in western Europe disagreed with some of Marx's and Lenin's ideas. They did not agree that the changes needed to get rid of the class system had to be violent. They hoped to win elections and then pass laws peacefully to improve conditions for the workers and to take control of industry from the capitalists. Socialists like this believed strongly in the western type of democracy (see page 24). They often called themselves **democratic socialists**. In Britain they supported the Labour Party. During the last seventy years, governments led by socialists of this type have held power in many countries.

Those socialists who followed Lenin and accepted all Marx's ideas began after 1917 to call themselves **Communists** or **Marxist-Leninists**. They insisted that the only way to break the power of the capitalists was by violent revolution, and they watched for the chance to start one. Communist parties later took control of several eastern European countries in the years 1945–8. They have since then been successful in China, North Korea, Vietnam and Cuba.

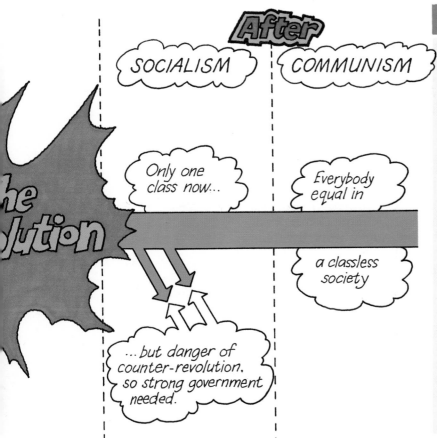

QUESTIONS

1 Explain why Karl Marx thought that there was going to be a revolution.

2 Explain the main difference between the ideas of communists and other socialists after 1917.

3 What sorts of people might be expected to:
   a accept Marx's ideas?
   b oppose them bitterly?

4 Lenin hoped for a world revolution in 1917–18. Use your knowledge of the First World War to explain why this seemed possible.

4.3 LENIN'S RUSSIA, 1917–24

Communist victory in Russia

When Lenin seized power in 1917, fewer than one Russian in five hundred was a Bolshevik. They faced what might have seemed an impossible task. At this time Kerensky and others, including some of the Tsar's generals, were collecting troops to attack and overthrow the Soviet government. They were known as the **Whites**, in contrast to the **Reds** they fought against. The government had no army, only a small **Red Guard**. Meanwhile the German army was advancing into Russia in the west with very little to stop it. Between 1917 and 1920 a number of other countries helped the Whites, as you can see from the map.

In 1918 the Bolsheviks set up the **Russian Communist Party**. By 1921 they had defeated all their enemies in Russia. By 1924, when Lenin died, the **Soviet Union** – made up of Russia plus fourteen other 'republics' – was firmly established in much the same form as it has today. How did the Communists achieve so much?

One thing that helped them was the collapse of Germany. In March 1918 Russia and Germany signed a peace treaty, the **Treaty of Brest-Litovsk**. This did not at first stop the Germans advancing into southern Russia. But in November came the defeat of Germany on the Western Front, the Kaiser's government collapsed and Germany was in disorder. This was not the start of the 'world revolution' that Marx had foretold and Lenin hoped for; but at any rate Germany was no longer a threat.

Another factor helping Lenin was the attitude of many people in countries like Britain and France which sent help to the Whites. Some political leaders, it is true, were frightened of the Russian Revolution spreading. They saw communism as a deadly danger to be crushed. Yet many people looked on socialism as a hope for the future and would not be likely to agree to a war to overthrow a socialist government. In any case, British and French soldiers had had enough of war and might refuse to fight. So the Western Allies gave the Whites only limited help.

War Communism

More important than both these factors for the Russian Communists' success were their own determination, skill and ruthlessness. Nothing mattered to Lenin and the Communist Party but the defence of the revolution. A new army, the **Red Army**, was built up quickly. It was brilliantly organized by **Leon Trotsky**, the most able of the Communist leaders after Lenin. Former officers of the Tsar had to be used, but over each was placed a reliable Communist to keep him in line with the wishes of the party.

To supply the army with weapons, all factories were taken over and told what to produce. Workers were forbidden to strike and compelled to work. Food was tightly rationed. Peasants were forced to hand over the food they had produced without any payment. If they refused they were shot. The policy was known as **War Communism**.

Many people objected to these policies, not surprisingly. So the Communists arrested the leaders of other political parties and

Russian poster of 1918. The message underneath says: 'Comrades! Join the Red Army.'

Starving peasant children in Russia, 1921.

closed down their newspapers. They set up a political police force, the **Cheka**, and gave it powers to shoot 'counter-revolutionaries'. It shot plenty.

The New Economic Policy

By 1921 it was clear that Lenin had succeeded, but the cost was fearful. War Communism had stopped trade almost completely. By 1921 money had lost its value in Russia, because there was nothing to buy. The peasants refused to grow food if it was just to be seized by the army. So famine spread, and with it disease. At least 5 million died – and probably more than twice that number.

In 1921 Lenin announced a change: the **New Economic Policy**. If the peasants were to grow the food that people needed, they had to be able to sell it, and had to have something to buy with the money. A limited return was made to the capitalist system of buying and selling for profit, and food became available again. Small factories and shops could make a profit once more, and business people were encouraged to start them up. A few Communists argued that all this was against the basic ideas of Marx. But Lenin persuaded them that, as long as the Soviet government kept full control of the big factories, the railways, the banks and foreign trade, it could still control the whole economic system.

Gradually the new economic policy began to work. By 1927 production was about back to the level of 1913.

QUESTIONS

1 a What countries attacked Soviet Russia in the years 1917–21?
b What countries took land from Russia at this time?
c Soon after the Peace of Brest-Litovsk, in March 1918, Britain and the USA sent troops to Russia. Why did they do this?

2 In 1918 the Soviet government moved from Petrograd to Moscow, which has been the capital ever since. Why do you think the move was made?

3 a 'War Communism was harsh and brutal.' What would you say in support of this statement?
b 'War Communism was necessary.' How would a supporter of the Communist Party have defended this statement?

Russia, 1918–23. ▼

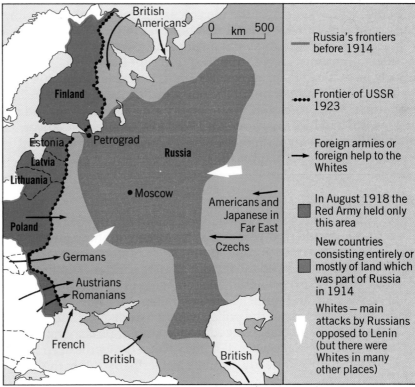

4.4 THE USSR UNDER STALIN

In 1923 the Soviet Communists renamed their country the **Union of Soviet Socialist Republics** (**USSR**). They had many serious problems. One was that the Industrial Revolution was only just beginning in Russia, and the working class was quite small. Marx's theory was that the industrial working class would take control first in one country and then in the whole world. The Communists had seized power in Russia in 1917 as leaders of the working class. But four out of every five Soviet citizens were peasant farmers, and most peasants had no education and had never heard of Marx. For them War Communism was a dreadful memory. Under the new economic policy they were beginning to improve their farms, and some, known as **kulaks**, were even getting rich. If there were more kulaks than Communists, how could the USSR become really socialist? You can see the different points of view of various Communist leaders in the cartoon.

Stalin and Trotsky

In 1924 Lenin died. The argument over policy that followed was a trial of strength between two men who were rivals for the leadership. Lenin's right-hand man since 1917 had been **Leon Trotsky**, a brilliant speaker, writer and organizer. **Joseph Stalin**, his rival, was the Secretary of the Soviet Communist Party. He had none of Trotsky's brilliance, but he made clever deals behind the scenes and got his friends into key jobs. The first question to be argued out was whether it was possible to have socialism just in the USSR, or whether the Communists should work for an early world revolution.

Stalin, who was against the idea of 'exporting' revolution, won the argument. Trotsky, a dedicated believer in world revolution, refused to accept this and went on arguing publicly for his own policy. Communists were supposed to accept the 'party line' loyally once it had been agreed. So Stalin was able to use this rule to have Trotsky turned out of the party in 1927, and in 1929 exiled from the USSR. Trotsky still went on arguing and writing, and in 1940 Stalin had him murdered. In 1928, now securely in power, Stalin sided strongly with those who wanted to build up Soviet industry rapidly, so this was the policy that went ahead.

The five-year plans

From 1928 to 1939 industry developed rapidly in the USSR. The Government made **five-year plans**. It worked out how much would be needed of each commodity, such as steel and coal and it then gave orders to build the factories, mines and machinery to produce them. Workers and managers were praised if they fulfilled the plan and punished if they failed. Mistakes were made, but on the whole the policy was an astonishing success. By 1939 the USSR had been changed from a land of peasant farmers into a great industrial power. For instance, it now produced more steel than Britain and nearly as much as Germany. Only the USA produced more.

Arguments within the Communist Party in the 1920s.

The Russian working class is small and weak, and the capitalists from the will probably attack us again soon. Let's spread the Revolution to get their workers on our side. Long live the world revolution!

TROTSKY   KAMENEV BUKHA

The industrial workers are only people we can rely on. Down with the kulaks! Let build more and more factorie quickly as we can. That'll m more workers and more gu to fight the capitalists.

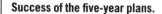

Success of the five-year plans.

4 .m. tonnes

5.05 m. kilowatt hours

35.4 m. tonnes

Before – 1927

Face facts! There's no chance of a world revolution for years. We have to build **socialism in the U.S.S.R. alone**.

We've had enough upheavals in the U.S.S.R. **Let's build socialism gradually.** The kulaks are growing the food that we need, so let's work with them.

STALIN

Collective farms

To feed the new town workers, Stalin determined to bring in a system of large farms, using modern farming methods. In these **collective farms** the peasants worked together to fulfil a production plan. They did not own the land so they could not sell the produce for themselves. Most peasants hated the system. Rather than hand over animals to the collective, they slaughtered them. Rather than sow crops for the collective, they sowed nothing. The result was another famine, in which many millions died. More than 3 million peasants were arrested and sent to **labour camps**. In this way Stalin got rid of the wealthy, independent-minded kulaks and forced the rest of the peasants into the collective system. The policy was brutal, but it worked. Soviet farming was still inefficient compared with farming in countries such as Britain, but it produced enough to feed the new factory workers.

Stalin's brutality towards opponents

Once the Communist party had agreed to these policies, anybody who opposed them was seen as an enemy of the party. Stalin's **secret police** (known as the **NKVD**) were sent to root out these 'enemies', bring them for trial and then either shoot them or put them into forced labour camps. Here several million people worked in the mines or on construction work. They often died on the job.

In 1934 it became clear to Stalin that some leading Communists were worried about the way things were going. Perhaps they were plotting to overthrow him as he had overthrown Trotsky. But Stalin controlled the NKVD so he could strike first. Between 1934 and 1939 well over half the leading members of the party were shot or sent to labour camps. So were 13 of the 15 generals of the Red Army and many of its other officers. Stalin was left in unchallenged power, surrounded by frightened yes-men.

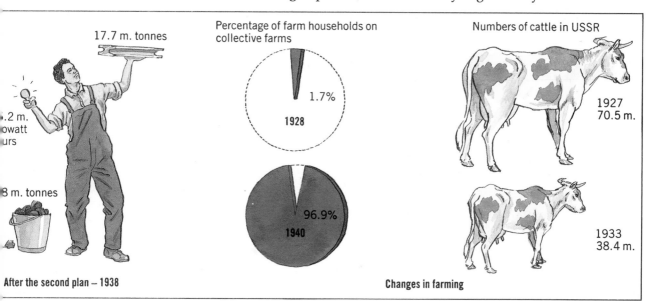

17.7 m. tonnes

.2 m. owatt urs

8 m. tonnes

After the second plan – 1938

Percentage of farm households on collective farms

1.7%
1928

96.9%
1940

Numbers of cattle in USSR

1927
70.5 m.

1933
38.4 m.

Changes in farming

EVIDENCE

4.5 STALIN: A REIGN OF TERROR?

SOURCE A

'Comrades, the pace must not be slackened. We must increase it. This is dictated to us by our obligations to the working class of the whole world. To slacken the pace would mean to lag behind; and those who lag behind are beaten. We are fifty to a hundred years behind the advanced countries. We must make up this lag in ten years. Either we do it or they crush us.'

Stalin, February 1931.

SOURCE B

'"How are things with you?" I asked one man. He looked around anxiously to see that no soldiers were about. "We have nothing, absolutely nothing. They have taken everything away." It was true. The famine is an organized one. Some of the food that has been taken away from them is being exported to foreign countries.

'It is literally true that whole villages have being exiled. I saw myself a group of some twenty peasants being marched off under escort. This is so common a sight that it no longer arouses even curiosity.'

'Manchester Guardian', 25 March 1933.

SOURCE C

'A quarter of a million souls, communists, kulaks, foreigners, convicts and a mass of blue-eyed Russian peasants building the largest steel works in Europe in the middle of the Russian steppe. Men froze, hungered and suffered, but the construction went on with a disregard for individuals and a mass heroism unparalleled in history.'

J. Scott, 'Beyond the Urals', 1942. Scott was an American who went to work on the new steel works at Magnitogorsk in the Ural mountains.

SOURCE D

'Nothing strikes the visitor to the Soviet Union more forcibly than the absence of fear. The plan removes at one stroke many of the more obvious fears. No fear of not enough money at the birth of a child cripples the Soviet parent. No fear for doctor's fees, school fees or university fees. No fear of underwork, no fear of overwork. No fear of wage reduction in a land where none are unemployed.'

Dr Hewlett Johnson, 'The Socialist Sixth of the World', 1939. Johnson was Dean of Canterbury Cathedral and known as 'the Red Dean'.

SOURCE E

'At the end of the day, there were corpses left on the worksite. The snow powdered their faces. One was hunched over beneath an upturned wheelbarrow: he had hidden his hands in his sleeves and frozen in that position. Two were frozen back to back leaning against each other. At night the sledges went out and collected them.'

Alexander Solzhenitzin, 'The Gulag Archipelago', 1974, a novel based on the writer's experiences as a prisoner in a Soviet labour camp in the years 1945–53.

SOURCE F

'Stalin discarded Lenin's methods. He abandoned the method of persuasion and argument for that of violence, mass repression and terror. Mass arrest and deportation of many thousands of people and execution without trial and without normal investigation created conditions of insecurity, fear and even desperation.'

Nikita Khrushchev, Soviet leader after the death of Stalin, speaking to the Party Congress in 1956. In the 1930s Khrushchev was a local Communist leader in the Ukraine.

SOURCE G

Poster, 1931. It says: 'The provision of plenty of crèches, kindergartens, canteens and laundries will ensure the participation of women in socialist construction.' Soviet laws said that women must have the right to a job, to paid maternity leave and to free health care.

SOURCE H

Soviet cartoon, 1933. In the top picture the figure looking at the 1928 five-year plan is saying: 'Day-dreams! Madness! Impossible!'

SOURCE I

Stalin with Soviet leaders in 1925, published in 1925.

Stalin and other Soviet leaders in 1925, published in 1947. The leaders missing in this picture were executed in 1936 and 1938.

EXERCISE

1 a Who is the figure in the top hat in Source H?
   b Explain the message of Source H.
   c Does Source C prove that this message was true?

2 Source D speaks of the 'absence of fear' and Source F of 'mass terror'. Does this mean one of the sources is wrong?

3 Look at Source I.
   a How can you explain the difference between the two photographs?
   b Would a historian find either of them a reliable source?
   c Would a historian find either of them useful?

4 How does Source A help to explain the brutal events described in Sources E and F?

5 a Choose a source which you consider to provide reliable evidence of conditions in the USSR in the 1930s and explain why you consider it reliable.
   b Choose another source which you think cannot be relied on for this purpose and explain your reasons.

5.1 THE WORLD MARKET AND THE COMMUNIST CHALLENGE

In 1914 much of the bread eaten in Britain was made from wheat grown in Canada. If you could have followed it from the Canadian field to the British table you would have seen thousands of people involved in growing, transporting, milling, baking and distribution. Even before it was grown or started its journey, other people had to make ploughs, ships and railways. And all of these people, from the plough manufacturer at the beginning to the shopkeeper at the end, had to buy the materials they needed and sell the goods they produced. A similar chain of buying and selling in many different countries was needed to produce most other goods. There was a complicated network of world trade: a **world market**.

Belief in free competition

What if this system went wrong? What if people made too few ploughs or corn mills, or grew too much wheat? The answer usually given to this question in 1914 was that, though the system might have its ups and downs, it could not go far wrong. Everybody at every point in the market system tried to make a profit out of what they did, and it was this that kept them in step. As long as there was **free competition** between different farmers, factories or shops, people would always buy whatever was of best value. If there was too little of anything, the price would go up, so people would see the need to make more. If there was too much, the price would go down, so less would be produced. In this way the world trading system would put itself right automatically. In 1914 this theory of free competition in the market seemed obvious common sense to most business people. Some people still accept this view today, though others disagree.

A market for shares and money

To set up or run a large business, such as a railway or a factory, you need **capital** – money to buy the necessary buildings and machines. This is usually raised by setting up a company and selling **shares** in it to people who have money to spare. These **shareholders** may get a **dividend** – a share of the profits of the company if it makes any. But if people think the company is likely to do well, the shares themselves will increase in value. Some people buy shares mainly with the idea of selling them again when they have risen in value and making a profit on the deal. The market in which shares are bought and sold is the **stock exchange**. In 1914 there was one in each major country, and they were all linked together by telegraph. You could buy shares in Russian or US companies in London. There was a world market in shares.

Governments often need to borrow money. One way they do this is by selling **bonds** on which they promise to pay interest. These are bought and sold just like shares, and in 1914 the world market in them was centred in London. For instance, between 1914 and 1917, Russian governments sold bonds in London and raised £757 million to help to pay for the war.

▲ A few links in the chain of buying and selling needed to produce a loaf of bread in 1914.

Buy my goods!

Mine are cheaper— buy mine!

Mine are best value!

Producers compete to sell their goods.

How the stock market works.

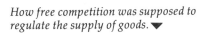

How free competition was supposed to regulate the supply of goods. ▼

The Communist challenge

Lenin and the Communists were opposed to the system of free competition in the market and to the world market in capital (see page 32). They stopped the market system working in Russia and set up a system of **state planning and control** of industry. Since 1917 there have been two rival economic systems, the market system and the Communist state system. The market system is much more widespread, but China and other countries set up state systems after 1949. The conflict between the two systems was an important reason for the division of the world into the two sides of the **cold war** after 1948 (see page 80). The question of whether they can work together peacefully is crucial for the future.

QUESTIONS

1 The diagram of the chain of buying and selling is very much simplified. For instance, it does not show that the corn mill needed machinery or that its workers had to wear shoes. Make a list of ten other items or people that are not shown in the diagram but must have existed in connection with it.

2 Look at the diagram of the stock market. Write an alternative set of speech bubbles for a time when the XYZ Company cannot sell its goods.

5.2 THE BOOMING 1920s

The United States

In the **USA** the First World War had been a time of prosperity, so in the 1920s there were plenty of people with money to invest. Wages were high compared with those in Europe, and people could afford to buy expensive items like cars. Most Americans were confident that they would go on getting richer. If they were short of money, they borrowed or bought goods on credit. This meant that there was a great demand for cars, radio sets, refrigerators and other products of new technology. You can see from the table how production went up during this **boom**. New companies were formed to make the goods that were in such demand, and many Americans saw this as an excellent chance to get rich quickly by investing their money. People made fortunes by buying shares one day and selling them the next when the price had gone up – they even borrowed the money to do it with. As long as the price went on rising, you could not lose. When anybody worried what would happen if share prices stopped rising, they were told that the market system would soon put things right.

During the boom of the 1920s the USA was by far the richest nation in the world. European countries anxious to repair war damage or to modernize their industry borrowed heavily from the USA. Between 1924 and 1928 Americans lent nearly £6,000 million to other countries. New York had taken over from London as the banking capital of the world. If anyone worried about how all this money could be paid back, the answer was that prosperity would soon grow in the borrowing countries so that they could easily repay what they owed.

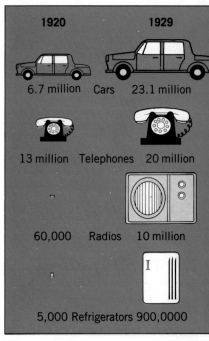

The Boom in the USA.

Germany

The 1920s were a time of recovery and prosperity for many European countries. But in **Germany** recovery was complicated by the Treaty of Versailles, which said that the country had to pay **reparations** of £6,600 million to the Allies. The only way to find so much money was by selling goods to earn it. But none of the Allies were keen to open their markets to a flood of German goods.

The Germans had from the start complained bitterly that the reparations were unfair, and in 1923 they stopped paying. The French replied by sending their army to seize control of **the Ruhr**, Germany's main industrial region, and to take coal and other goods to make up for the unpaid money. In reply the Germans went on strike, and the German economy began to grind to a halt. With few goods in the shops, prices rose rapidly. The German government made matters worse by continuing to print large amounts of paper money, which was soon worth nothing. Goods worth one mark in 1913 cost more than 700,000 million marks in November 1923. People's life savings were wiped out overnight, and whole market systems seemed about to collapse.

Economic collapse was avoided partly by the German government giving way and agreeing to pay reparations in small instalments. The other reason was US money. In 1924 an

QUESTIONS

1 In the 1920s Americans would be keen to buy shares in companies producing certain goods. Make a list of such goods and head it 'Shares likely to rise in value'.

2 Make a list of other goods in which shares would be likely to fall in value.

3 Look at Source A.
   a For how long would Ford car workers have to work for their wages to be equal to the price of a car?

SOURCE **A**

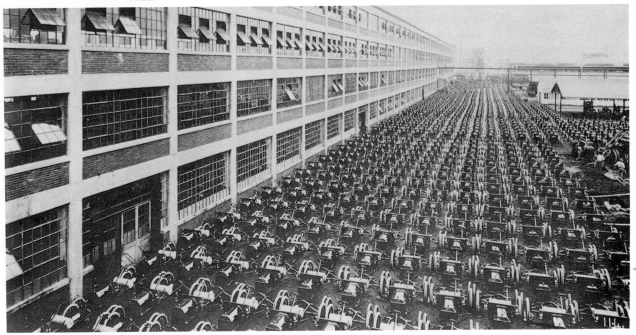

Mass production of cars: a Ford factory in the USA. Henry Ford made 15 million of his famous Model T. In 1925 he sold them for $290 (£59.60) each. A Ford worker earned $34 a week.

American banker, Charles Dawes, worked out the **Dawes Plan** for reparations. By 1932, when this system was scrapped, Germany had paid off £370 million. In the same period it borrowed £4,000 million, mainly from the USA.

Great Britain

Britain did not share in the boom of the 1920s, partly because of increased **foreign competition**. The country's great wealth in the nineteenth century had depended on its position as 'workshop of the world'. But the Industrial Revolution had now spread to many other countries. India and Japan could make cotton cloth much more cheaply than Britain; Germany could mine cheaper coal; the USA could make cheaper cars. These countries had newer and more up-to-date machinery, and some paid much lower wages. British factories found it hard to compete.

The other main source of Britain's wealth before the First World War had been its worldwide trade. But world trade in the 1920s' was less than it had been before the war. This was because of **protectionism**: most nations were keen to protect home industry against competition from abroad, so they imposed high customs duties on imported goods. For instance, the USA did this in 1922. Britain was the only major country which kept its markets open to imported goods from all other countries. If anyone worried that this might harm British industry, the answer was that the market system would work properly only if there was free trade and free competition (see page 40). After a few more years of peace and prosperity, it was said, the world trading system would get back to normal as it had been before the war, and Britain would be prosperous again.

b How might this affect the sales of cars?

c How might the number of cars sold affect the price?

4 a What percentage of its reparations bill had Germany paid off by 1932?

b Does this mean that the reparations were a mistake?

5 What arguments might have been put forward in Britain in the 1920s (i) for and (ii) against high customs duties on imported foreign goods?

5.3 THE SLUMP OF 1929–32

CAUSATION

The boom of the 1920s ended with a bang in 1929. The **Slump** (or **Great Depression**) which began then reached its worst about the year 1932. Between 1929 and 1932 world trade shrunk by two-thirds, and at least 30 million people lost their jobs. Banks went out of business, so many people lost their savings. The discontent and despair which this caused led to major political changes. For instance, in Germany it helped to bring Hitler to power (see page 50).

Too many goods
It began in the USA. One way to explain it is to say that US farms and factories were producing too many goods – more than people could afford to buy. Since about 1925 farms had been growing more food than they could sell. This meant that prices fell, and farmers and farmworkers had less to spend on factory-made goods. But until 1929 this did not have much effect on the factories in the towns. In the USA of the 1920s it was very easy to borrow money. People bought radios and refrigerators on hire purchase or borrowed from the banks to buy combine harvesters or cars.

The Wall Street crash
In 1929 this easy borrowing suddenly stopped, and instead the banks asked for their money back. This was because of the **Wall Street stock-market crash** of October 1929.

During the years 1925–9, as the price of **shares** went up and up, people scrambled madly to buy them, often with money borrowed from the banks. If the price stopped rising and fell even a little, these people had to sell quickly so as to pay back what they had borrowed. If a lot of them sold at the same time, prices were sure to fall. In October 1929 this is what happened. Suddenly there was a mad scramble to sell, and prices collapsed completely. Many people were ruined. Many banks failed to get their money back and had to go bankrupt.

This financial collapse soon affected industry. People now had no money to spend, so they stopped buying cars and radios. Factories making these things closed down, and workers were laid off. Now they in turn had no money to spend in the shops, and this made matters worse still. The USA, the richest country in the world, seemed to be in deep trouble. By 1933, 13 million Americans were unemployed, more than 4,000 banks had closed, and 20,000 companies had gone bankrupt.

The World Slump
US banks had lent money to help Germany to recover from the war and from reparations. They had also lent millions of dollars to other countries all over the world. In 1929 this lending stopped almost completely; the banks now began to ask for their money back. So in all these other countries the same results followed as in the USA. Banks collapsed, factories were closed, workers were sacked, and trade shrank. In this way the crisis that had started in the USA spread to the whole world market. The only country which was little affected was Communist Russia.

SOURCE A
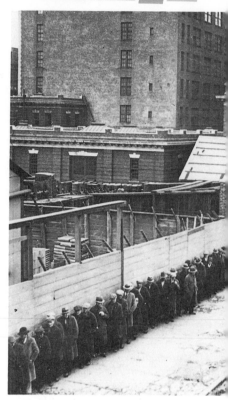

Unemployed men queue for food in the USA, 1931. There was no unemployment benefit in the USA.

SOURCE B
'In Oregon I saw thousands of bushels of apples rotting in the orchards. At the same time there are millions of children who, on account of the poverty of their parents, will not eat one apple this winter. The roads of the West and Southwest teem with hungry hitchhikers. The camp-fires of the homeless are seen along every railroad track.'

Oscar Ameringer, evidence to Congressional Committee, 1932.

President Hoover does little to help

The President of the USA from 1929 to 1933 was **Herbert Hoover**. He was leader of the Republican Party, the party of business people. He believed that it was not the government's job to interfere with banks and business. He thought that the government should not help the unemployed or the hungry. There was, he insisted, nothing seriously wrong with US business. The free market system would put things right if the government left it alone. So during the worst years of the Slump the US government did very little to help people, and things got steadily worse.

Boom. . . and Slump.

EXERCISE

1 It was very easy to borrow money in the USA in the 1920s. How did this make matters worse in 1929–32?

2 Many factories closed during the Slump. How would closing a factory affect:
   a the people who worked there?
   b the people who owned shares in it?
   c the people who supplied it with raw materials?
   d the people who bought its finished goods?
   e the shops where its workpeople and their families usually shopped?
   f the firms which supplied those shops?
   Explain what the effect would be at each step.

3 There have been many other smaller slumps or 'recessions' before and since 1929, but none quite so serious.
   a What other events of the period 1914–29 made this one specially serious?
   b How did they do this?

4 The Slump affected people's ideas about capitalism and socialism (see pages 40–1).
   a How might it have influenced the ideas of people mentioned in Sources B and C?
   b How might it have influenced people in the USSR or Germany?

SOURCE C

'More than 100,000 applications have been received at the Soviet Russian New York Office for 6,000 jobs. Applicants are skilled workers at machine construction, on the railroads, in steel mills, automobile factories, or the building industries. Three principal reasons are (1) unemployment (2) disgust with conditions here, (3) interest in the Soviet experiment.'

'Business Week' magazine, October 1931.

5.4 THE NEW DEAL

EVIDENCE

In 1932, at the depths of the Slump, **Franklin D. Roosevelt**, leader of the Democratic Party, was elected President of the USA. Within a hundred days he had passed through Congress laws to bring in what he called the **New Deal**. Roosevelt agreed with Hoover that there was nothing basically wrong with the US economic system. But he was far better at persuading people that this was so. 'The only thing we have to fear', he said, 'is fear itself.' Like Hitler he was one of the first world statesmen to use radio effectively to get his ideas and his own self-confidence across to millions of people. Roosevelt disagreed completely with Hoover about what the government should do. Although he was rich himself, he had great sympathy for the poor people who were in such distress, and he insisted that it was the government's job to help them as much as possible. One way of doing this was to bring in strict **regulation** of the **banks** and **stock market**. Another was to get farmers to produce less crops, so that the price would rise to a reasonable level again. He spent $7,000 million of taxpayers' money on **public works** like roads and dams, to create jobs. He brought in old-age **pensions** and **unemployment insurance** and forced employers to work with the trade unions and to bargain with them over wages.

SOURCE B

'Dear Mr President, This is just to tell you that everything is all right now. The man you sent found our house all right and we went down to the bank with him and the mortgage can go on for a while longer. You remember I wrote about losing the furniture too. Well, your man got it back for us. I never heard of a President like you.'

Letter to President Roosevelt. As part of the New Deal the government lent money to people who could not keep up their mortgage payments.

SOURCE A

Unemployment in the USA, 1925–45.

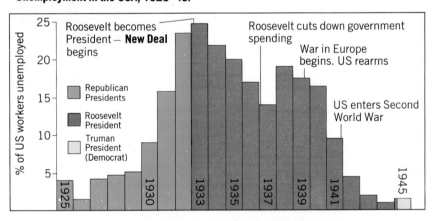

The New Deal was very popular with ordinary Americans, and Roosevelt was re-elected in 1936 and again in 1940 and 1944. But many business people were horrified. In their opinion the New Deal went against the system of free market capitalism that had made them (and the USA) rich. Congress had given Roosevelt and his government far more power than any earlier President, and the Republicans argued that this was a danger to freedom. In 1935–6 they were able to get the Supreme Court (the highest US court) to overthrow part of the New Deal. For instance, the New Deal had fixed minimum wages and maximum hours of work for many millions of workers. In 1935 the Court declared this to be against the US constitution. But many other parts of the New Deal, like the pensions scheme and the control of farm prices, became permanent parts of the US system.

SOURCE C

A dam being built on the river Tennessee. The Tennessee Valley Authority was part of the New Deal. It used government money to build dams and power-stations, prevent soil erosion and get people into jobs. By 1940 this once-derelict area had become prosperous.

In some ways the New Deal was only partly successful. But it was a complete success in restoring the confidence of Americans in their way of life. Some people in 1933 thought that if things went on getting worse there might be a revolution in the USA. The New Deal may have prevented this from happening.

SOURCE D

This poster was part of a campaign by US business firms in 1936.

SOURCE E

A farmer and his sons in a dust storm, Oklahoma, 1936.

EXERCISE

1 Study the graph showing US unemployment. Which of the following statements can be supported from the graph? Explain your answer.
   a The New Deal solved the unemployment problem in the USA.
   b The New Deal helped to reduce unemployment in the USA.
   c Rearmament and war really solved the unemployment problem.

2 Do you think the writer of Source B was in favour of the New Deal? Explain your answer.

3 Many US business people were against the New Deal. Why do you think some firms paid for posters like Source D?

4 Source E is a photograph taken in 1936. Does this mean that the New Deal was a failure?

5 Sources D and E give very different impressions of the United States in 1936. Does this mean one of them must be useless to the historian? Give reasons for your answer.

6 Source A is based on official US figures. Does this mean it cannot be biased? Give reasons for your answer.

7 Which of the sources on this page is most useful for the study of the New Deal? Explain your answer.

5.5 DICTATORS AND DEMOCRACY IN EUROPE, 1919–39

Britain Unsuccessful attempts by fascist leader Sir Oswald Mosley to gain power 1931–9

Germany Adolf Hitler (1933–45) dictator

USSR 1929–55 Stalin in complete power

■ Dictatorships 1919–39

■ Democracies

Estonia 1934
Latvia 1934
Lithuania 1926

Poland Army seizes power 1926; Josef Pilsudski dictator 1926

Portugal Army seizes power 1926; Salazar dictator 1932–68

Romania
King Carol makes himself sole ruler 1938

Iron Guard (Romanian fascist)

Bulgaria King Boris makes himself dictator 1934, supported by army

Greece Metaxas dictator 1934

Hungary also a dictatorship most of this period

Spain Civil War 1936–9; army seizes power 1939; Franco dictator 1939–75

Italy Mussolini dictator 1922–43

Yugoslavia King Alexander makes himself dictator 1929, supported by army

Mussolini's party symbol, the 'fasces', an Ancient Roman symbol of power

QUESTIONS

1 Using the map, make a list of the dictators, with the dates when they came to power.

2 Underline those who took power after the Slump began in 1929.

3 How might the Slump have influenced the rise of these dictators?

4 Look back at page 24. Which countries were very undemocratic before the First World War? How might this have helped dictators to take power afterwards?

5 What kinds of people would be likely to have supported the fascists?

Democracy means 'people power'. For a country to be a democracy, all of its people must have a vote. But to use the vote effectively, you need some other things as well:

- **Freedom of speech and of information**, so that you can read what books and newspapers you like, make up your own mind and say what you think.

- **Freedom to join or form political parties**, to oppose or support the government if you want to.

- **Personal freedom**, the right not to be arrested, imprisoned, bullied or threatened by anybody, whether the police, your landlord or your employer.

In a **dictatorship** all the people may have a vote, but the government is run by one man (the dictator) or by a small group. Dictators usually take control of the press, radio and television and perhaps of education in the schools. They usually ban political parties opposing them. They often arrest and imprison people who oppose them. They sometimes torture and kill them.

A dicatorship that claimed to be democratic

If you check this definition of dictatorship against the description of Soviet Russia under Lenin and Stalin in pages 34–7 you will find that their system was clearly a dictatorship. They called it **'the dictatorship of the proletariat'** (or working class). But they also said that any country which had a class system could not possibly be a democracy, because the ruling class was bound to control things (see page 32). So the 'classless society' that they hoped to build would be the only real democracy. Most of the Communist countries today call themselves 'people's democracies' for this reason.

Fascists

It was **Mussolini**, the Italian dictator, who called his followers **fascists**, but the word is often used to describe others who had (or still have) similar ideas. It is a mistake to think that the fascist dictators were all the same, but many of them did have the following ideas in common:

- They bitterly opposed communism and socialism.

- They banned political parties other than their own.

- They banned trade unions and co-operated with landlords and factory owners.

- They liked the idea of using force and often seized power violently.

- They thought war was noble and admired the army.

- They stood up strongly for their nation against all others. Many of them hated other races of people, such as the Jews or blacks.

5.6 THE RISE OF HITLER

When the Kaiser gave up his throne in 1918, Germany became a republic. The **Weimar Republic**, as it was called, was democratic but weak. In the years 1919–23 several groups tried to overthrow it by force. Communists hoped to copy the recent success of Lenin's Red Guards in Russia. Many of those opposed to communism, often ex-soldiers with no jobs and little hope, joined private armies or *Freikorps*. One of these unemployed anti-communist ex-soldiers was **Adolf Hitler**.

Hitler had been a 'drop-out' in Vienna before the war. In 1914 he joined the German army, and this gave him something to live for – a burning sense of German greatness and power. When defeat came in 1918, Hitler, like many other Germans, could not accept it. Germany must have been betrayed, perhaps by the Jews, perhaps by the Communists, perhaps by the politicians who now ran the Weimar Republic. Hitler and others like him formed a new party, the **National Socialist German Workers' Party** (**Nazis** for short). Its aim was not to win votes and elections but to seize power by force, so it built up a private army of thugs and ex-soldiers. They wore brown shirts and were known as the **SA**, short for *Sturm Abteilung* (storm-troopers).

The main aim of the Nazi Party was to abolish the Treaty of Versailles and unite all Germans, including those in Austria and Czechoslovakia, in one country. In this new Germany, Jews would not be allowed rights as citizens. The Nazis also promised to give German workers a share in the profits of industry, to improve old-age pensions and to do other things to help the poor.

In 1923 Hitler believed that his chance had come. The German currency collapsed during quarrels with the Allies over reparations (see page 27). Many people lost their savings. Hitler thought he could take advantage of the discontent in **Munich** where he lived. Seizing control there, he announced that the Nazis were setting up a new German government. But he had little support in the rest of Germany, and the army, much to his surprise, supported the Weimar government against him. He was arrested, tried and sent to prison.

Hitler's trial made him a national figure. He was in prison for only nine months, during which time he wrote a book, *Mein Kampf* ('My Struggle'), to spread his ideas. He also decided to change the tactics of the Nazi Party. From now on it would try to gain control by standing for election to the Reichstag like the other parties.

In the years 1924–8 Germany became prosperous again, and people were more contented. Perhaps democratic Germany would settle down peacefully with its neighbours. Then in 1929 came the world **Slump** (see page 44). You can see from the graph what happened. By January 1933 more than 6 million Germans were unemployed. The Communists said that capitalism was failing and that the time had come for a revolution. But although the Communists gained support, Hitler gained even more. In November 1932 he was leader of the largest party in the Reichstag

SOURCE A

'So it had all been in vain. In vain all the sacrifices. In vain the death of two millions. Had they died for this, so that a gang of wretched criminals could lay hands on the Fatherland?'

Hitler, 'Mein Kampf', 1924.

SOURCE B

'I am not a criminal. There is no such thing as high treason against the traitors of 1918. It is not you, gentlemen, who pass judgement on us. History will judge us as Germans who only wanted the good of their people and Fatherland, who wanted to fight and to die.'

Hitler speaking at his trial in 1923.

Adolf Hitler.

and claimed that he should be Germany's **Chancellor** (Prime Minister). In January 1933 he was sworn in.

Once in power, Hitler destroyed the Weimar Republic. In February 1933 the Reichstag building was burned down, and Hitler succeeded in laying the blame on the Communists, though it seems likely that the Nazis set it on fire themselves. They certainly got the benefit, since they used the scare to arrest Communists, to ban their newspapers and to let the SA loose to beat up anti-Nazis. Six days later came the last election shown on the graph. When the new Reichstag met, Hitler brought forward a law giving him the power of a dictator – the right to issue emergency laws without asking anyone. The Reichstag passed this **Enabling Act** by 441 votes to 94 on 23 March 1933. German democracy was dead.

SOURCE D

'The elections will certainly be the last for the next ten years, probably even for the next hundred years.'

Herman Goering, a leading Nazi, speaking to a meeting of bankers and business men in March 1933. They gave DM 3 million for election expenses.

SOURCE C

Seats won in elections to Reichstag 1928–33

Nazi seats

Communist seats

Unemployment in Germany 1928–33

Unemployment and election results in Germany, 1928–33.

Election poster, 1932: 'We want work and bread. Elect Hitler.'

QUESTIONS

1 a Explain what Hitler meant by 'criminals' in Source A and 'traitors' in Source B.
b What kinds of people would be likely to have agreed with him?

2 What kinds of people was the poster, Source C, designed to influence?

3 Look at the graphs.
a How successful was Hitler by 1928?
b What connection can you suggest between the two graphs?

4 Look at Source D and at the graphs. Why should bankers and business men have supported the Nazis?

5 a 'The German people voted Hitler into power.'
b 'Hitler got into power by tricking the German people.' Is either of these statements true, or are they both true? Explain your answer.

5.7 ONE NATION, ONE RACE, ONE LEADER

Germany, 1933–9: growth of a police state

Hitler's system of government in Germany was very simple: he was the leader, and his will was law. He banned all political parties except his own, and all trade unions. The same principle applied inside the Nazi Party itself. Ernst Röhm, leader of the SA, disagreed with Hitler and wanted to bring the army under party control. Others wanted to attack the rich. In June 1934 Hitler had Röhm and several hundred other people murdered by his personal bodyguard, the SS. After that he was unchallenged.

Germany became a **police state**. Anybody who opposed the Nazis actively was arrested. Special prisons, **concentration camps**, were set up. A political police force, the **Gestapo**, was given powers to arrest anyone suspected of even speaking against Hitler. People were imprisoned, beaten up and hanged with no chance of a fair trial. Before 1939 there were never more than about 25,000 prisoners in the concentration camps, but that was enough to silence most other Germans.

Controlling people's ideas

Joseph Goebbels was Hitler's **Minister of Propaganda**. His organization ran all the radio stations and also some of the newspapers, while censoring the rest. In this way he made sure that the people of Germany heard plenty about the successes of the Nazis and nothing about their brutality. The Nazi Party often organized marches and rallies, which were carefully stage-managed to impress the people and make them proud to be Germans and Nazis.

Hitler took special care to control the minds of young people. He wanted the next generation trained not to think for themselves but to dedicate themselves without question to the Nazi Party. In the schools, history textbooks were rewritten to show the wickedness of the Jews and the unfairness of the Treaty of Versailles. All young people, except Jews, were supposed to join the **Hitler Youth** or the **League of German Maidens**. In these organizations they were taught to look forward to the honour of fighting for the Fatherland or of bearing sons who could fight. They took part in political marches and rallies, went camping and followed other outdoor pursuits. They enjoyed the comradeship and the excitement.

An end to unemployment

Germany had 6 million unemployed in 1933. Hitler solved this problem partly by **public works** and partly by building up the **armed forces**. About a million people were set to work to build motorways and bridges; and by 1939 there were 1.4 million men in the forces. But most of the new jobs were in **armaments**. There were big government orders for guns, planes and tanks. The factory owners had to make what they were told to, but their factories were busy; strikes were forbidden by law, and profits were high. As for the workers, they had long hours and low wages. On the other hand, they had jobs and could eat. In 1939 there were only 300,000 unemployed.

SOURCE **A**

SOURCE **B**

Attacks on the Jews
Anti-Semitism was not new. It dated back in Europe to the Middle Ages. In Hitler's Germany it was developed into a complete racial theory. This was that the Germans and north Europeans (or 'Aryans') were a 'master race', born to rule over the other 'slave races'. The Jews were singled out as a 'poison race' who had plotted against Germany (and the world) and would corrupt it if not checked.

The theory was complete nonsense in both biological and historical terms, but this did not stop it being taught in schools and universities. It supplied an excuse for the increasing persecution of Germany's half-million Jews. They were beaten and bullied. Germans were forbidden to marry them or to work as servants in their homes. The SA organized a boycott of Jewish shops. Synagogues were smashed and Jewish leaders imprisoned. About a quarter of a million German Jews were able to escape to other countries. The rest stayed and suffered – their situation got worse and worse as time went on.

Support for Hitler
A few brave Germans openly protested against Nazi actions and were sent to concentration camps. Others were secretly horrified. But most looked the other way and saw a different side of Nazism. Hitler stood for order and discipline, for a strong and proud Germany. Many people in positions of power or authority in Germany – landowners, business leaders, judges, army officers, teachers – agreed strongly with the idea of discipline and order. Before 1933 they had been worried at the weakness of the Weimar Republic and frightened of communism. But by 1939 Germany appeared strong and united. Other countries in Europe copied some of Hitler's methods (see page 48). Hitler had already overthrown the Treaty of Versailles (see page 58). Goebbels's newspapers were full of this sort of news, saying nothing about the concentration camps. So it is not very surprising that most Germans supported Hitler with enthusiasm.

A Nazi rally, 1935.

The Volkswagen or 'People's Car'. Hitler set up a factory to make these cars in 1938. The poster reads: 'Save 5 marks a week if you want to ride in your own car. Information about prices and how to pay available at any Strength through Joy establishment.' Thousands of workers started paying, but no cars were produced until after the Second World War.

QUESTIONS

1 Some Germans were better off as a result of Hitler's policies, and others were worse off. How might each of the following have been affected?
  ● a factory worker,
  ● a housewife,
  ● a factory owner,
  ● an army officer,
  ● a school pupil.
  Explain your answers.

2 Study the poster, Source B. No German worker who joined this scheme got a car. Do you think that the poster would have succeeded in encouraging Germans to support Hitler?

3 Look back at page 46 on the New Deal in the USA.
  a What problems did both Hitler and Roosevelt face?
  b In what way did they both try the same methods?
  c In what way were their methods different?

5.8 FAILURE OF THE LEAGUE OF NATIONS

Japan attacks China

Japan has never been part of another country's empire. Even in the late nineteenth century, when the Europeans controlled most of the rest of the world, they did not control Japan. Instead the Japanese copied European methods. They built up their own army, navy and industry on European lines, and they also copied the European idea of building an overseas empire. They captured Korea, Taiwan and Port Arthur in China (see map). During the First World War, Japan was on the Allied side and expected to be able to increase its control of China as a reward. But Britain and the USA would not agree to this, mainly because they wanted to trade freely in China themselves.

The young officers of the Japanese army thought, like Hitler, that war was glorious and noble. They believed that their country, like Germany, had been cheated in the 1919 peace settlement. In 1929 the world Slump hit Japan just as hard as it hit Europe. Half the country's factories closed down, and many farmers were ruined. It seemed to the young officers serving in Port Arthur that it would be easy to seize a large part of China by force. Japan could then go on to solve its problems by building up a large empire, like the British Empire.

The officers knew that there was no chance of the government accepting this plan. So in 1931 they picked a quarrel with the Chinese on the border and attacked without asking permission from Tokyo. They rapidly overran large parts of **Manchuria**. The Japanese government and the Emperor were horrified at first, but the people of Japan were wildly enthusiastic. The government then gave its approval, and the army went on to capture the whole of Manchuria.

These events had two important results. In Japan they encouraged the army and those politicians who wanted to go on with military conquest and expansion. In 1937 they began an all-out attack on the rest of **China** which helped to cause the Second World War. The second result was the effect on the **League of Nations**. China and Japan were both members of the League. If the League could not stop one of its members attacking another, it was obviously not much use. The League made careful enquiries and in 1933 announced that the Japanese were in the wrong. Japan promptly left the League. Nothing else was done.

Italy attacks Abyssinia

Japan and Germany were not the only countries to think that the peace settlement of 1919 was unfair. So did **Italy**. The Italians had fought hard on the Allied side and had gained little at the peace.

Like Hitler and the Japanese officers, **Mussolini** thought that war was noble and glorious, and in 1935 he saw a chance of easy success. **Abyssinia** (now called Ethiopia) was small, weak and backward. Although independent, it was sandwiched in between Italian, British and French colonies. In October 1935 Mussolini attacked Abyssinia with planes, tanks, bombs and poison gas – all the modern weapons. The Abyssinians, with their out-of-date rifles, stood no chance.

Japanese overseas conquests.

SOURCE **A**

British cartoon by David Low, 1932.

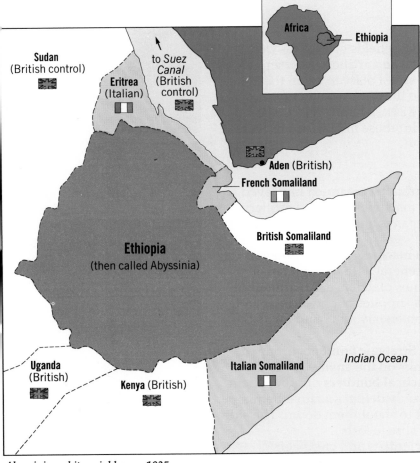

Abyssinia and its neighbours, 1935.

Abyssinia was a member of the League of Nations and appealed for help. This set a problem for the governments of Britain and France. They were beginning to worry about possible danger from Germany so they wanted Italy's friendship. On the other hand, most people in Britain and France could see that the Italian attack was wicked and brutal. So at the League meeting Britain and France voted for **sanctions**. This meant cutting off some trade with Italy. But they made sure that they did not cut off the trade which would have stopped the Italian planes and tanks overnight – the trade in oil. At the same time they secretly suggested to Mussolini that he should be satisfied with half of Abyssinia. But the secret leaked out, and Mussolini went ahead regardless and took the whole country.

SOURCE B

THE LEAGUE ? PAH !
THE LEAGUE IS CONTEMPTIBLE !
THE LEAGUE CAN DO NOTHING !

Mussolini, drawn by Low, 1935.

QUESTIONS

1 How similar were the reasons behind Japan's attack on Manchuria and Italy's on Abyssinia?

2 How similar were the reactions of the League to the two attacks?

3 Could the events in Manchuria have affected Mussolini's decision to attack Abyssinia?

4 What influence was the League likely to have after 1936?

5 a Do you think that Low's cartoons are fair?
  b What influence might cartoons like Low's have had?

6 What reasons can you suggest for the failure of the League?

6.1 TECHNOLOGY AND WAR

CHANGE

The First World War

The weapons that dominated the battlefields of 1914–18 were the **machine-gun** (invented in the 1860s) and **artillery** for firing high explosives (invented in 1866). The safest place to be on these battlefields was in a deep **trench**, so the armies could not move easily – it was a static war (see page 20). Aircraft were first used for war in 1914 and tanks in 1916. But these new weapons were still at an early stage of development.

The Second World War

In the 1920s and 1930s tanks and aircraft were much improved. When war broke out again in 1939 machine-guns and artillery were still important, but it was the tanks and aircraft that dominated the battle of 1939–45.

Inside a **tank** you were safe from machine-gun fire and you could travel at up to 20 mph. So a general with enough tanks could punch a hole in the enemy lines of defence. An **armoured division**, with lorries to carry all its supplies of petrol, food and ammunition, could cut in behind an enemy army and force it to surrender (see first diagram).

Aircraft were used in two ways. **Strategic bombers** dropped high-explosives or incendiary bombs on the enemy's war factories or civilian population. **Tactical bombers** dropped them on enemy troops or warships. The only defence against bombers was to have enough **fighter aircraft** to shoot them down. The side without air cover would be almost sure to lose.

During the Second World War scientists and engineers designed many **new weapons**. Among these were long-range rocket weapons and the atomic bomb, the first nuclear weapon. These new weapons were used at the end of the war, and the two atomic bombs dropped on Japan may have forced it to surrender in 1945. But the main importance of rockets and nuclear weapons lay in the years after 1945.

Since 1945

Nuclear weapons have not been used again since 1945, though they have been developed a great deal. There have been about two hundred local wars during this period, still dominated by tanks and aircraft. But the terrible threat of nuclear weapons has hung like a nightmare over the world.

At first, nuclear bombs had to be carried by manned bombers, which would take hours to get to their target and might get shot down on the way. Then, in the 1960s, long-distance rockets were developed. They can carry a nuclear warhead 5,000 miles or more in less than half an hour. These **intercontinental ballistic missiles (ICBMs)** can hit a target anywhere in the world. There is no reliable way of shooting them down, and no certain defence against them. Instead each country possessing nuclear weapons has missiles hidden in safe places (such as in deep-sea submarines). Then, even if the home country is destroyed, they can still be used to strike back and destroy the enemy country. This is called **mutually assured destruction ('MAD')**.

Armoured division

Supply lines

Supply lines

Enemy defence lines

Tank breakthrough.

SOURCE **A**

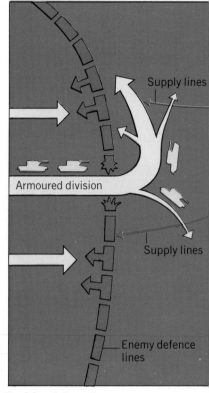

Lancaster bomber, 1944. The RAF's main strategic bomber, it could drop about 5 tonnes of high explosives. One thousand Lancasters might take part in a raid.

SOURCE **B**

Hospital in Hiroshima after the bomb, 1945. The atom bomb dropped here had the power of 15,000 tonnes of high explosives. It killed about 70,000 people outright. Perhaps as many more died later from burns or radiation sickness.

EXERCISE

1 a Make a list of the weapons mentioned in this unit. Against each write the dates of invention or development.

b What effect did each weapon have on the way wars were fought (or not fought)?

c Which of the new weapons was most important? Explain your choice.

2 If a defence minister wanted money for new weapons in 1910 or 1935 or 1965, what arguments might he have used?

3 'This has spoiled war!' was the comment of a German officer in 1945 when he heard of the atomic bomb. Can you explain what he meant?

Since the 1960s it has been likely that a major war would turn much of the world into a radioactive desert, killing most people and animals. This is so horrible a prospect that all the countries concerned claim that they have nuclear weapons only as a **deterrent**, to warn off possible attackers.

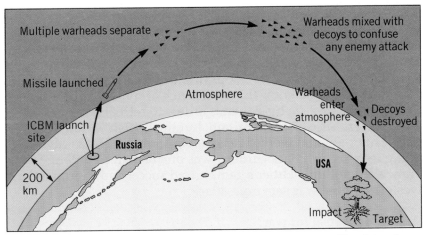

ICBMs can carry several warheads, each aimed at a different target. They have the power of between 40 and 1,600 Hiroshima bombs.

6.2 GETTING READY FOR WAR AGAIN?

Disarmament

People have often hoped for a peaceful world with no weapons and no wars. This hope was strong in the 1920s, after the horrors of the trenches. In 1928 the world's major nations signed a treaty, the **Kellogg–Briand Pact**, promising not to start a war by attacking their neighbours. In 1932–3 the League of Nations organized a conference to discuss plans for **disarmament**. But instead in 1933 Europe began to rearm. What went wrong?

One answer is that Hitler came to power in Germany. The Treaty of Versailles allowed Germany a very small army of only 100,000 men, and left its frontier wide open to French attack. Hitler made it clear to the League's conference that the first step would have to be an increase in Germany's army. The French would never agree to this. France felt safer with the Versailles system. So the disarmament conference failed, and Hitler announced that Germany was leaving the League.

Rearmament

Hitler was determined to restore Germany's military strength. It took time to build planes and tanks and to train men, but by 1935 Germany's new air force and growing army were strong enough for Hitler to take a risk. He openly announced that he had broken the Versailles treaty limits on German weapons; that his air force was as strong as the RAF; and that he was now going to bring in conscription – another breach of the treaty. Germany had a larger population than France, so in a few years the German army would be bigger than the French. France and Britain, however, saw no immediate danger and did nothing. In 1935 Britain even agreed that Hitler could break another of the Versailles limits by building a number of battleships. In the years 1935–9 Germany built up its forces as fast as it could. So did Italy. France and Britain followed suit and began to modernize their defences. Most people were horrified at the idea of another war, but Europe was **rearming** fast.

Hitler moves troops into the Rhineland

The Treaty of Versailles had forbidden Germany to keep troops in the **Rhineland** on its frontier with France. The idea was to make it impossible for Germany to defend itself against a French attack. In March 1936 Hitler broke this part of the treaty by sending a small number of troops into the Rhineland. It was a gamble, because he knew that the French army was still stronger than his, and he gave his generals orders to retreat if the French attacked. France consulted Britain, but the British would not help. Hitler's action seemed reasonable enough. 'He is only going into his own back garden,' was one British comment. So France did nothing. Hitler's gamble had succeeded. Germany's western frontier was safe from attack.

A dress rehearsal for war?

The other important event of 1936 was the beginning of the **Spanish Civil War**. This was caused mainly by Spain's internal

SOURCE D

Do not misunderstand me when the government say that they are looking to our defences. I give you my word that there will be no great rearmament.'

British Prime Minister Stanley Baldwin, election speech, November 1935. Baldwin's party won the election.

SOURCE E

'German and Italian rearmament is proceeding much more rapidly than rearmament can in England. In three years Germany will be ready.'

Hitler, in private conversation with Mussolini's son-in-law, Count Ciano, October 1936.

▼ *In 1937 Guernica, a small Spanish town, was destroyed by German bombers. It showed the world what bombs could do.*

problems, but it soon got mixed up with wider events. The Spanish government consisted of Socialists and Communists. **General Franco**, who led an army rebellion against them, held many of the same ideas as Hitler. Above all he was against communism. Germany and Italy sent troops and supplies to Franco, and this was probably the main reason for his success in 1939. The USSR sent some help to the Spanish government, but more came from private individuals from many lands. They considered the Spanish war to be a war for freedom and democracy against fascism. Hitler and Mussolini saw Spain as a useful testing ground for their new weapons.

The British and French governments found it difficult to know what to do, so they decided to keep out. They persuaded Germany, Italy and the USSR to sign an agreement to send no help to either side. The Germans and Italians signed but went on helping Franco as before, and the USSR went back to helping the Spanish government. The British and French sat back and did nothing, and by April 1939 General Franco had won.

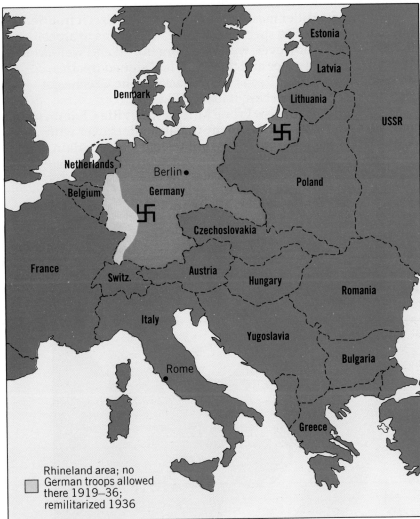

Germany and its neighbours in 1935.

Rhineland area; no German troops allowed there 1919–36; remilitarized 1936

6.3 **FOUR STEPS TO WAR, 1938–9**

Step one – Austria

Austria is a German-speaking country, and many Austrians, like Hitler himself, looked upon themselves as Germans. There were also many German-speaking people in other parts of eastern Europe, such as Czechoslovakia. Hitler's idea was to unite all Germans in one country ruled by himself from Berlin. He called it **Greater Germany**. In March 1938 he took the first step.

Hitler arranged for the local Nazis in Austria to demand union with Germany, and he sent troops to the border to threaten the Austrian government and make it agree. Instead it decided to organize a **plebiscite** (a vote) on the matter. Hitler promptly moved his troops in. He announced that Austria was now part of Germany, arrested all who disagreed and then held his own plebiscite. Ninety-nine percent of the votes were for union with Germany.

Step two – Czechoslovakia: the Sudetenland

In the **Sudetenland** area of **Czechoslovakia** most people were German speakers. In the summer of 1938 they demanded union with Germany. Hitler massed his troops on the Czech frontier and made threatening speeches to force the Czechs to agree. Czechoslovakia, however, was a well-organized and well-armed democracy. Both France and the USSR had signed treaties promising help if the Czechs were attacked. The Czechs got ready to defend themselves. It looked like war.

At this point the British Prime Minister, **Neville Chamberlain**, took the lead. He flew to Germany to talk matters over with Hitler. Hitler kept up his threats, but he told Chamberlain that

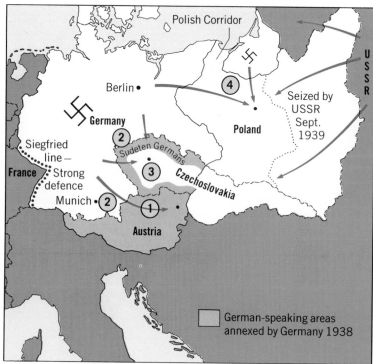

Four steps to war.

David Low cartoon, July 1936.

'Nightmare Waiting List', David Low cartoon, September 1938.

David Low cartoon, September 1939.

the Sudetenland was 'his last territorial demand', and Chamberlain believed him. At a conference held at **Munich**, Germany, France, Italy and Britain agreed that the Czechs would have to give up the Sudetenland to Germany. Then they called in the Czechs and told them that, if they refused, and decided to fight, the French would not help them. The Czechs had no choice but to give way. Hitler moved his troops in, among cheering crowds of Sudeten Germans. When Chamberlain returned to Britain he announced that he had brought back 'peace in our time'. He thought that his policy of giving Hitler what he wanted, or **appeasement**, had prevented war.

Step three – Czechoslovakia: the remainder

Czechoslovakia's frontier defences were entirely in the areas now lost to Germany. Hitler waited only until the spring of 1939 before moving his troops into the rest of Czechoslovakia and breaking it up entirely. So much for his 'last demand'. Even Chamberlain was now alarmed. It seemed very likely that Hitler's next victim would be Poland. The **'Polish corridor'** was the only piece of land taken from Germany at Versailles that Hitler still had to recover. So Britain and France now publicly promised to help the Poles if Hitler attacked them. It was not very clear how they could do this, but they hoped that the threat of war might be enough.

Step four – Poland

Everybody could see that a German attack on **Poland** was likely in the summer of 1939. The prospect worried the Soviet government a great deal. The USSR knew that Hitler was bitterly anti-communist. It knew too that he had vague plans for what he called *Lebensraum* or 'living space'. This meant the right of Germans to settle throughout eastern Europe and southern Russia and to gain economic control there.

Because of these fears, in April 1939 Stalin offered to join Britain and France in a military alliance against Germany. But there were serious complications: the Poles hated and feared Stalin's USSR, and the British and French governments were strongly anti-communist. Then, while the British and French were wondering what to do, the seemingly impossible happened. Hitler and Stalin made an agreement, the **Nazi–Soviet Pact** of August 1939. They agreed not to fight each other and also, in secret, decided to draw a line down the middle of Poland and take half each.

There was little to stop Hitler taking his half straight away. He moved his armies in on 1 September 1939. The Poles had no chance against them. It seemed to Hitler that he had called the bluff of Britain and France and that there was nothing they could do to help Poland. But to Hitler's surprise they kept their promise and declared war on 3 September. This made no difference to the speed with which Germany and the USSR gobbled up Poland – it took them about a month. In the long run, however, the world was never to be the same again.

QUESTIONS

1 Each one of the four 'steps to war' made the next one easier for Hitler to take. Explain how this was so.

2 Hitler knew that Britain and France had promised to help Poland in 1939, but he thought they would not keep their promise. What earlier events might have encouraged him to think this?

3 Study Source A.
  a What names of countries might be written instead of the question marks?
  b Who was the cartoonist criticizing? Explain your answer.

4 Study Source C.
  a Why are Hitler and Stalin insulting each other?
  b Why are they bowing so politely?
  c Whose is the body over which they are bowing? Explain your answer.

5 Historians have used the following factors to explain the coming of war in 1939: mistakes in the Treaty of Versailles; Hitler's aggressive policy; appeasement; distrust between the USSR and non-communist countries. Choose the factor which you consider most important and explain your choice.

6.4 **MUNICH: PEACE WITH HONOUR?**

EMPATHY

At the **Munich Conference** of 1938 the British Prime Minister, **Neville Chamberlain**, helped Hitler to take control of the **Sudetenland**, the German-speaking region of Czechoslovakia. In 1939 Hitler seized the rest of that country and went on to attack Poland and start the Second World War. It is hard for us, knowing about this, to see how a British Prime Minister could have co-operated with Hitler in 1938.

SOURCE A

'Germany wants peace. The principal effect of every war is to destroy the flower of the nation. Germany needs peace and desires peace!'

Hitler, speech to the Reichstag, May 1935.

SOURCE C

We, the German Führer and Chancellor and the British Prime Minister, have had a further meeting today and are agreed in recognising that the question of Anglo-German relations is of the first importance for the two countries and for Europe.

We regard the agreement signed last night and the Anglo-German Naval Agreement as symbolic of the desire of our two peoples never to go to war with one another again.

We are resolved that the method of consultation shall be the method adopted to deal with any other questions that may concern our two countries, and we are determined to continue our efforts to remove possible sources of difference and thus to contribute to assure the peace of Europe.

▶ *Agreement signed by Hitler and Chamberlain at Munich, 30 September 1938.*

SOURCE B

'Whatever one may think of Hitler's methods, there can be no doubt that he has achieved a marvellous transformation in the spirit of the people. As to his popularity, especially among the young of Germany, there can be no doubt. The old trust him; the young idolize him. The idea of a Germany intimidating Europe forms no part of the new vision. The Germans no longer have any desire to invade any other land.'

David Lloyd George, former British Liberal Prime Minister, quoted in the 'Daily Express', November 1936. Lloyd George had just visited Germany and met Hitler.

SOURCE D

Downing Street, 30 September 1938. Chamberlain waves back to the cheering crowd. He told them: 'I believe it is peace for our time.'

SOURCE E

'When I think of those four terrible years, and I think of the millions of young men who were cut off in their prime, the 13 million who were maimed and mutilated, the misery and suffering of the mothers and the fathers, the sons and the daughters of those who were killed – then I am bound to say to all the world: "In war, whichever side may call itself victor, there are no winners but all are losers." It is these thoughts that have made me feel it my duty to strain every nerve to avoid a repetition of the Great War.'

Prime Minister Neville Chamberlain, speaking to supporters in 1938.

SOURCE F

'How horrible, fantastic, incredible it is that we should be digging trenches and trying on gas-masks here, because of a quarrel in a far-off country between people of whom we know nothing.'

Neville Chamberlain, radio broadcast, 22 September 1938.

SOURCE G

'We have sustained a total and unmitigated defeat. All the countries of Middle Europe will be drawn one after another into the vast system of Nazi policies. Do not suppose that this is the end. It is only the beginning.'

SOURCE H

'Czechoslovakia lost territories which it would probably have been wiser not to have included at Versailles in the Czech State. I wrote to Mr Chamberlain when it was all over: "Millions of mothers will be blessing your name tonight for having saved their sons from the horrors of war." The verdict of history will assuredly be that the Prime Minister was right. I wrote at the time: "The day may come when we may be forced to fight Germany again. If we have to do so I trust that the cause may be one in which the morality of our case is so clear as to ensure us the full support of the British people." This would not have been the case in September 1938.'

Nevile Henderson, British Ambassador in Berlin in 1938, writing in 1940.

SOURCE I

Woman of 40: 'Things will be a lot better now, thank God. Chamberlain had done it for once, hasn't he? This'll stop it.'

Man of 45: 'He's done the right thing. He tried to mediate, and that was wanted by everybody. Who wants a bloody war? Let 'em fight it if they do.'

Man of 70: 'I think he's doing wrong. He should have gone to Czechoslovakia first. I'm an old soldier. Why shouldn't the Czechs fight for their country? Why should we allow a bully like Hitler to dominate Europe? Let's fight him and finish with it.'

Mass Observation, interviews with ordinary British people, September 1938.

◀ *Winston Churchill MP, speaking about Munich in the House of Commons, October 1938.*

EXERCISE

1 Do you think Chamberlain regarded the Munich Agreement as a success? Give reasons for your answer.

2 Why do you think the crowd (Source D) welcomed Chamberlain back from Munich so enthusiastically?

3 Winston Churchill (Source G) and the 70 year-old man (Source I) did not approve of the Munich Agreement. Do you think they both had the same reasons?

4 Look back at Source B on page 60. What opinion did the cartoonist have about the Munich Agreement?

5 'Chamberlain was stupid. Everyone could see that Hitler had to be stopped. Munich was the time he should have done it.'
 Is this a valid judgement of the situation in 1938? Give reasons for your answer.

6.5 HOW IMPORTANT WAS HITLER IN CAUSING WAR?

CAUSATION

How important was Adolf Hitler to the outbreak of the Second World War? Did he control events, or was he swept along by them? There were some factors in world history in the 1920s and 1930s that were much more powerful than any one person. For instance, some people in many countries were bitterly opposed to the terms of the Treaty of Versailles. Another 'impersonal factor' was the horror of the war that many people felt. Yet another was the world Slump and the massive unemployment of the early 1930s. During the 1930s these, and other factors like them, combined in a pattern that led to war in 1939. What part did Hitler play in this deadly pattern?

This question can be split up into three others:

- What personal qualities made Hitler such a powerful leader?

- Did Hitler's personal decisions give events an unexpected twist?

- Did events work out the way Hitler expected?

Look back at pages 48–63 and use your knowledge of the period and the sources on this page to work out your answers.

SOURCE A

'A man who is born to be a dictator is not compelled: he wills it. It is his duty to step forward.'

Hitler at his trial in Munich in 1923.

SOURCE B

Nazi election poster. The words read: 'Yes! Führer (Leader), we follow you!'

SOURCE C

'I don't know how to describe the emotions that swept over me as I heard Adolf Hitler. When he spoke of the disgrace of Germany I felt ready to spring on any enemy. His appeal to German manhood was like a call to arms; the gospel he preached, a sacred truth. I forgot everything but the man. Then glancing around me I saw that his magnetism was holding these thousands as one. The intense will of the man, the passion of his sincerity, seemed to flow from him into me. I experienced an exultation that can be likened only to religious conversion.'

A Nazi's memories, 1948.

SOURCE D

'Unless I have the inner conviction – *this is the solution* – I do nothing. Not even if the whole Nazi Party tries to drive me into action.'

Hitler, reported by a German writer, H. Rauschnigg, who knew him well, 1939.

SOURCE E

'I will give unconditional obedience to the Führer of the German Reich and people, Adolf Hitler, the supreme commander of the armed forces, and will be ready as a brave soldier to stake my life at any time for this oath.'

Oath taken by all officers and men in the German army after Hitler became Führer in 1934.

SOURCE F

Recruiting poster for the Hitler Youth, 1939. It reads: 'Youth serves the Führer. All 10-year-olds in the HJ' (Hitler Youth).

SOURCE G

'The forty-eight hours after the march into the Rhineland were the most nerve-wracking in my life. What would have happpened if anybody but myself had been at the head of the Reich? Anyone you care to mention would have lost his nerve. What saved us was my unshakable obstinacy.'

Hitler in conversation, 1942.

SOURCE H

'Germany's problems could be solved only by means of force. Our first aim must be the overthrow of Czechoslovakia and Austria simultaneously in order to remove the threat to us in any possible operation against Britain and France. It is while the rest of the world is preparing its defences that we are obliged to take the offensive. Germany has the right to a greater living space than other peoples. It is Hitler's unalterable resolve to solve Germany's problem of space at the latest by 1943–5.'

Report of a meeting of Hitler with German army generals, November 1937. The generals complained that Hitler's plans were too dangerous. The generals were sacked.

SOURCE I

'From now on I take over personally the command of the whole armed forces.'

Announcement by Hitler, February 1938.

EXERCISE

1 Study Sources A, B and C. In each case:
  a What does it show about Hitler's character or skills?
  b How might this have helped Hitler?

2 What do Sources B, E and F tell you about Hitler's position in Germany? Explain your answer.

3 Read about Hitler's occupation of the Rhineland in 1936 (Source G and page 58).
  a Is it possible to see Hitler' personal influence on these events?
  b How important was this in the train of events leading to war in 1939?

4 Read about the attack on Czechoslovakia in 1938 (Source H and page 60).
  a Is it possible to see Hitler's personal influence on these events?
  b How important was this in the train of events leading to war in 1939?

5 Read about the Nazi–Soviet Pact of 1939 (page 61).
  a Is it possible to see Hitler's personal influence on these events?
  b How important was this in the train of events leading to war in 1939?

6 a What worked out the way Hitler expected in Source H?
  b What worked out differently from the way he expected in Source H?
  c Would you say that Hitler controlled these events or was he swept along by them?

7 To what extent can Hitler be blamed for the outbreak of war in 1939?

6.6 SUCCESS FOR THE AXIS, 1939–42

Blitzkrieg ('lightning war')

By 1939 the German army and air force were well trained in the new methods of fighting using tanks and planes (see page 56). They were expert in this 'war of movement' which Hitler called **blitzkrieg** ('lightning war'). Germany knocked out **Poland** in a few weeks in September 1939. Six months later, in the spring of 1940, Hitler struck in the west. First he overran the neutral countries **Denmark, Norway, Holland** and **Belgium**. Then he sliced through the old-fashioned French and British armies, captured Paris and forced **France** to make peace. All this took less than three months. When Mussolini saw that Hitler was winning, **Italy** joined in the war on Germany's side.

The British army had been defeated in France, but the Royal Navy still controlled the English Channel. In June 1940 it was able to rescue the soldiers from the beaches of **Dunkirk**, although leaving their heavy weapons behind. Britain now stood alone. Hitler had most of Europe either under his control or on his side, and in 1940 he made an alliance with Italy and Japan, the Berlin–Rome–Tokyo **Axis**. Behind him was a triumphant army, well equipped with the latest weapons. Britain, on the other hand, now had to start to build a new army and design and make new weapons; the prospects looked bleak.

If Britain were to stand any chance the whole country would have to work together. Parliament saw that to win the war Britain needed a Prime Minister who could unite the nation. Neville Chamberlain (Prime Minister until May 1940) was the wrong man. He was a man of peace who had tried hard to appease Hitler. **Winston Churchill**, who now became Prime Minister, was a man of fighting spirit. He had warned people against Hitler for years and had always been against appeasement. Now he was able to persuade people by speeches and broadcasts that victory was possible if they all pulled together. The whole nation accepted his lead. Churchill saw to it that plans for new armies and weapons were made quickly and carried out efficiently.

Battle of Britain and the Blitz

Hitler knew that to end the war he would have to get his victorious army across the English Channel. But first he must get control of the air. Otherwise the Royal Navy and the RAF would easily sink the ships carrying his invading army. Luckily for Britain, among the few effective weapons the country had were some excellent fighter planes, Hurricanes and Spitfires, and pilots who knew how to fly them. There were just enough. During most of August and early September 1940 the **Battle of Britain** raged in the skies above Kent and the Channel. By mid-September Hitler saw that he was losing more planes than he could afford, and he gave up the idea of invading Britain. He had met his first defeat.

Now Hitler sent his bombers to attack London and other cities. British people called it **the Blitz**. In 1940–1 this did a great deal of damage, but Britain's war production still increased. The Blitz killed about 60,000 people, but it made the British more determined than ever to win the war.

Air-raid damage London, September 1940.

QUESTIONS

Look at the map.

1 Make a list of the countries conquered by the Axis. Put in the dates.

2 Make a list of the Axis powers and their allies.

3 Suggest reasons why some countries wanted to ally with Hitler and Mussolini? (See page 48.)

4 What reasons can you suggest for the successes of the Axis?

Germany attacks the USSR

In June 1941 Hitler turned to the east. He had always hated communism and hoped to gain control of the rich supplies of oil and other raw materials in the **USSR**. So now he unleashed his blitzkreig against the Red Army. You can see from the map how much the Germans conquered in 1941–2 and how near they came to capturing Moscow and Leningrad.

Why did they fail? One reason was the Russian winter. The Soviet troops knew how to move and to fight in sub-zero temperatures that froze the oil in the engines of the German tanks. Another reason was the determination of the Soviet people. Some of them were fighting to defend communism, others simply to defend their country. But all were horrified at the brutal behaviour of the Germans in the territory they controlled (see page 72).

Yet another reason why the Red Army was able to halt the Nazi advance was the help it began to get from Britain and the USA. Churchill had always been a bitter enemy of communism, but when Hitler attacked the USSR he did not hesitate to make an alliance with Stalin. Britain promised to send as many weapons and other supplies as it could. Soon the USA began to do the same.

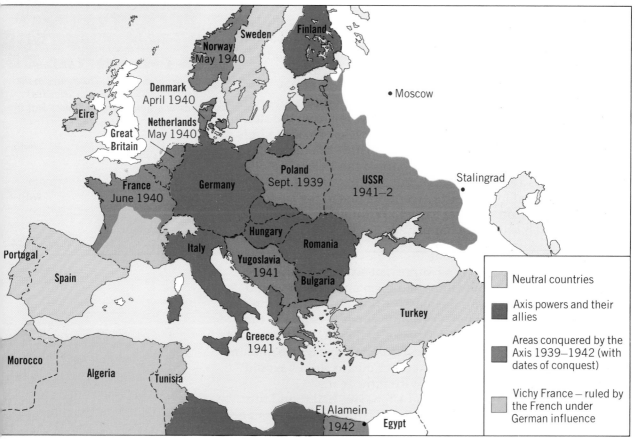

Europe and North Africa, 1939–42.

6.7 SUCCESS FOR THE ALLIES, 1942–45

The Allies

In 1942 **Britain**, the **USA** and the **USSR** became firm allies in the fight against Hitler's Germany. (See page 70 for the reasons why the USA joined in the war.) For the next three years the Allies worked together for victory. Disagreements about communism or capitalism were not allowed to get in the way of the war effort, although they soon came to the surface again when the fighting was over.

Success in Europe and North Africa

The Allies agreed that Germany was the main enemy and had to be tackled first. It was the Soviets who took the main weight of the fighting. They destroyed a large German army at **Stalingrad** in the winter of 1942–3 and after that forced the Germans steadily back. Meanwhile the British won the **Battle of Alamein** in November 1942, and with US help drove the Axis armies out of Africa. Then in June 1944 British and US armies landed in **Normandy** and drove the Germans out of France. By May 1945 the Axis armies in Europe had all surrendered, and Hitler had shot himself.

Producing the weapons

By 1942 the Allied commanders had learned how to use modern weapons like tanks and planes. To win the war they needed a huge supply of these. It was the massive production of the USA that made victory certain in the end. Factories in Britain and the USSR worked long and hard and turned out far more than seemed possible. But many Soviet and British factories were damaged by German attacks, and they were short of raw materials and workers. In the USA there was plenty of everything and no war damage. US industry had recovered from the slump of the 1930s, and the government ordered weapons of all kinds in immense quantities. There was now a wartime boom in production much greater than the boom of the 1920s. Out of the factories poured a stream of tanks, guns, ships, trucks, planes – everything needed for war. They went not just to the US forces but to those of the other Allies as well. Without this the victories of 1942–5 could hardly have happened.

Battle of the Atlantic

You can see from the map how important **sea-borne supplies** were to the Allies. If supply lines had been cut, Britain would have had to surrender, and the massive Soviet attacks in the east could hardly have happened. Germany's main weapon in the Atlantic was the submarine. 'Wolf packs' of these **U-boats** attacked Allied shipping with their torpedoes, sinking more than 6 million tonnes of shipping in 1942. It looked at times as if they would win the Battle of the Atlantic and with it the war.

By 1943, however, the British and US navies had found the answer. With **radar** they could locate the U-boats. **Long-distance aircraft** could sink them with depth charges. Warships with spotter aircraft could protect **convoys** of merchant ships. Some losses continued, but the grave danger was over.

SOURCE **A**

Soviet poster, 1944. The figures in the background are men who defended Russia against German attacks in the Middle Ages, in 1812 and in 1917–18.

Bombing Germany

In 1942–5 the British and US air forces attacked Germany. Their bombing raids were far heavier than those of the German Blitz on Britain. A thousand bombers at a time could destroy the centre of a city like **Berlin** or **Hamburg**. About eighty German cities were totally or partly destroyed, and 600,000 civilians were killed. As in Britain, the survivors gritted their teeth and carried on. In 1943–4, in spite of the raids, Germany produced three times as many weapons as in 1941. But by 1945 things were different. As the Allied armies came nearer, the bombing got heavier still, and German war production began to collapse.

Allied advances in North Africa and Europe, 1942–5. ▼

QUESTIONS

1 Study Source A.
  a What do you think the written message is?
  b What feelings is the artist appealing to?

2 a Make a list of the factors that enabled the Allies to win battles in the years 1942–4.
  b Which of these do you consider most important? Give your reasons.

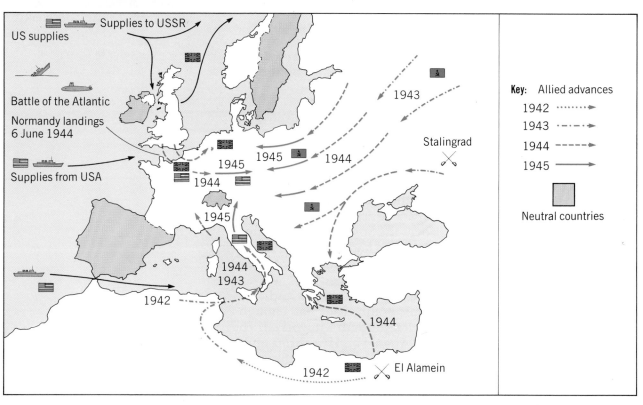

US supplies

Supplies to USSR

Battle of the Atlantic

Normandy landings 6 June 1944

Supplies from USA

1945

1944

1945

1944

1945

1944
1943

1942

1943

Stalingrad

1944

1944

1942

El Alamein

Key: Allied advances
1942 ·········▶
1943 ·–·–·▶
1944 ------▶
1945 ———▶

Neutral countries

6.8 THE WAR IN THE FAR EAST

Japanese plans for expansion

Japan was very successful in the attack on China which it had launched in 1937, two years before war broke out in Europe. By 1941 the Japanese had taken control of large parts of eastern China. They saw this as the start of a larger plan to seize key points throughout the Far East and establish economic control, as the Europeans had done in their empires. They called the plan the **Greater East Asia Co-Prosperity Sphere**. Two obstacles stood in their way: the British Empire and the US navy.

In 1940 the first of these seemed to be collapsing. The British were in deadly danger in their own islands and could not send large forces to the other side of the world. But the USA was far richer and more powerful than Japan and had a large Pacific fleet based at **Pearl Harbor** in Hawaii. The USA was strongly opposed to Japanese military expansion and might use its fleet to prevent it.

In the **Axis Treaty** of 1940 Hitler promised to help the Japanese if any country (meaning the USA) attacked them.

Pearl Harbor – the USA declares war

In December 1941 Japanese bombers, without any warning, attacked the US fleet at Pearl Harbor. They hoped to smash US naval power in the Pacific completely. They sank three battleships and destroyed most of the aircraft, but the aircraft-carriers, vital for war in the Pacific, were not damaged. The USA immediately declared war on Japan, as did Britain. Hitler kept his promise by declaring war on the USA.

It would take time for the USA to build up the power to strike back, and the British had more pressing dangers to face nearer home. So the war in the Far East began with sweeping Axis victories, just as the war in Europe had done. Nothing could be done to stop the Japanese capturing the areas shown on the map.

Allied successes 1942–5

The war in the Far East consisted mainly of **'island-hopping'**. First the US forces gained control of the western Pacific Ocean and the air above it, and then they drove the Japanese out of the islands they had conquered. By early 1944 the USA had air bases near enough to start bombing Japan itself. By June 1945 the Japanese had been driven out of all the islands apart from their own. There were still unbeaten Japanese armies in **China**, but now that the war in Europe was over the Soviets were getting ready to attack them there. British troops had driven the Japanese out of most of **Burma**, and Britain too was getting ready to take part in the final attack on Japan.

Meanwhile in the USA a massive team of scientists and engineers was developing the **atomic bomb**. They had enough material for three bombs. One was a test bomb – it worked. The other two were dropped on 6 and 9 August on **Hiroshima** and **Nagasaki**. You can read more about these bombs and the damage they did on page 76. On 15 August Emperor Hirohito of Japan gave his troops orders to surrender. The war was over.

QUESTIONS

1 Make a list of the countries or parts of countries captured by Japan, with the dates.

2 Japan was much poorer and weaker than the USA in 1941. Why then would the Japanese have attacked Pearl Harbor?

3 Does Source A show that the attack was a success?

Look back at pages 66–9 before you answer questions four to seven.

4 The war in Europe had important effects on the war in the Far East. Choose two examples of these effects and explain your choice.

5 Draw a time chart of the main events of the Second World War from 1939 to 1945, marking in the Axis successes and the Allied successes.

6 Choose one Axis success which might be thought of as the key to others. Explain your choice.

7 Choose the Allied victory which you consider to have been most important. Explain your choice.

SOURCE **A**

The Japanese attack the American fleet at Pearl Harbor. Notice the Japanese plane which has just dropped its bomb.

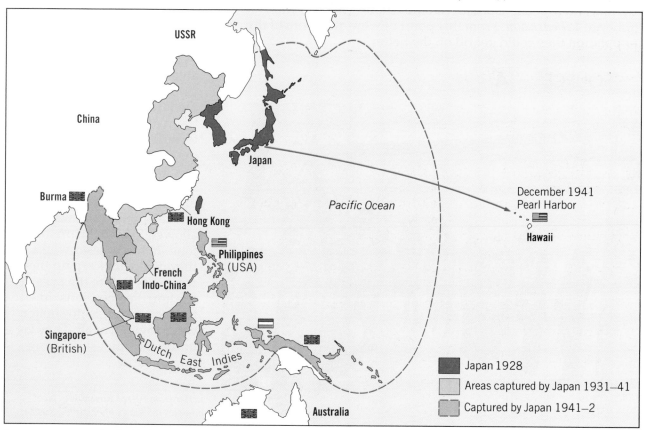

Japanese conquests in the Far East, 1931–42.

6.9 EUROPE UNDER THE NAZIS

EMPATHY

Hitler and the Nazis ruled most of Europe for nearly five years. They had two main aims. The first was to strengthen Germany at all costs so that it could win the war. The second was to lay the basis for a 'new order' in which the German 'master race' would dominate.

Slave workers
Wartime Germany needed millions of extra workers in farms, mines and factories. In the early years of the war some came freely from western Europe. But after 1941 more and more were brought by force. By 1944 there were more than 7 million **slave workers**, one in five of all workers in Germany. About half were Russians. They lived in labour camps near the factories and were given just enough food to be able to work.

Prisoners of war
British and other west European **prisoners of war** were on the whole treated fairly by the Nazis. East Europeans, such as Poles and Russians, were not. The lucky ones became slave workers in Germany. Altogether the Germans took about 5½ million Russian prisoners, of whom 3 million died.

Clearing 'living space'
The Nazis planned to give Germany permanent control of eastern Europe and to set up German colonies there. This was their policy of *Lebensraum*. From this point of view, the more of the population they could get rid of, the better.

SOURCE A

Russian civilians hanged by the Germans.

SOURCE B

'I found these women suffering from open festering wounds. There were no medical supplies. They had no shoes. The sole clothing of each consisted of a sack with holes for their arms and head. Their hair was shorn. The camp was surrounded by barbed wire and closely guarded by SS guards. The amount of food in the camp was extremely meagre and of very poor quality.'

A doctor at the Krupp munitions works, giving evidence describing slave workers, in 1945.

SOURCE C

'The fate of the Soviet prisoners is a tragedy. Of 3,600,000, only a few hundred thousand are still able to work fully. A large part of them have starved, or died because of the weather. Camp commanders have forbidden food to be put at the disposal of prisoners; instead they have let them starve to death. Even on the march to the camps, the civilian population was not allowed to give the prisoners food. In many cases when they could not keep up they were shot before the eyes of the horrified civilians. In numerous camps no shelter was provided at all. They lay under the open sky during rain or snow.'

Letter from Alfred Rosenberg, Nazi minister in charge of occupied Russia, to General Keitel at Hitler's headquarters, February 1942.

SOURCE D

'At Auschwitz the incoming prisoners would be marched past one of the doctors, who would make spot decisions as they walked by. Those who were fit for work were sent into the camp. Others were sent immediately to the extermination plants. Children of tender years were always exterminated since because of their youth they were unable to work.'

Rudolf Hoess, commandant of the Auschwitz death camp, giving evidence at his trial in 1945.

The Jews – the 'final solution'

It was the **Jews** who suffered most in Hitler's Europe. As each country was conquered, anti-semitic laws were brought in. Jews were herded into **ghettos** or sent to **concentration camps**. Then in the summer of 1941, as the Germans advanced into the USSR, Hitler gave orders for the systematic extermination of the Jews in Europe – the Nazi's **'final solution'**. The first method tried was to send SS troops behind the army to round up the Jews and machine-gun them, or gas them in portable gas chambers. Later the Nazis worked out a more 'efficient' method. Five massive **death camps** were built in Poland. **Auschwitz** was one of them.

In these camps there were factories to make weapons for Germany, with living accommodation for those who were judged fit enough to work. Nearby were large gas chambers to kill those considered unfit, and ovens to burn the bodies of the dead. Once these death-camps were in working order, Jews were sent there from all over Nazi-controlled Europe. Some were tricked with stories about a new homeland for the Jews; others were just taken by force. Source D tells you what happened when they arrived. Only the strongest survived for long. Between 1 million and 3 million Jews were killed at Auschwitz alone. Some 6 million died altogether.

SOURCE E

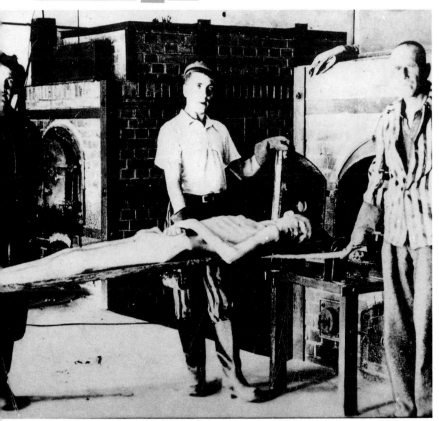

One of the ovens for corpses at Auschwitz.

EXERCISE

1 When Hoess gave evidence (Source D), he was on trial for his life. Why do you think he decided to say what he did?

2 Sources A and E are photographs taken by Germans. Does this mean they were proud of what they were doing?

3 How might the policies described in this unit have affected the view most people in conquered countries had of the Nazis?

4 In April 1942 the *Reichstag* passed a resolution saying: 'The nation is conscious of the wisdom, justice and kindness of its leader.' Does this mean members *cannot* have known about slave workers, the treatment of prisoners of war, and the 'final solution'? Give reasons for your answer.

6.10 WHY DID THE ALLIES WIN THE WAR?

SOURCE A

'The Russian danger is our danger, and the danger of the United States, just as the cause of any Russian fighting for his hearth and home is the cause of free people in every quarter of the globe.'

Winston Churchill, radio broadcast, 22 June 1941.

SOURCE B

'The only thing that ever really frightened me during the war was the U-Boat peril . . .'

Describing what he thought when he heard of the Japanese attack on Pearl Harbor: 'So we had won after all. Britain would live. Hitler's fate was sealed. As for the Japanese, they would be ground to a powder. I went to bed and slept the sleep of the saved and the thankful.'

Winston Churchill, 'The Second World War', 1950.

SOURCE C

'The gratitude of every home in our island, in our Empire and indeed throughout the world, except in the abodes of the guilty, goes out to the British airmen who are turning the tide of world war by their prowess and by their devotion. Never in the field of human conflict was so much owed by so many to so few.'

Winston Churchill, speech in the House of Commons, 20 August 1940.

SOURCE D

'If Great Britain goes down, we would be living at the point of a gun. There can be no appeasement with ruthlessness. A nation can have peace with the Nazis only at the price of surrender. We must be the great arsenal of democracy.'

US President Roosevelt, radio broadcast, 29 December 1940, after agreeing to sell weapons to Britain. Most US citizens at this time were against joining in the war.

SOURCE F

Revellers in London celebrate victory in Europe, May 1945.

SOURCE E

The USSR's Red Flag is raised over the Reichstag in Berlin.

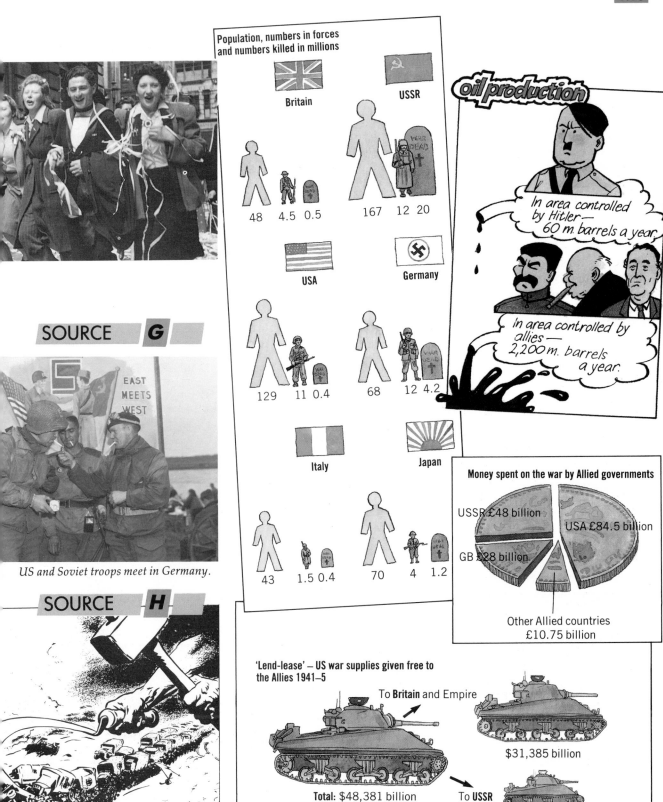

SOURCE **G**

US and Soviet troops meet in Germany.

SOURCE **H**

HAMMER AND SICKLE

British cartoon, 4 January 1943.

Population, numbers in forces and numbers killed in millions

Britain — 48 4.5 0.5
USSR — 167 12 20
USA — 129 11 0.4
Germany — 68 12 4.2
Italy — 43 1.5 0.4
Japan — 70 4 1.2

oil production

In area controlled by Hitler — 60 m. barrels a year.

In area controlled by allies — 2,200 m. barrels a year.

Money spent on the war by Allied governments
USSR £48 billion
USA £84.5 billion
GB £28 billion
Other Allied countries £10.75 billion

'Lend-lease' – US war supplies given free to the Allies 1941–5
To Britain and Empire $31,385 billion
Total: $48,381 billion
To USSR $10,982 billion

The resources used to fight the Second World War.

6.11 WHY DID THE ALLIES DROP THE ATOM BOMB?

EMPATHY

On 6 August 1945 a US plane dropped the first atomic bomb on the city of **Hiroshima**. It killed more than 70,000 people in a flash, and about as many died a lingering death later. Three days afterwards a second A-bomb killed another 40,000 people in **Nagasaki**.

It had taken three years to make these bombs. Scientists and engineers and more than 30,000 other people in factories and laboratories all over the USA had spent most of the war on **Operation Manhattan** – the code-name for the bomb project. Why did the Allies work so hard to make such dreadful weapons? And when they were ready, why did they drop them on cities, killing so many ordinary Japanese civilians?

The answer to the first question is straightforward: Germany was known to be making nuclear weapons too. Before the war there was nothing secret about nuclear physics, and scientists in all countries could see from discoveries made in 1938–9 that a nuclear bomb might be possible. Hitler often boasted of his 'secret weapons' that were to win the war for Germany, and the Allies knew from their spies that the Germans were working on a nuclear bomb. They were determined to make it themselves first.

Why drop the bomb?

The second question is more difficult. Three months before the bomb was ready, Germany surrendered. The USSR promised to join in the attack on Japan which was bound to come soon. Japan would not stand a chance. Then, on 12 July 1945, nearly a month before the first atomic bomb was dropped, the Japanese asked for peace talks. So why drop the bomb at all? To answer this question you need to look at it from the point of view of people involved in the decision at the time (Sources A to F).

SOURCE A

'Any weapon that would bring an end to the war and save a million casualties among American boys was justified, and we were talking about people who hadn't hesitated at Pearl Harbor to make a sneak attack destroying not only ships but the lives of many American sailors . . . I would have been satisfied had the Russians determined not to enter the war against Japan. I believed the A-bomb would be successful and would force the Japanese to accept surrender on our terms. I feared what would happen when the Red Army entered Manchuria.'

James Byrnes, US Secretary of State in 1945.

SOURCE B

'The decision whether or not to use the atomic bomb to compel the surrender of Japan was never even an issue. There was a unanimous, automatic, unquestioned agreement (on the use of the bomb) around our table; nor did I hear the slightest suggestion that we should do otherwise.'

Winston Churchill, describing the meeting of Allied leaders at Potsdam, 18 July 1945.

Count-down to surrender, 1945	
12 July	Japan asks for peace talks.
17 July	Test bomb. It works.
17–26 July	Allied leaders meet at Potsdam. They decide: • USSR to declare war on Japan in August, • Japan must surrender completely or be destroyed.
28 July	Japan refuses to surrender.
2 August	Japan asks again for talks.
6 August	Hiroshima bomb.
7 August	Japanese army opposes surrender.
8 August	USSR declares war on Japan.
9 August	Nagasaki bomb.
14 August	Emperor of Japan orders surrender.

Two other air raids		
Tokyo	14 March 1945	197,000 killed and missing
Dresden	13–14 February 1945	120,000 killed and missing

EMPATHY

SOURCE C

British prisoners of war in a Japanese camp in Burma. According to a British medical officer they were treated 'like animals'.

SOURCE D

'No demonstration, such as over a desert island, was likely to bring the war to an end. The final decision of when and where to use the atomic bomb was up to me. I regarded the bomb as a military weapon and never had any doubt that it should be used. The top military advisers recommended its use.'

US President Harry S. Truman, who gave the order to use the bomb.

SOURCE E

'It is my opinion that the use of this barbarous weapon at Hiroshima and Nagasaki was of no material assistance in our war against Japan. The Japanese were already defeated and were ready to surrender because of the effective sea blockade and the successful bombing with conventional weapons.'

SOURCE F

'The experience of Russian scientists in nuclear research is entirely sufficient to enable them to retrace our steps within a few years. The race for nuclear armaments will be on in earnest not later than the morning after our first demonstration of the existence of nuclear weapons. The military advantage and saving of American lives achieved may be outweighed by a wave of horror and revulsion sweeping over the rest of the world.'

Report to the US government by an advisory committee of scientists, 1945.

◀ Admiral Leahy, US navy, adviser to President Truman in 1945, writing in 1950.

SOURCE G

'It was a horrible sight. Hundreds of injured people who were trying to escape passed our house. The sight of them was almost unbearable. Their faces and hands were burnt and swollen; and great sheets of skin had peeled away from their tissues to hang down like rags on a scarecrow. This morning they had stopped. I found them lying on both sides of the road so thick that it was impossible to pass without stepping on them.'

Diary of Dr Tabuchi, a Japanese doctor, 7 August 1945.

EXERCISE

1 It was part of the code of honour of Japanese soldiers to commit suicide rather than surrender. How do you think this may have influenced the events of August 1945?

2 What might the following people have thought or felt when they heard the news on 6 August 1945? Look at the table 'Two other air raids' and at the figures in pages 66–9 as well as at the sources.
   • an Allied soldier.
   • families in Britain.
   • families in the USA.

3 Why were Churchill (Source B) and Truman (Source D) so certain that the decision to drop the bomb was right?

6.12 THE UNITED NATIONS ORGANIZATION

The Second World War, like the First, sickened and horrified people with its brutality, so they wanted to make sure that it would not happen again. The League of Nations, which had been set up in 1919 to keep the peace, had clearly failed. In 1945 the victorious Allies tried again by setting up the **United Nations Organization (UN)**.

The League had failed for two main reasons. First, some of the most powerful countries, like the USA, or Germany after 1933, were not members. Second, it had no 'teeth' – it could only ask its members to take action to keep peace. It was like trying to stop robberies without a police force, by just asking the neighbours if they would be kind enough to help.

The UN avoided the first of these weaknesses. All the Allies agreed to join, and later on so did the defeated countries and all others of any size. In 1945 there were 50 members; and in 1987, 157. But the second of the League's weaknesses was harder to avoid. It was the governments of the most powerful countries, the four wartime Allies, that first suggested the UN and they have dominated it ever since. These governments were not likely to give up their own national power by letting the new world organization have much power of its own. So they placed the main power of the UN in the hands of the **Security Council**. This had nine members (now fifteen). Five of these – the USA, USSR, China, Britain and France – are **permanent members**, and no action can be taken if any one of these five votes against it. This is called the **veto**. It means that the UN can be effective if all five agree on something, but not if they do not.

Unfortunately they have in fact disagreed bitterly on most things ever since. Even in 1945 the Soviet Union and its non-communist Allies had a deep distrust for each other, and this soon led to the **cold war**. At the same time the nuclear arms race began, and within twenty years the two **superpowers** (the USA and USSR) had enough bombs to destroy each other several times over in an hour or two. No international organization could have strong enough 'teeth' to deal with this sort of danger.

This does not mean that the UN was or is a failure. There have been some issues on which the great powers could agree. Many of the problems of the years since 1945 have been connected with the break-up of the overseas empires previously controlled by countries such as Britain (see page 94). The USA, USSR and China, and most people in Britain and France, all welcomed this break-up. The **UN Trusteeship Council** took over the mandates system from the League, and helped former colonies to gain their independence.

Another success of the UN has been in sending **UN forces** to a trouble spot where the great powers are not trusted, such as the Congo (now Zaire). A UN army can be made up by borrowing soldiers from member nations – usually the smaller neutral ones such as Ireland or Sweden. These troops have been used to patrol cease-fire lines and have played an important part in keeping the peace.

SOURCE A

'We, the people of the United Nations, are determined to save succeeding generations from the scourge of war, which twice in our lifetime has brought untold sorrow to mankind, and to reaffirm faith in the fundamental human right, in the dignity and worth of the human person, in the equal rights of men and woman and of nations large and small, and to establish respect for treaties and international law, and to promote social progress and better standards of life in larger freedom.'

UN Charter, 1945.

SOURCE B

UN troops in the Congo, 1961. A UN army of 20,000 men helped to keep order in the newly independent Congo (now Zaire).

SOURCE C

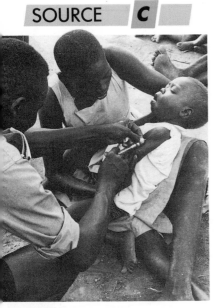

A WHO doctor vaccinating a child, 1976. In 1967 the WHO began a world campaign against smallpox; by 1980 the disease had been stamped out.

SOURCE D

World is declared to be free of smallpox

A formal declaration that smallpox had been eradicated was made yesterday at the thirty-third World Health Assembly in Geneva.

Announcements that smallpox was on the point of eradication have been made several times in the last four years as the World Health Organization thought that its intensified eradication programme was coming to an end. But the announcements have always been followed by renewed outbreaks, most notably in the Horn of Africa during the war between Somalia and Ethiopia.

A total of 3,229 cases were notified in Somalia in 1977 but since October 26 of that year no further cases, other than a laboratory-associated outbreak in the United Kingdom, have come to light.

'The Times,' 9 May 1980.

The **General Assembly** of the UN is a meeting of all its members which takes place at least once a year at the UN headquarters in New York. Each member country, great or small, has one vote, and there is no veto. The Assembly therefore sometimes passes resolutions which one of the great powers opposes. But before any action can be taken as the result of a resolution, the Security Council has to agree, and a permanent member can always veto this. However, the great powers are keen to get world public opinion on their side, and they try not to go openly against resolutions of the Assembly.

The Assembly elects the **Secretary-General** of the UN. He or she (all have been men up to now) leads the permanent staff of the UN. The Secretary-General also acts if there is any danger to peace by holding talks with both sides or with other governments, by arranging a cease-fire or by planning and organizing UN forces.

Most of the work of the UN is not concerned with peace-keeping, but with the day-to-day running of the 'global village'. The **Economic and Social Council** links together the work of fifteen organizations, mostly set up by the UN, but some taken over from the League and others even older. One is the **World Health Organization** which helps poor countries with health care and organizes a worldwide battle against epidemics. Another, the **World Bank**, lends money to help poor countries to develop. Other organizations allot radio and television frequencies, promote cultural and educational exchanges and arrange world air control systems and shipping regulations. The complicated business of the global village would be impossible without them.

QUESTIONS

1 Read Source A. Which parts of it may refer to the actions of Hitler before or during the war?

2 In what way was the UN stronger than the old League of Nations?

3 In what way was it still very weak?

4 Use an encyclopaedia to make a complete list of the 'special agencies' of the UN, such as the World Health Organization, and describe what each of them does.

7.1 THE COLD WAR

Two points of view.

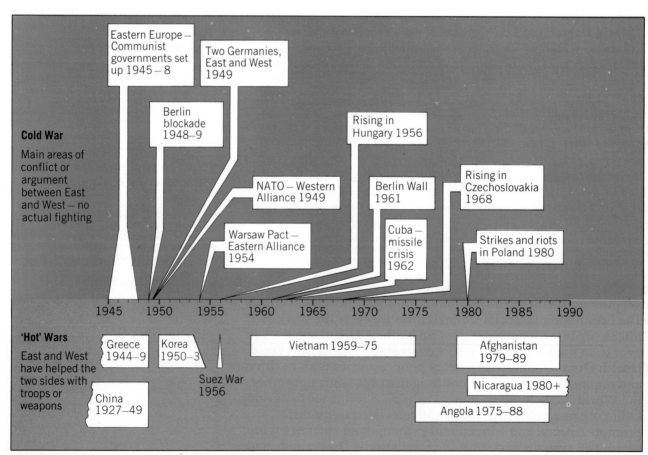

Cold war and 'hot' wars.

At the beginning of 1945 the USSR, the USA and Britain were friends and allies, fighting together against Germany and Japan. Four years later, in early 1949 the USA and Britain formed an armed alliance, **NATO**, to defend themselves *against* the USSR. People were beginning to talk about a **cold war**. By this they meant hostility of all kinds except the actual shooting of a 'hot' war. In the forty years since then, in almost every important international argument, the USSR and its allies have been on one side, and the USA and its allies on the other. There have been more than two hundred 'hot' wars in that time. In some of these, such as the wars in Korea, Vietnam and Afghanistan, one side has been backed by the USSR and the other by the USA. So these local wars have been aspects of the worldwide cold war.

Why did the cold war begin? Why has it gone on for so long? If we are to make much sense of world history as a whole during this time, we need to understand the causes and the effects of the cold war.

There have been times during the forty years of the cold war when it has seemed to become less bitter. People have talked of a 'thaw'. One of these periods was in the 1960s, and for convenience this unit deals only with events before then. But the basic conflict still continued, and most of the remaining units of the book deal with events that were influenced in one way or another by the cold war.

The coming of the cold war

Why did the wartime Allies become peacetime rivals? During the Second World War all members of the Alliance agreed that the main aim was to defeat the Axis. They often disagreed about how this was to be done, but they could still work together because they agreed on a common purpose. But when the war ended, there was no clear common purpose left. Instead there was an urgent problem that caused disagreement.

In many newly liberated or ex-enemy countries there was in 1945 great disorder, and trade and industry were in ruins. New governments had to be set up as soon as possible. Who was to set them up? In some cases former rulers or politicians had fled during the war and now hoped to return to power. For instance, there were two 'governments in exile' for Poland, a Communist one in Moscow, and a non-communist one in London. In many countries there were resistance fighters who had helped to overthrow the enemy and who now demanded a say in the running of their country. Many of these resistance fighters were communists who hoped to bring about a revolution when they took power. This was the case in China, Vietnam, Yugoslavia and Greece.

QUESTIONS

1 Look at 'The view from Moscow' in the drawing.
  a What Marxist theory might lead Stalin to think like this?
  b What earlier historical events might he point to, to show that these fears were realistic?
  c How might the explosion of the atomic bombs in August 1945 affect Stalin's fears?

2 Look at 'The view from the West' in the drawing. Why should the possibility of the spread of communism in Europe and in the Far East worry many Americans?

3 In 1945 new governments had to be set up all over liberated Europe.
  a How would Stalin want this to be done? Explain his reasons.
  b How would Churchill or Truman want this to be done? Explain their reasons.

4 a Make a list of the causes of conflict between the USSR and the Western Allies in 1945.
  b Which of these could be called long-term causes because they went back for many years?
  c Did these causes make conflict inevitable in 1945?
  d Does the cold war still continue today? Are any of the 1945 causes of conflict still present today?

7.2 CLOSING THE IRON CURTAIN

When the fighting stopped in 1945 the Red Army found itself in control of much of eastern Europe. It had advanced up to a line agreed between the Allies at the meeting at **Yalta** in February 1945.

The people of eastern Europe were nearly all thankful to see Hitler overthrown. Some of them were Communists who welcomed the Red Army with open arms. But other people in these countries disliked and feared the USSR. For instance, Poland had a long and bitter history of conflict with Russia, going back four hundred years. So the Soviets were bound to meet with difficulties.

When new governments were formed in these countries in 1945, the USSR saw to it that the Communists had many of the important jobs, but other parties were also given a share. The new governments began to carry out changes like taking land and industry from private owners and so weakening or overthrowing the old upper class.

Now look at the larger map. By 1948 all the countries which the USSR controlled had a **one-party government** controlled by the Communists, just like the USSR itself. How was this done? The Soviet government and the Red Army helped the Communists to take control of the police, the radio and the newspapers. They interfered with elections if they seemed to be going against them, and they arrested people who opposed them.

In March 1946 Winston Churchill attacked these actions in a famous speech in which he said: 'An iron curtain has descended across the Continent.' The wartime Alliance was coming to an end, and the cold war was beginning. From the information in this unit you can get an idea how and why the Iron Curtain was closed. But you can see from the dates on the map that in 1948 and 1949 the cold war got very much worse. To understand this you must read about events in Germany on page 84.

Areas held by Allied armies when Germany surrendered in 1945.

The last wartime agreement

At **Yalta** in February 1945, Churchill, Stalin and Roosevelt agreed that:

Germany would be treated as one country. Each of the Allies would occupy part of Germany. Germany would be completely disarmed. The Allies would take machinery and goods from Germany to repair damage to their own countries. Half the total taken was to go to the USSR.

Poland would lose land in the east to the USSR and gain land in the west from Germany. The USSR could set up a mainly Communist government in Poland, but promised to hold free elections soon.

Other liberated countries were to be helped to set up their own democratic governments.

War against Japan: the USSR was to join in this war.

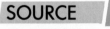
SOURCE A

◀ *Churchill, Roosevelt and Stalin pose for an official photograph at Yalta, 1945.*

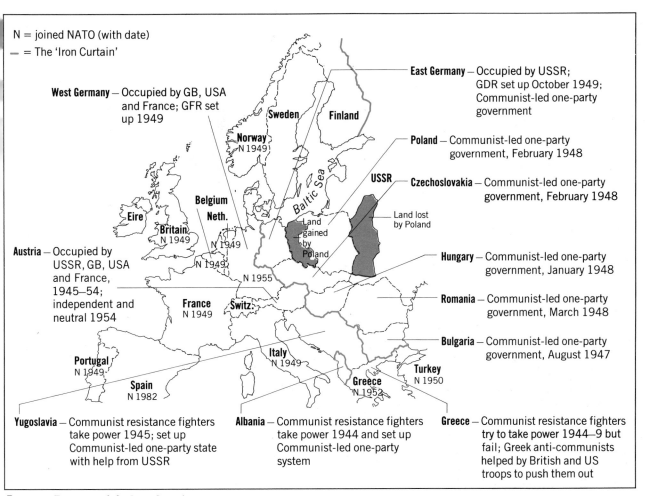

N = joined NATO (with date)

— = The 'Iron Curtain'

West Germany — Occupied by GB, USA and France; GFR set up 1949

Sweden

Finland

Norway N 1949

East Germany — Occupied by USSR; GDR set up October 1949; Communist-led one-party government

Poland — Communist-led one-party government, February 1948

Czechoslovakia — Communist-led one-party government, February 1948

USSR

Land lost by Poland

Belgium

Neth.

Eire

Britain N 1949

N 1949

N 1949

Land gained by Poland

Baltic Sea

Austria — Occupied by USSR, GB, USA and France, 1945–54; independent and neutral 1954

France N 1949

Switz.

N 1955

Hungary — Communist-led one-party government, January 1948

Romania — Communist-led one-party government, March 1948

Bulgaria — Communist-led one-party government, August 1947

Portugal N 1949

Spain N 1982

Italy N 1949

Greece N 1952

Turkey N 1950

Yugoslavia — Communist resistance fighters take power 1945; set up Communist-led one-party state with help from USSR

Albania — Communist resistance fighters take power 1944 and set up Communist-led one-party system

Greece — Communist resistance fighters try to take power 1944–9 but fail; Greek anti-communists helped by British and US troops to push them out

Post-war Europe and the Iron Curtain.

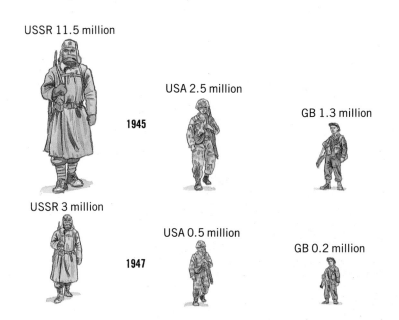

USSR 11.5 million

USA 2.5 million

GB 1.3 million

1945

USSR 3 million

USA 0.5 million

GB 0.2 million

1947

Armed men in Europe, 1945–7.

QUESTIONS

1 What parts of the Yalta agreement were carried out in the arrangements shown on the larger map?

2 What part of the Yalta agreements were broken by those arrangements?

3 Look at the smaller map and at the diagram showing Allied Forces in Europe. How could they be used to explain why some of the agreements were broken?

4 What other explanation might there be for this?

7.3 GERMANY IS SPLIT IN TWO

At Yalta and in later discussions the wartime Allies had agreed on zones of occupation in Germany and Austria. The Soviets began to dismantle factories and machinery in their part of **Germany** in order to use it to repair damage in the USSR. They also seized food and other goods produced in Germany as part of the **reparations** to which they were entitled. But this caused a serious problem for the Western Allies. The western zones, especially the British one, had always depended on food supplies from the east. Now none came – how were people to be fed? The problem was made worse by the arrival in the western zones of about 10 million extra Germans fleeing from the areas controlled by the USSR. Until all these people could be set to work, how could they buy food?

In 1946 food had to be provided free, but it was obvious that the sooner industry and trade could be started again the sooner this problem could be solved. So the Western Allies set about restoring the economy in their own zones. They linked the three zones (British, US and French) together, and encouraged industry, agriculture and transport. The owners of the factories and farms were the same business people and landowners who had been there in Hitler's time. This restoration of the economic system in the western zones was helped very much by the US-funded **Marshall Plan**. The Western Allies also began to set up a new system of government, and finally in May 1949 the three zones were put together to form the **German Federal Republic** ('West Germany'). The USSR protested that this was breaking the Yalta agreements. But when it saw that its protests were no use, it organized a German government for its own zone. The **German Democratic Republic** ('East Germany') was set up in October 1949.

" IF WE DON'T LET HIM WORK, WHO'S GOING TO KEEP HIM

David Low cartoon, 12 July 1946. The men arguing are the Foreign Ministers of the four wartime Allies.

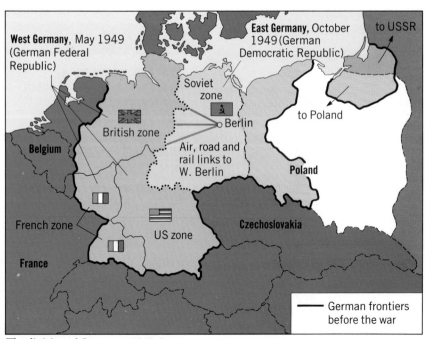

The division of Germany, 1945–9.

West Germany, May 1949 (German Federal Republic)

East Germany, October 1949 (German Democratic Republic)

to USSR

Soviet zone

British zone

Berlin

Belgium

Air, road and rail links to W. Berlin

to Poland

Poland

French zone

US zone

Czechoslovakia

France

German frontiers before the war

he Marshall Plan

lost countries had been ruined by the war. Even Britain, a
ountry only slightly damaged compared with others, could not
ake ends meet at the end of the war without borrowing from
e USA. But for the USA the war had been a time of great
rosperity, with industry and agriculture working flat out. It was
ready the richest country in the world in 1939; now it was in a
ass by itself. The USA had lent money to the British and to the
oviets and had paid (through the United Nations) most of the
ost of helping the refugees in Germany.

In 1947, **George Marshall**, the US Secretary of State, proposed
new plan. Europe would set up an organization which would
ake plans for rebuilding the economy of the continent. Any
ountry joining the organization could get help, and the USA
ould pay the bill. The USSR refused to join and prevented the
ast European countries under its control from joining. Between
)48 and 1952 the USA paid out $13.15 billion in **Marshall Aid**.

he Berlin blockade

erlin was 150 miles inside the Soviet zone. In early 1945 the
oint occupation of Germany's capital by all the Allies seemed a
ensible temporary arrangement until a new government for the
vhole of Germany could be set up. Nobody thought that
Germany would be split in two and that the 'temporary'
rrangement might last for half a century or more.

As a communist Germany began to take shape in the east, and
capitalist one in the west, Berlin became a problem for both.
he Western Allies allowed the new political parties from their
ones to operate in Berlin. They encouraged capitalist industry in
erlin and trade with the west.

In 1948 the USSR and the Western Allies quarrelled about a
ew currency which was being introduced in the western zones.
s part of this dispute the Soviets stopped all traffic by rail and
oad through their zone from the west to Berlin. It looked as if the
llies would have to give up their plan to keep Berlin linked to
ne west, or else try to fight their way to Berlin and risk starting
third world war. But the Soviets' blockade did not stop the
Vestern Allies. From July 1948 until May 1949, for 318 days, the
JS and British air forces organized the **Berlin airlift**, supplying
Vest Berlin by air with food, coal and goods of all kinds – 1.5
nillion tonnes in all. In the end the USSR had to admit that its
)lockade had failed. On 12 May 1949 it allowed traffic between
Berlin and the west to run freely again.

NATO

n April 1949, towards the end of the Berlin blockade, the
Western Allies agreed on a new military alliance. The USA,
Canada, Britain, France and eight other West European nations
greed that if any of them were attacked they would all join
ogether against the attacker. They set up the **North Atlantic
Treaty Organization (NATO)** to plan joint military action against
possible Soviet attack.

QUESTIONS

1 Marshall Aid was a US offer to
   help to pay to rebuild war-
   damaged countries including
   the USSR, which had been
   very badly damaged.
   a Stalin refused the offer.
      What reasons can you
      suggest for this?
   b One communist country,
      Yugoslavia, did accept. How
      can this be explained? (See
      page 83.)

2 Read the following two
   explanations of the coming of
   the cold war:
   ● 'Stalin's aim was to spread
      communism as widely as
      possible. This made the
      Red Army a danger. The
      USA and western Europe
      had to defend themselves
      against this danger.'

   ● 'The Western Allies were not
      carrying out the Yalta
      agreement to weaken
      Germany. They were
      planning instead to rebuild
      German industry an use it in
      an attack on communism,
      backed by US capitalists.
      The USSR was forced to
      defend itself and eastern
      Europe against this danger.'
   a What events of the years
      1945–9 might be used to
      support the first
      explanation?
   b What events of the years
      1945–9 might be used to
      support the second
      explanation?
   c What earlier events might be
      used to support either
      explanation?

7.4 THE COMING OF THE COLD WAR

EVIDENCE

SOURCE A

'A shadow has fallen upon the scenes so recently lighted by the Allied victory. Nobody knows what Soviet Russia and its Communist international organization intends to do in the immediate future, or what are the limits, if any, to their expansive tendencies. From the Baltic to the Adriatic an iron curtain has descended across the Continent. Behind that line lie all the capitals of the ancient states of Central and Eastern Europe, in what I must call the Soviet sphere. The Communist parties, which were very small in all these eastern states of Europe, have been raised to power far beyond their numbers. Police governments are prevailing in nearly every case. This is certainly not the liberated Europe we fought to build up.'

Winston Churchill speaking at Fulton, USA, March 1946.

SOURCE B

(In March 1947 the British government told US President Truman that it could not afford to go on helping the Greek government in its civil war against Greek Communists. Truman, in the following speech, asked the US Congress to send help. This began a US new policy of sending money and troops to support anti-communist governments.)

'Greece is today threatened by the terrorist activities of several thousand armed men, led by Communists. Greece must have assistance if it is to become a self-supporting democracy. The government of the United States has made frequent protests against coercion and intimidation, in violation of the Yalta agreement, in Poland, Romania and Bulgaria.

'At the present moment in world history nearly every nation must choose between alternative ways of life. One way is based upon the will of the majority, free elections, individual liberty, freedom of speech and religion. The second way of life is based upon the will of a minority forcibly imposed upon the majority. It relies upon terror and oppression, a controlled press and radio, fixed elections and the suppression of personal freedoms.

'I believe it must be the policy of the United States to support free peoples who are resisting attempted subjugation by armed minorities or by outside pressure. The free peoples of the world look to us for support.'

President Truman, speaking to Congress, 12 March 1947.

SOURCE C

'The Marshall Plan is merely a variant of the Truman Doctrine. It faces the European countries in need of relief with the need to give up their right to plan their national economy in their own way. This plan is an attempt to split Europe into two camps. An important feature of this plan is an attempt to confront the countries of Eastern Europe with a "bloc" of countries including Western Germany. The intention is to make use of German heavy industry as a base for American expansion in Europe, in disregard of the national interests of the countries which suffered from German aggression'.

Andrei Vyshinsky, Soviet Foreign Minister, speech to UN General Assembly, 18 September 1947.

SOURCE D

'After the Second World War, American policy makers could see communism only in terms of a military threat. In creating NATO they had drawn a line arbitrarily across Europe against an attack no one was planning. After the war the Soviet Union did not want or need to overrun other countries. The Atlantic Pact (the NATO treaty) was unfortunate because it was quite unnecessary.'

George F. Kennan, former US Ambassador to Moscow, speaking in 1965.

SOURCE **E**

◀ *Soviet fears expressed in a cartoon, about 1950: Western 'mother-hens' hatching a new Nazi 'chick'.*

SOURCE **F**

Western German cartoon, about 1950. It reads 'thanks to our liberators'.

EXERCISE

1 How do the cartoons support the arguments in the written sources?

2 Does the fact that the sources support each other make them more reliable?

3 Which (if any) of the sources are likely to be unbiased? Explain your answer.

4 Does the fact that some sources are biased make them of no use in helping us to understand the causes of the cold war?

5 Which of the speakers or writers was in a good position to know the aims of his own side?

6 Which of them was in a good position to know the aims of the other side?

7 Use the sources and your knowledge of the background to explain the coming of the cold war.

7.5 THE COLD WAR SPREADS TO THE FAR EAST

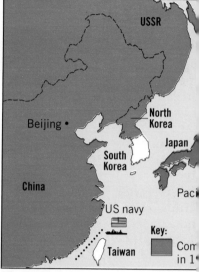

The Far East, 1949.

How Korea was divided
Korea is the nearest part of the mainland of Asia to Japan, and the Japanese had controlled it since 1905. In 1945 when Japan was defeated, the USSR and the USA agreed in a friendly way to occupy half of Korea each, north and south respectively. Nobody intended this to last long. But, just as in Europe, the Soviets gave support and encouragement in their half of Korea to the local Communists, and the Americans to landowners and business people who opposed communism. As a result, two governments were set up in 1948, Communist in the north and anti-communist in the south, though both claimed to be the rightful government for the whole of Korea. In June 1949 the USA and the USSR agreed to withdraw their troops. It looked as if the Koreans would be left to sort out their own problems.

The USA and China
At about the same time as it withdrew from Korea, the USA also stopped supporting the anti-communist leader **Chiang Kaishek** in **China**. Then, in September 1949, the Communist **People's Republic of China** was set up. Chiang Kaishek fled to **Taiwan**, an island off the south coast of China. Many Americans blamed their own government for permitting this Communist success.

US elections were due in November 1950, and the US Democratic Party was accused of being 'soft on communism'. So in 1950 the Democratic **President Truman** needed to prove that this was not true. One way to do this was to refuse to accept the Communists as the rightful rulers of China, and to support Chiang. Truman sent warships to stop the new Chinese government getting control of Taiwan, and used US influence to keep Chiang in control of the Chinese vote in the United Nations.

The USSR had never given much help to the Chinese Communists, but now it protested at Truman's actions. The Soviets refused to attend any UN meetings while Chiang controlled the Chinese vote there.

The Korean War begins
It was at this point, in June 1950, that the North Koreans suddenly attacked the South. They had a good army, armed with Soviet weapons, and it was clear that they could quickly conquer South Korea. Within a few days President Truman sent US troops from Japan to Korea. At the same time a meeting of the UN Security Council was called. Since the USSR refused to attend, the Council was able to agree to condemn the North Korean attack as 'aggression', and to ask member nations to help the South. A UN force was formed; sixteen nations, including Britain, sent troops to fight in Korea.

China enters the war
By the beginning of October 1950 the UN forces, mainly Americans, had driven the North Koreans out of South Korea. They then went on to invade the North and soon reached the

Korea, 1950–51.

SOURCE A

'It seems strangely difficult for some to realize that here in Asia is where the Communist conspirators have chosen to make their play for global conquest. Here we fight Europe's war with arms while diplomats there still fight it with words. If we lose the war with communism in Asia, the fall of Europe is inevitable.'

US General MacArthur, speech to Congress, April 1951.

orean border with **China**. Up to this point neither China nor the USSR had taken any part in the fighting, though the USSR supplied weapons to the Koreans. But now the Chinese sent in a powerful army and by January 1951 they had driven the UN forces well back into South Korea.

The US **General MacArthur** commanding the UN forces wanted to meet this attack by bombing China itself, perhaps with atomic bombs. Britain, the most important of the USA's allies, objected strongly. President Truman decided instead to give up the idea of driving the Chinese out of North Korea. When MacArthur objected to this and called loudly for an attack on China, Truman was furious – it was his job to lay down policy and a general's job to obey orders. In April 1951 he sacked MacArthur.

The end of the fighting

Although some fighting continued in Korea for another two years, there were no more large-scale attacks. After much argument a line was drawn between the two Koreas, roughly where it had been when the war began. Even then it was only a **cease-fire agreement**, not a peace treaty. From that day to this the two Korean governments have each claimed to rule the whole country.

SOURCE **B**

A wounded Korean girl carries her sister to safety. About 4 million people were killed or wounded in this war. About a million of those killed were Korean civilians.

QUESTIONS

1 Why did the North Koreans invade South Korea in June 1950?

2 Why did US President Truman send troops straight away?

3 Clement Attlee, Prime Minister of Britain, visited President Truman in December 1950. The Chinese were forcing the UN troops to retreat in Korea. General MacArthur wanted to stop this by bombing China itself, using the atomic bomb. What arguments might Attlee have used against this?

4 Read Source A. MacArthur suggests that the Korean War is part of a worldwide communist plot. What evidence might be used to support this point of view?

5 Choose one of the following statements and explain why you agree or disagree with it.
   a The Korean War strengthened the United Nations by showing that aggression could be stopped.
   b The only important effect of the Korean War was to kill or wound 4 million people.
   c The Korean War made the cold war much more bitter.

7.6 THE COLD WAR BECOMES WORLDWIDE

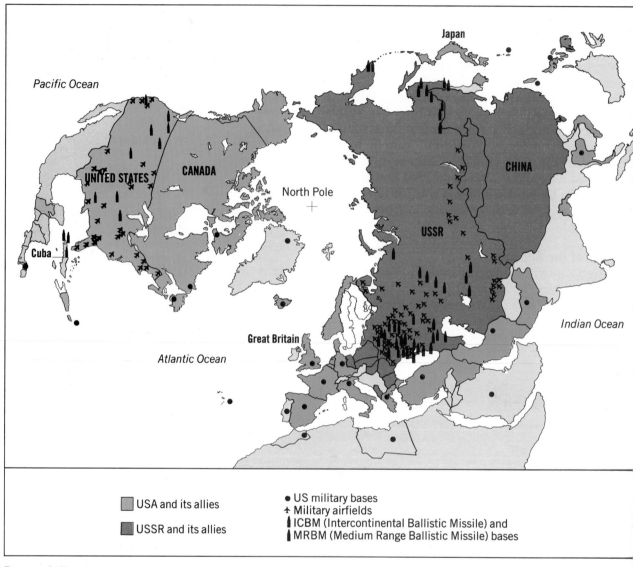

USA and its allies

USSR and its allies

- US military bases
- ✛ Military airfields
- ▮ ICBM (Intercontinental Ballistic Missile) and
  MRBM (Medium Range Ballistic Missile) bases

Bases and alliances, 1960. ▲

▼ *The balance of armaments, about 1960*

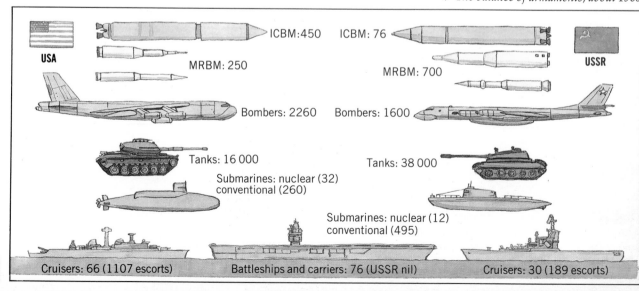

USA

ICBM: 450

MRBM: 250

Bombers: 2260

Tanks: 16 000

Submarines: nuclear (32)
conventional (260)

Cruisers: 66 (1107 escorts)

ICBM: 76

MRBM: 700

Bombers: 1600

Tanks: 38 000

USSR

Submarines: nuclear (12)
conventional (495)

Battleships and carriers: 76 (USSR nil)

Cruisers: 30 (189 escorts)

...ases, bombs and alliances

...fter the Korean War the government of the **USA** made no
...erious attempt to overthrow communism in China or Europe.
...stead it followed a different policy, known as **containment**.
...his meant doing everything it could to prevent communism
...preading any further, but not attacking the communist
...ountries. The main way this was to be done was by
...rengthening the US armed forces, and making them ready to
...ake rapid action anywhere in the world against communist
...ttacks. To do this the USA needed allies and friends all over the
...orld, countries that would allow US bases to be built on their
...erritory to deal with any attack. By 1960 the USA had built up the
...orldwide system shown on the map.

The **USSR** watched this with great alarm. The extra US
...eapons and bases were said to be for defence and not attack.
...ould the Soviet generals be sure of this? Then in 1954 **West
...ermany** joined NATO and begin to build up an army. What
...ould this have reminded the Soviets of? Generals in every
...ountry are paid to prepare for wars and to make sure that the
...ight weapons are there when they are needed. So the USSR and
...ts East European allies built up their armed forces with great
...nergy. In 1955 they formed the **Warsaw Pact** and set up a joint
...efence system. The Warsaw Pact countries were much poorer
...han the NATO countries, but they tried hard to build up as
...many modern weapons. The diagram shows the balance as it
...vas in about 1960.

SOURCE A

*US hydrogen bomb explosion, Bikini
Atoll, Pacific Ocean, 1956.*

SOURCE **B**

SPACE AGE IS HERE
Soviet satellite circling world in 95 minutes

Headline in the 'Daily Express', 1957.

The spread of nuclear weapons		
	A-bomb	*H-bomb*
USA	1945	1951
USSR	1949	1953
Britain	1952	1957
France	1960	1968
China	1964	1967

QUESTIONS

1. Study the map and the
   information about weapons in
   1960.
   a Could it be said that one
   side was clearly safer than
   the other?
   b If you were in charge of US
   or USSR forces, where (if
   anywhere) would you expect
   an attack?
   c If you were in charge of US
   or USSR forces, where (if
   anywhere) would you want to
   set up a new base or airfield?

2. In the early 1960s ICBMs
   (intercontinental ballistic
   missiles, with a range of
   20,000 km or more) came into
   use. What effect would this
   have had on the safety of either
   the USA or the USSR?

3. Would the news item in Source
   B have worried a US general?
   Give reasons for your answer.

7.7 CUBA, 1962 – NEARLY A 'HOT' WAR

Long-range missiles which could attack from halfway across the world were only just coming into use in the 1960s. Before this the USA had plenty of bases from which its shorter-range missiles could attack Moscow; but the USSR had none within range of US cities. In 1962 the Soviet leader **Nikita Khrushchev** tried to change this by siting missiles in **Cuba**.

Cuba is an island only ninety miles off the coast of the USA. Until 1959 it was ruled by Batista, a dictator who had seized power by force. The Cubans were mostly poor peasants or workers on sugar plantations, and much of the land and industry was owned by US companies and business people.

In 1959 **Fidel Castro**, a young lawyer, led a revolt against Batista, overthrew him and formed a goverment. Castro was not a member of the Communist Party, but he agreed with many Communist ideas, and he began to carry out one of them which was certain to be popular. He nationalized the large sugar plantations, formerly owned by Americans. The USA promptly stopped buying Cuban sugar, so Castro turned instead to trade with the USSR and Eastern Europe. Then in 1961 US **President J. F. Kennedy** allowed a group of anti-communist Cubans who had fled to the USA to invade Cuba. When they landed, nobody

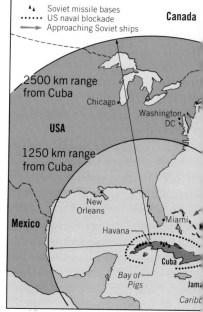

Cuba and the North American mainland

SOURCE A

US air photograph of Cuba, 1962, with labels added by US intelligence officers.

supported them and they were easily rounded
up by Castro's army.

The Cubans had already bought weapons from the USSR. Now they seemed to need them more than ever, and more began to arrive – with the US air force keeping a close watch from the sky. In October 1962 a US air photograph showed that Soviet technicians were building **missile bases** in Cuba. Once any missiles arrived, they would be a threat to many US cities. So before the missiles could be landed President Kennedy ordered the US navy to blockade Cuba, stopping all ships going there. If the Soviet ships carrying the missiles refused to stop, it seemed likely that the US navy would sink them, leading almost certainly to a war between the USA and the USSR, a war using nuclear weapons. This was the moment when the cold war came nearest to thermonuclear heat.

While the world held its breath, Khrushchev made a suggestion. If the US government would agree not to attack Cuba, and to end the blockade, the Soviet government would take away the missiles and destroy their sites. On 28 October, Kennedy agreed, and the world breathed again. The Cuba crisis was over.

QUESTIONS

1 How reliable is Source A?

2 In 1962 the USSR offered to arrange for Soviet missiles to be sited in Cuba. What arguments for and against would have gone through Castro's mind?

3 In October 1962 the US blockade of Cuba began. What fears, hopes and plans would either Kennedy or Khrushchev have had then?

4 Both Kennedy and Khrushchev claimed to have 'won' the Cuba crisis. Which, if either, do you think came off best?

SOURCE B

Missiles on a Soviet ship on its way to Cuba, 1962.

8.1

THE END OF EMPIRE

In 1939 the empires of European countries were even bigger than they had been in 1914 (see map, page 16). They included well over a quarter of the world's people. Yet by 1969, only thirty years later, these empires had all vanished. This change is one of the most important described in this book. How can it be explained?

Education encouraged independence movements

The European empires brought **education** to some of the colonial people. Schools teaching in European languages were set up. Missionaries taught Christianity. In the 1920s and 1930s a few successful students from the colonies studied at universities in Britain, France and other European countries. There they learned to be doctors, teachers and engineers, but they learned some other things too.

One was ideas of **democracy** – that people should control their own governments. This went with the idea of **self-determination** – that people had the right to a government of their own nationality. These ideas had been applied in Europe in 1919 (see pages 24–5), but not to Europe's empires.

What question would the colonial students have asked when they learned about this? What might they have told their friends when they got back home?

Another set of European ideas that colonial students found interesting were those of the **socialists** and **Communists**. Lenin had argued that empires were a way by which the capitalists of the European countries forced the colonial people to work for them for low wages. In this way the poor people in the colonies helped to make the rich people in Europe richer than ever. When the colonial students got back home, what might they have suggested to people working on plantations or in the mines and factories?

The war weakened Europe

Europe almost tore itself to pieces in the Second World War. When the dust settled after 1945, the world was dominated by the USA and the USSR, the two superpowers. **Britain** was one of the victors, and had armies and navies throughout the world, but it could not afford to keep them there for long. Before 1939 Britain had become rich by selling goods all over the world and by investing money abroad, living to some extent on the profits of these investments. But during the war Britain had been far too busy fighting to be able to export goods for sale. So the war had been paid for partly by selling off the overseas investments and partly by borrowing money. After 1945 Britain owed vast amounts and had few investments to bring in income. How could it pay its way in the world, much less pay the cost of keeping a worldwide empire under firm control?

Other former European colonial powers, such as **France** and **Belgium**, faced the same problem on a smaller scale.

SOURCE **A**

'If we could clear out every mission station in the country and stop all this fostering of higher native education, we would much sooner become an asset to the Empire. We are simply committing suicide.'

'We are in this country because we represent a higher civilization, because we are better men. It is our only excuse for having taken the land. For us to turn round now and ask the natives to help in directing the government of ourselves is ridiculous.'

Southern Rhodesian white colonist, about 1930.

Population of imperialist countries and their colonies, 1939.

◀ *Japanese leaflet dropped on Indian soldiers during the Second World War.*

The war encouraged independence movements

When the Japanese attacked in 1941, the European empires in the Far East collapsed. The people in these areas often disliked the Japanese, and fought against them, but Japan had at any rate shown that the Europeans could be defeated. When the war ended, the people in some parts of east Asia, for instance in **Vietnam** and **Indonesia**, refused return to European rule.

Colonial people learned about modern warfare

During the war some colonial people learned to fight by organizing guerrilla warfare against the Japanese. For instance, the Communists in **Vietnam** did this. When the French tried to resume control in 1945, the Vietnamese put up a tough fight. In the vast British Empire control had always depended on native troops. The Indian army, with a few British senior officers, had been the main support for British power in the East for a hundred years. During the Second World War it had fought on the British side, and in 1945 it was well equipped. What might it do if India asked for independence and Britain refused?

The British Commonwealth

Almost all the people in Canada, Australia and New Zealand were white settlers of European origin. Most of them were British and were used to the idea of voting and having control of their own affairs. They were proud to be British, and many had fought in Europe in the world wars. But they were not prepared to take orders from the London government.

In the 1920s and 1930s the British had changed this part of their Empire into a **Commonwealth**. Canada, Australia and New Zealand become **dominions** instead of colonies. This meant that they were completely independent of the British government in London, but agreed to continue to work together as friendly equals. This caused very little difficulty, and the arrangement still exists. In the parts of the British Empire where most people were black, matters were different. One of them, **South Africa**, was allowed to become a self-governing dominion without giving the blacks any share in power. **India** was another country where there was a great deal of conflict. Its leaders demanded independence, but in the 1920s and 1930s the British refused.

QUESTIONS

1 Four reasons for the ending of European empires are suggested in this unit.
   a Which of them were entirely due to the Second World War?
   b Which of them were partly influenced by the war?
   c Which of them were happening in any case, even without the war?

2 The writing on the poster, Source B, is in Urdu.
   a Why should the Japanese drop leaflets instead of bombs on Indian troops?
   b What do you think the leaflet says?

3 a Read Source A. Why was the writer so opposed to the education of colonized people?
   b What justification does the writer give for the existence of the white colony in Rhodesia?
   c What answer to this might be given by a black person living there?

8.2 # INDIA UNDER THE BRITISH RAJ

The British had come to **India** to increase their own power and wealth. To do this they had built railways and ports and started cotton factories and tea plantations. Britain also brought a new legal system and set up schools and universities for the richer Indians. So there were good opportunities in British India for Indian landowners, business people, lawyers and government officials, and the British were proud of what they had done.

Indians demand independence, 1919
Educated and well-off Indians may have benefited from these opportunities, but they hated being second-class citizens in their own land. They were proud of their own ancient culture, and found the British attitude of racial superiority humiliating. The First World War, and the Treaty of Versailles with its idea of **self-determination**, encouraged them. So did the Russian Revolution of 1917. Why not an independent India?

   The British were prepared to set up local councils to which Indians could be elected, and even talked about gradually giving more and more power to Indians in the future. But from 1919 Indians were led by men who wanted to take immediate control of their own country.

Massacre at Amritsar, 1919
In 1919 a strike led to riots in the town of Amritsar. Indian rioters killed five Englishmen and beat up a woman missionary. **General Dyer**, the local army commander, banned all meetings there. In spite of this the local people flocked to a mass meeting in the town square. Dyer decided that the time had come to teach the Indians a lesson, and he ordered the troops to fire. 379 people were killed and a thousand wounded. Afterwards Dyer ordered that all Indians passing the place where the missionary had been attacked must crawl on their bellies. The British government later dismissed Dyer and condemned his action, but many British people approved of it. A public subscription for him raised £30,000.

Gandhi
In 1919 **Mahatma Gandhi** became leader of the Indian nationalist movement. He was an Indian lawyer with a London University degree, and he respected British ideas of justice and fairness. But he thought that British control, though it might help wealthy Indians get richer, made things worse for the great mass of India's poor. He had enormous sympathy for the poor and showed it by living simply himself. His idea was to build up a mass political party, and use strikes and protest meetings to force the British to grant independence as soon as possible. In the 1920s Gandhi succeeded in building up a mass party, the **Congress Party**, with branches in every village. He encouraged even the 'untouchables', the lowest-caste Indians, to look on themselves as people with rights, able to stand up to the British and proud to be Indians.

   One of Gandhi's most important ideas was **non-violence**. The

SOURCE A

'There are few Indians, even of the highest rank, who have not had the experience of gross insult when travelling by railway because Englishmen refused to sit in the same carriage as a native.'

Sir Henry Cotton, 'New Indian'.

SOURCE B

'We did not conquer India for the benefit of the Indians. I know it is said at missionary meetings that we conquered India to raise the level of the Indians. That is cant. We conquered India as an outlet for the goods of Great Britain. We conquered India by the sword and by the sword we hold it.'

Sir W. Joynson-Hicks, Home Secretary, 1928.

SOURCE C

British cartoon, 1933.

SOURCE D

Lord Minto, Viceroy of India, at an official ceremony in 1905.

strikes and protests often led to violence, and Gandhi could see that this played into the hands of the British, who controlled the police and the army, as Amritsar had shown. He himself hated violence, and he decided to fight the British with what he called 'soul force' in a campaign of **civil disobedience**. He told his followers never to resist by force. They were to allow themselves to be arrested and imprisoned. But they were to use all forms of peaceful protest – marches, meetings and strikes. They were to refuse to buy British goods, to refuse to pay British taxes, to refuse to co-operate with the British government in any way.

Britain makes concessions

Gandhi's policy was highly successful. He was often imprisoned, and so were thousands of his supporters, and he was not always able to prevent violence. But the Congress Party became stronger and stronger as more and more Indians came to feel that they were members of a proud nation and had a right to run their own country. In 1931 the British invited Gandhi and other Indian leaders to discussions. In 1935 they brought in a new system of elected governments for the various provinces of India. Britain was to keep central control in its own hands, but the plan included an **all-India parliament** to give advice.

QUESTIONS

1 Look at Source D. What does this picture tell you about the British in India?

2 Look at Source C.
   a Explain the message of the cartoon.
   b Was the cartoonist for Gandhi, against him, or neither? Explain your answer.

3 **a** What would Edwin Montagu (Source E) have probably thought about the events at Amritsar in 1919?
   b What would Sir W. Joynson-Hicks (Source B) have probably thought?

4 What effect, if any, do you think Amritsar would have had on:
   a ordinary Indian people in other areas?
   b people in other countries such as the USA?

5 Look at Source F. Why might these people have had their photograph taken breaking the law?

6 What concessions did the British make in India in 1935? Explain why they did this.

SOURCE E

'The policy of His Majesty's Government is that of increasing the association of Indians in every branch of the administration, and the gradual development of self-governing institutions.'

Edwin Montagu, Secretary for India, speaking in the House of Commons, 1917.

SOURCE F

Indians defying the British tax laws by making salt, 1930.

8.3 INDEPENDENCE FOR INDIA AND PAKISTAN

The Muslims of India

British India had many religions. About two-thirds of the people were **Hindus**, and a quarter **Muslims**. Gandhi believed strongly in equal rights for all religions, but he was a devout Hindu himself, and so were most members of the Congress Party. Muslims could see that the Congress Party would be likely to win the elections for an all-India parliament. Would a mainly Hindu India be fair to Muslims? They had their own political party, the **Muslim League**, and they began to talk about insisting on a separate country, **'Pakistan'**, which they could be sure of controlling themselves.

Britain promises independence

In 1939 the British government took India into the war as part of the British Empire. Gandhi and the Congress Party refused to support the war – what they wanted was independence. Then in 1942, when the Japanese had overrun most of the rest of Britain's Empire in the East, Britain promised to give India independence when the war was over. Gandhi was not satisfied with a promise for the future, and instead began a campaign to make the British leave straight away. The British put him in prison.

In 1945 a Labour government came to power in Britain. The Labour Party had always sympathized with Gandhi and with the idea of Indian independence. So the government announced that it intended to give self-government to India as soon as possible. For two years the British tried hard to get the Muslim League and the Congress Party to agree to work together. But the distrust between them was too deep. In 1946 a series of riots and massacres took place in the areas where Muslims and Hindus lived close together. Thousands were killed on both sides, and refugees carried tales of horror into other areas, causing the hatred and fear to spread.

Independence and the bloodbath

These disturbances ruined any chance there might have been of a single independent India for people of all religions. So in 1947 the British simply announced that they were leaving India within a year. In fact it took only six months for Congress and the Muslim League to set up separate governments for the two new independent countries, **India** and **Pakistan**, and to agree how to divide the subcontinent between them. In August 1947 Britain handed over control, and the British Empire in India was at an end. But neither India nor Pakistan wanted to cut off all their links with Britain, and both agreed to join the Commonwealth as self-governing dominions.

Plenty of Hindus and Muslims lived on the 'wrong' side of the new frontiers. People were suspicious of these minority groups, and they in turn were terrified of being attacked. Amid scenes of riot and slaughter worse than before, about 10 million people fled across the new frontiers. Perhaps as many as a million were killed in the process. Gandhi used his enormous influence on the Hindus to prevent some of the violence, but in 1948 he was killed himself – by a Hindu extremist.

SOURCE A

'How can you ever dream of Hindu–Muslim unity? We have no intermarriages. We have not the same calendar. The Muslims believe in a single god and the Hindus worship idols. The Hindus worship animals. No Hindu will take food from a Muslim. They consider cows sacred – we want to eat them. There are only two links between Muslims and Hindus: British rule and the common desire to get rid of it.'

M. A. Jinnah, leader of the Muslim League, 1943.

SOURCE B

Gandhi in 1947 with Lord Mountbatten, the last Viceroy of India, and Lady Mountbatten.

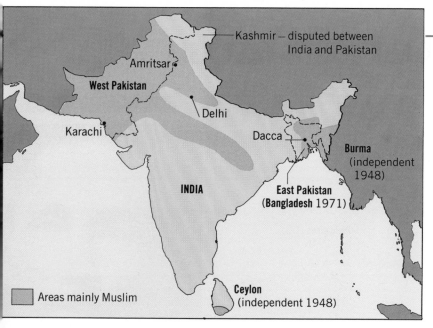

Kashmir – disputed between India and Pakistan

Amritsar

West Pakistan

Delhi

Karachi

Dacca

Burma (independent 1948)

INDIA

East Pakistan (Bangladesh 1971)

Ceylon (independent 1948)

Areas mainly Muslim

The Indian subcontinent.

India and Pakistan since 1947

The Prime Minister of India from 1947 to 1964 was **Jahawarlal Nehru**. Like Gandhi he had a British education and admired the British system of democracy. He and the other Congress leaders had spent long years in British prisons, but they knew how to organize a mass political party and run elections. India also had plenty of skilled civil servants, judges and army officers. Since 1947 India has had many problems, but the democratic system set up in 1947 has stood the strain well.

Pakistan has not been so successful. As you can see from the map, it was divided into two parts, with India in between. It has also had serious border conflicts with India. In 1971 East Pakistan, with Indian support, broke away to become the independent country of **Bangladesh**. Pakistan has never been able to agree on a satisfactory system of democracy, and since 1957 has been ruled mainly by the military.

SOURCE C

Victims of the rioting in the Punjab, India, 1947.

QUESTIONS

1 a Why do you think Gandhi insisted that India should be given independence in 1942?

b Why did the British refuse in 1942 though they gave way in 1947?

2 Look at the map. How can it be used to explain the violence that took place before and after the partition of India?

3 a What reasons does Jinnah give in Source A for wanting a separate Pakistan?

b Do the events of 1947 prove that he was right?

4 In what ways did the events of the years 1919—47 help to prepare India for self-government?

5 Look back at page 94.

a List the four reasons suggested there for the decline of European empires.

b What events or sources here and on pages 96—7 show each of these reasons affecting India under British rule?

c Choose the one of these reasons which you think was most important for India and explain your choice.

8.4 INDEPENDENCE FOR SOUTH-EAST ASIA

Key: Ex-colonies with date when they became independent
- British
- French
- Dutch

China

Canton

Hong Kong (British)

Macao (Portuguese)

Philippines (US) 1946

Burma 1948

Hanoi

Rangoon

Laos 1954

North Vietnam 1954

Manila

Thailand

South Vietnam

Cambodia 1954

Saigon

N. Borneo Sarawak 1963

Malaya 1957

Singapore 1963

I n d o n e s i a 1949

The countries of South-East Asia gain independence, 1946–63.

SOURCE A

Ho Chi Minh, Communist leader of the Vietnamese. He had worked as a cook in Paris in the 1920s.

SOURCE B

As the Japanese surrendered in 1945. British and US troops marched into the areas of **South-East Asia** that Japan had conquered. It looked at first as if they would hand back control to the Europeans who had governed these areas before the war. This happened without much difficulty in the British possessions of **Hong Kong** and **Singapore**. But in most parts of the region groups of local people had been fighting their own guerrilla wars against the Japanese. The leaders of these movements had often been educated in Europe or the USA. Now they wanted to get control of their own countries. By about 1960 they had got it.

The Philippines   The USA had always claimed to stand for the freedom of colonial peoples. In 1946 it handed over control of the Philippines to a Filipino government, though keeping for itself a large military and naval base and retaining great influence on the government.

Indonesia   As the Japanese left, the Indonesians set up their own government. The Dutch sent troops and made an attempt to restore their pre-war control, and there was a short struggle. But the Indonesians, under their leader **Dr Sukarno**, were well organised, and in 1949 the Dutch withdrew and accepted the independence of Indonesia.

Malaya, 1949: British police question a Chinese Malayan peasant.

Vietnam Opposition to Japan in Vietnam had been led by the Communists under **Ho Chi Minh**. In 1945 they formed their own government in Hanoi, the capital. The French, determined to restore France's greatness, tried to overthrow Ho Chi Minh and set up instead a Vietnamese government they could control. A bitter war lasted for six years (1948–54); in the end the French were beaten and a French army had to surrender. The struggle for independence in Vietnam was complicated by the beginning of the cold war (see pages 84–7). Communist China gave help to Ho Chi Minh, and the USA gave help to the French. In 1954, after the French surrender, Vietnam was divided into two. Ho Chi Minh's Communists ruled the northern half, and anti-communist Vietnamese the south.

Malaya As in Vietnam, the opposition to Japanese rule in Malaya had been led mainly by the Communists. In 1945 the British returned, but in 1948 the Communists began a rebellion which was to last twelve years. In Malaya, Communists were mostly of Chinese origin. There were racial tensions between Chinese and Malays, and many Malays helped the British, so the rebellion was defeated. At the same time the British helped the Malays to organize a government of their own. In 1957 Malaya became an independent country within the Commonwealth.

What the end of empire meant
The overseas empires that came to an end in these years had worked in two ways:
- **Political** The 'imperialist' country ruled over the 'colonial' one, collecting taxes, running the police and the army and organizing the government.
- **Economic** Banks and business firms from the imperialist country owned railways, plantations, factories and mines in the colony and made a profit from them.

When a colony became independent it usually got political but not economic independence. It now ran its own police, army and government, but the railways, plantations and so on often still belonged to people in the imperialist country.

The USA and empires
The USA disliked empires. In the eighteenth century, after a war of independence, it had won its freedom from Britain. Americans were proud of this and glad to see other colonies gaining independence. The USA had taken over the Phillipines from Spain after a war in 1898, but most US citizens were against the idea of controlling an empire.

The USA was strongly in favour, however, of its banks and business people trading and investing money all over the world. After 1945 the USA was by far the richest country in the world. Its people had money to invest in oil wells, factories, plantations and mines in many countries, including many of the newly independent countries. The USA did not take over direct political control of other countries, but it had a great deal of **economic control**. The Communists called this 'US imperialism'.

SOURCE **C**

The first Prime Minister of Singapore, Lee Kuan Yew. He studied at Cambridge University after the war, and started a political party in Singapore in 1954. He was still Prime Minister in 1988.

QUESTIONS

1 The Second World War greatly increased the power, wealth and influence of the USA. How might this have affected the European empires?

2 The gaining of independence by former colonies was often complicated by disagreements between Communists and others.
   a Give examples of this.
   b Why might communism have been an attractive idea to colonial people seeking freedom?
   c Why might the USA have been specially keen to prevent ex-colonies turning Communist?

8.5 INDEPENDENCE FOR AFRICA

Africa north of the Sahara

The Arab countries of **North Africa** were part of the proud and ancient **Islamic** civilization. When they saw the European colonies in India and the Far East gaining independence, they naturally wanted it for themselves. Some of them, such as Morocco, Tunisia and Egypt, already had a good deal of self-government under France or Britain. All of them had educated leaders, who had learned the European ideas of equality and democracy, and could organize political parties as Gandhi had done in India.

In **Egypt** it was the officers of the army, led by **Colonel Nasser**, who spearheaded the movement for independence. They seized power in 1952, set up a mass political party and demanded that Britain should withdraw its army from its bases beside the Suez Canal. In 1954, with Egyptian people solidly against it, Britain had to agree.

In **Tunisia** and **Morocco** there were similar nationalist movements against the French, who gave way as the British had done in Egypt. In 1956 both countries became independent.

Although Egypt was now independent, the British and French still owned the **Suez Canal**. As well as being of great strategic importance in case of war, the canal made a good profit. In 1956 Nasser announced that Egypt was taking over ownership and control. Britain and France objected strongly, and sent troops to take back the canal. But before they got very far, there was a financial crisis in Britain, and the only way to solve it was to borrow from the USA. The US government flatly refused to lend, so the British and French armies were forced to withdraw. Nasser had stood up to the two leading imperialist countries, and he had won.

Meanwhile in **Algeria** there was more trouble. The Arab population formed a nationalist movement, but here in Algeria there were large numbers of French settlers who were determined to remain citizens of France. These settlers held most of the good jobs and ran the country. They knew that they would be a minority in an independent Algeria, so they fought with bitter determination against decolonization. The Algerians could never hope to beat the French army, so they used guerrilla warfare, and murdered and bombed French civilians to frighten them into leaving. The French army fought with great brutality, often beating and torturing suspects, and this sickened people in France and throughout the world. In 1962, after six years of conflict, even the French settlers saw that they had lost. President de Gaulle of France agreed to Algerian independence.

Africa south of the Sahara

There was no way of stopping ideas of independence and democracy from spreading to the rest of Africa. When people heard about Gandhi in India or the success of independence movements in North Africa, they thought, 'Why not us too?'

But there were two special problems in **central and southern Africa**. The European empires had broken up the traditional

Cartoon of 1959 by the British artist Ronald Searle.

Algerians celebrate their independence, 1962.

African way of life without giving the Africans much chance in the white people's world. The Europeans brought work to some, but it was mainly unskilled work in mines or on plantations. The whites kept the skilled jobs for themselves. So the level of African education was very low – most black Africans could not even read. This made it difficult for them to organize an independence movement.

The second problem was that the European colonies included many different tribes and races of Africans who had not much in common with each other. In the Belgian Congo, for instance, seventy-five different African languages were spoken. How could the people of an area like this be persuaded that they belonged to a single nation? How could they be persuaded to work together to establish and run one?

As you can see from the map, between 1957 and 1980 the whole of Africa except South Africa and Namibia became independent. In general, this happened peacefully. Many people in Britain and France now felt strongly that colonial people should have their freedom. Those who disagreed knew from the wars in Vietnam, Suez and Algeria that it would be difficult to hold colonized people down by force. Yet there were still some attempts to do this, as you can read in the next unit.

QUESTIONS

1 Make a list of the countries shown on the map which gained independence. Against each write the name of the European country to whose empire it had belonged, and the date of independence.

2 Look at Source A.
 a What was the artist's opinion about colonies in Africa?
 b What effect might a cartoon like this have had?

3 Find Gibraltar, Malta, Cyprus, the Suez Canal and Aden on the map.
 a Britain had controlled these places so that it could control the route to . . . where?
 b Why was this less important in the 1950s and 1960s than it had been earlier?

4 What effect might the failure of the British in Suez and the French in Algeria have had throughout Africa?

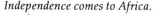
Independence comes to Africa.

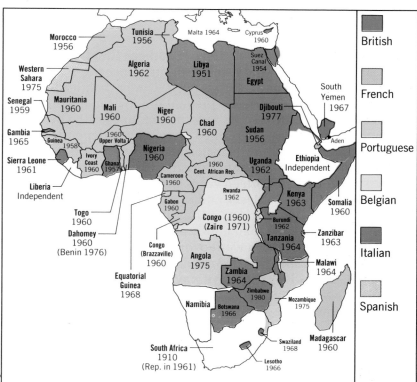

8.6 CONFLICT IN CENTRAL AND SOUTHERN AFRICA

White settlers

Whatever the people of Europe thought about freeing their Africans colonies, matters looked very different through the eyes of the **white settlers**. In some parts of **central and southern Africa** whites had gained control of much of the best farmland. They had built railways and were building power-stations and modern cities. They had plenty of experience in running these things, and they often looked on the uneducated Africans as children or as people belonging to an inferior race. The whites enjoyed a standard of living far higher than that of the blacks or of ordinary people in Europe.

South Africa

The most extreme example of white domination was **South Africa**, where 2.5 million whites ruled over 12 million blacks. Since 1909 they had been a self-governing dominion in the British Commonwealth. Only the whites could vote, so they were able to pass strict laws to keep control in their own hands.

Kenya

In **Kenya** the white settlers were only 1 per cent of the population. For ten years they resisted the idea of a black government. The Africans were led by **Jomo Kenyatta**, a graduate of London University who was leader of the Kikuyu tribe, the largest in Kenya. A Kikuyu organization called **Mau Mau** turned to violent methods. Many Africans were killed, and so were about seventy whites. The British arrested Kenyatta and many of his followers, and some were brutally treated in prison camps. But by the end of the 1950s the British government in London came to think that independence was inevitable. Kenyatta was released, won an election and in 1963 became the first Prime Minister of independent Kenya.

Southern Rhodesia

About 8 per cent of the population of **Southern Rhodesia** were European settlers. They had run the country since the 1920s, and had built up prosperous tobacco exports. Under their leader, **Ian Smith**, they were determined to prevent the African majority from ever getting control of the government. In 1965 the British government was just as determined not to give independence to a country run by a small white majority. The white Rhodesians declared independence without British agreement. This illegal independence lasted for fifteen years. Britain asked the United Nations to condemn Rhodesia, and to order UN member states to cut off trade with it. Many countries, such as South Africa, ignored this order, and it had hardly any effect. Much more important was the guerrilla warfare organized by the Africans under **Robert Mugabe**. This did not defeat the whites but it wore them down, and in 1979 they gave way and accepted a constitution which gave the blacks control. In 1980 Robert Mugabe became Prime Minister of **Zimbabwe**, as Rhodesia is now called.

SOURCE A

'We could not possibly hold by force our territories in Africa. The march of men towards freedom can be guided but not halted. Of course there are risks in moving quickly. But the risks of moving slowly are far greater.'

Ian Macleod, British Colonial Secretary, 1959.

SOURCE B

'We have seen the awakening of national consciousness in peoples who for centuries have lived in dependence on some other power. Fifteen years ago this movement spread through Asia. Today that same thing is happening in Africa. The wind of change is blowing through the continent, and, whether we like it or not, this growth of national consciousness is a political fact.'

British Prime Minister Harold Macmillan, speaking in South Africa, 1960.

SOURCE C

Jomo Kenyatta, who led Kenyans to independence in 1963. ▶

SOURCE **D**

SOURCE **E**

White Rhodesian soldiers question villager, 1965.

Street scene in Leopoldville, Congo (now Kinshasa, Zaire), 1960.

Angola and Mozambique

The nationalists in the Portuguese colonies of **Angola** and **Mozambique** began their campaign for freedom in the 1950s. **Portugal** was itself not a democracy but a military dictatorship. The Portuguese government saw little need to worry about public opinion and sent massive armies to put down the nationalists. But in 1974 the Portuguese people overthrew the dictatorship, and one of the first actions of the new democratic government was to grant independence to its colonies.

The Congo

The **Congo** was ruled by **Belgium** until 1960. All the important jobs were held by Belgians, and there were no Africans trained to do them. In 1960 they handed over power to **Patrice Lumumba**, leader of the largest nationalist party. There were several other parties, some representing particular tribes or regions of the country. Once the Belgian army officers had gone, order broke down; it looked as if the country would fall to pieces. Lumumba asked the United Nations for help, and the UN sent expert advisers and troops. The UN force was too weak to control the situation, and members of the Security Council could never agree on what it should do. But it did help to get the new government started and to prevent total chaos. The struggle went on for five years. Many people were killed, including Lumumba himself. In 1965 **General Mobutu**, leader of the new Congolese army, seized power and made himself dictator. It was he who changed the name of the country to **Zaire**. In 1988 he was still President.

QUESTIONS

1 What effect might events in the Congo (Source E) have had on the attitude of the Rhodesian soldiers in Source D?

2 a Make a list of the sorts of people who might have favoured independence for African colonies in the 1950s and 1960s.
  b What arguments might they have used?

3 a Make a list of the sorts of people who might have opposed independence.
  b What arguments might they have used?

4 Read Source À.
  a What 'risks of moving quickly' might Ian Mcleod have been thinking of?
  b What 'risks of moving slowly' might there have been?

5 Read Source B. Macmillan was speaking to white South Africans. How do you think they would have felt about what he said?

9.1 RACIAL PROBLEMS IN THE GLOBAL VILLAGE

Ideas of racial supremacy

In 1914 the white people of Europe and North America ran the world. Some, like the British, controlled large empires whose people were mainly black. As well as being black they were mainly poor. The whites' empires and trade had weakened the old African and Indian way of life, and offered the blacks only hard work for low pay in unskilled jobs. There were some exceptions to this, but on the whole the white people from Europe had a far higher standard of living than the black people of the colonial lands. Many whites looked down on blacks and believed that the white races were in some way superior. Some of the black people were so used to being pushed around that they even accepted this themselves.

The USA had no colonial empire, but about 11 per cent of its people were descendants of the black slaves brought from Africa in earlier times. Although slavery had been abolished in 1863, the US blacks were poor and badly educated and mostly did unskilled work for low wages. So in the USA there was the same sort of gulf between black and white as in Africa or India, with the whites in control, usually looking down on the blacks as inferior and determined to keep them 'in their place'.

These ideas of racial supremacy had no scientific evidence to support them. But that did not stop a great many whites accepting them without thinking much about it.

Migration spreads the problem to new areas

During the twentieth century improvements in transport have made it easy for large numbers of people to move to new parts of the 'global village'. During and after the Second World War many black people moved from areas where wages were low and jobs hard to find to others where they would have a better chance. For instance, many people from the Caribbean, from India, from Pakistan and from Bangladesh came to Britain. In the USA many black people from the southern states moved into the industrial cities of the northern USA, such as Chicago. These newcomers usually had to move into the poorest housing and take the worst-paid jobs. They often found themselves competing for these with the poorest of the white people who lived there already. This caused conflict. Many whites, who already looked down on the blacks as 'inferior', now feared them as rivals. Blacks were often forced to live close to each other for safety in the poorest parts of the city, the '**black ghettos**'.

World opinion turns against racialism

At the same time as racial problems were spreading to new areas, it became clear to more and more people that ideas of racial supremacy were dangerous, as well as being nonsense. Hitler's idea of a 'master race' was directed mainly against the Jews, but he showed how easy it was to whip up racial hatred, and what brutalities it could lead to. The Allies' victory in 1945 looked like a victory for democracy and for equal political rights.

SOURCE A

'As to the Negroes, they have a most profound respect for the white man. As long as he keeps them at worshipping distance they are all right.'

Southern Rhodesian quoted in F. Fox, 'The British Empire', 1929.

SOURCE B

'In 1939 I came up with the idea of starting a shop and tried to get a licence. Indians apparently had little difficulty, but for Africans it was nearly impossible. Nairobi was full of such pinpricks in those days: railway-station lavatories marked EUROPEANS, ASIANS and NATIVES; hotels we could not enter except as servants, and even certain kinds of beer that we could not drink.'

W. Itote, Mau Mau General, 1967.

SOURCE C

SOURCE **D**

'Whites only' beach in South Africa.

QUESTIONS

1 What would the person quoted in Source A think of the author of Source B?

2 What would the author of Source B think of the person quoted in Source A?

3 **a** What feelings or attitudes are shown by the faces and gestures of the people in Source C?
   b Why should some people in Britain in 1984 feel and think like this?
   c How useful is this photograph as evidence for the study of racial attitudes in Britain?

4 Look back at page 53. What similarities and differences are there between Hitler's attitude to the Jews and the attitudes of white people to black people shown in this unit?

From 1948 onwards the mainly black people of the former colonies threw off the control of the white Europeans and set up their own nations. Most people in most countries came to accept the ideal that people of every colour, race and religion should have equal rights.

This does not mean that racial discrimination disappeared. It takes time for people to forget their prejudices and fears. In any case, the blacks in most countries still had the worst jobs, the lowest pay and the worst education; thus a gulf remained between their way of life and that of the whites. But there have been some real improvements in the years since 1948. You can read about the **civil rights movement** in the USA on page 108. Even in countries like South Africa, where a white minority still runs the country, the black people have shown that they are no longer willing to submit to white supremacy.

National Front supporters Britain, 1984. The banner says 'Keep Maidstone white'.

9.2 THE USA TACKLES ITS RACIAL PROBLEMS

SOURCE A

Whites lynch a black man, USA, 1919.

SOURCE B

White Americans stop a black girl going to school, Little Rock, 1957. The day after this, US soldiers forced the local whites to open the school to blacks (see Source C.)

From 1875 to 1957 the US Congress passed no laws to try to improve the position of black Americans, but in 1957–68 it passed many, and real improvements were made. Why did this happen at that time? Unit 9.1 suggests one answer to this. This unit will help you to think of others.

1954   The US **Supreme Court** ruled that it was illegal for any state schools to be for whites only. Most southern states found ways to dodge this and keep their 'whites only' schools.

1955–6   Black people in **Montgomery, Alabama**, refused for a year to ride in segregated buses (those with 'white only' seats). They won. **Martin Luther King**, a Baptist minister, became leader of the black civil rights movement.

1957   The state of Arkansas openly broke the law by keeping blacks out of a state school at **Little Rock**. President Eisenhower sent US troops to protect the black students and get them into school.

1957   Congress passed a **Civil Rights Act** to try to make sure that blacks could vote. Southern whites found ways to stop it working.

1957–63   Many protest marches and black sit-ins in 'whites only' eating places. Martin Luther King led a civil rights march of 250,000 people to Washington in 1963.

1960–8   More **Civil Rights Acts** passed. These made any racial segregation in public places illegal; and made it impossible for the southern whites to stop blacks voting. In 1963 only 35 per cent of the blacks who could have voted had their names on the register of voters; by 1969 the figure was 65 per cent.

SOURCE C

'In connection with the disgraceful occurrences of today at Central High School in the city of Little Rock, I will use the full power of the United States to prevent any obstruction of the law and to carry out the orders of the court. Every right-thinking citizen will hope that the American sense of justice and fair play will prevail. It will be a sad day for this country – both at home and abroad – if schoolchildren can safely attend their classes only under the protection of armed guards. Our enemies are gloating over this incident and using it everywhere to misrepresent our nation.'

US President Dwight D. Eisenhower, September 1957.

1964   Martin Luther King awarded **Nobel Peace Prize**.

1964–8   The **Black Power** movement launched by people angry at the limited success of King's non-violent movement. Many riots and much violence, mainly in the northern cities.

1968   Martin Luther King **assassinated** by a white gunman. This led to riots in which fifty people were killed and 20,000 arrested.

1970s and **1980s**   Little more trouble over civil rights. Black mayors elected in many US cities, such as Chicago. Some blacks get good jobs, but many in the city ghettos still poor, unemployed and without hope.

SOURCE   F

'He got the peace prize, we got the problem. I don't want the white man to give me medals. If I'm following a general and he's leading me into battle, and the enemy tend to give him rewards, I get suspicious of him.'

Malcolm X, Black Power leader, speaking of Martin Luther King in 1964. In 1965 Malcolm X was murdered.

SOURCE   D

◀ *Racial tension in Chicago, USA, August 1963.*

SOURCE   E

'We have waited more than 340 years for our God-given rights. The nations of Asia and Africa are moving with jet-like speed towards gaining political independence, but we still creep at horse-buggy pace towards gaining a cup of coffee at a lunch counter.

'It is easy for those who have never felt the stinging darts of segregation to say, "Wait." But when you have seen vicious mobs lynch your mothers and your fathers; when you have seen hate-filled policemen curse, kick and even kill your black brothers and sisters; when you have seen the vast majority of your 20 million Negro brothers in poverty in the midst of an affluent society – then you will understand why we find it so difficult to wait.'

'Non-violent resistance has a way of disarming an opponent; it weakens his morale and at the same time it works on his conscience. Violent resistance will place Negroes in a position where they confront a far larger adversary than it is possible to defeat.'

Martin Luther King, 1964 and 1965.

QUESTIONS

1   What can you tell from Sources A and B about the attitudes of some white Americans to black people?

2   Use the sources and your historical knowledge to explain why black Americans demanded equal rights so strongly in the 1950s and 1960s.

3   Use the sources and your historical knowledge to explain why many white Americans supported the civil rights movement.

9.3 BLACK AND WHITE IN SOUTH AFRICA

Since 1945 most of Africa has accepted the idea of equal rights for people of all races. But the white people of **South Africa** have strengthened their control and developed a system of racial segregation far more complete than before. It is called **apartheid**. Why has this happened? Why have events in South Africa been so different from those in other parts of the world?

The main reason is that there are four black South Africans for every white, so a democratic South Africa would be ruled by its black majority. The most powerful section of the white population are bitterly opposed to this. These are the **Afrikaners**, people whose ancestors came to Africa from the Netherlands in the seventeenth century; but they long ago stopped thinking of themselves as European colonists who could go 'home'. They are a tough and determined people who have built up their own nation with its own language, Afrikaans. For over a century they struggled against the British Empire, succeeding in holding on to their land and their traditions.

One of the strongest Afrikaner traditions was an attitude of fear of and contempt for black people. In the nineteenth century the whites had fought bitter wars with the blacks in South Africa, had taken land from them and made them first slaves and then labourers. Afrikaners looked down on blacks as inferior and were convinced that a mixture of the races would destroy the Afrikaner way of life.

In 1948 the **Afrikaner Nationalist Party** won South Africa's whites-only election. The party has been in power ever since, gradually developing its policy of Apartheid or racial separation. Much of this was not new – it tightened up a system of segregation which was already in existence. For instance, ever since 1913 black people had not been allowed to own land except in certain **'native reserves'**. These were small and poor, so people had to travel away to work in the white-owned mines, factories and farms. Here wages were low; black men had to live away from their families and send back money for them to live on. Apartheid built on this system. The plan was that the native reserves were to be enlarged slightly and renamed **homelands**. They cover about 15 per cent of the country – the poorest lands. Since 1963 all blacks (70 per cent of the population) have been looked on as citizens of one or other of ten homelands, and can be sent 'home' if they have no work in the white areas. Each of the homelands was to have its own elected black local government under the overall control of the white central government.

Apartheid under attack

Black South Africans at first resisted apartheid by means of peaceful protest marches and demonstrations. In 1960 the **African National Congress (ANC)** told people to march to the police stations and hand in or burn the **pass books** which blacks were supposed to carry at all times. At the town of **Sharpeville**, 10,000 joined in. How could the police arrest them all? The Sharpeville police's answer to this problem was to open fire on the crowd – killing 67 people. In 1962 the government passed laws giving it

The apartheid system

Black people not allowed to:
- Vote or be MPs.
- Marry or have sex with whites.
- Live in white areas.
- Use 'white' cinemas, buses, hotels or beaches.
- Go to 'white' schools.
- Travel without a passbook.
- Own land in 'white' areas.

SOURCE

'We have had to take up arms because that is the only answer. There was no other course open to us. The Afrikaner knows only one language, violence. And that is why we are seeing the violence in the townships today.'

Winnie Mandela, wife of imprisoned ANC leader Nelson Mandela, interviewed in 'Woman' magazine, 8 February 1986.

SOURCE

Dead and wounded at Sharpeville, March 1960.

power to imprison people without trial and to ban opposition movements. It banned the ANC. Other marches or similar protests have been dealt with in a similar way. For instance, in 1976 about five hundred blacks were killed by the police putting down a series of protests which started in the town of **Soweto**.

By the 1970s the banned ANC could count on support from the newly independent black African countries to the north (see the map on page 103). It began to train guerrilla fighters there and to plan a campaign of violent resistance to apartheid. Up to now it has not had much effect.

Prosperity causes problems

South Africa's racial problem has not prevented it from becoming the richest and most powerful country in Africa. It has plenty of **gold** and other **minerals** and in the last thirty years has set up many modern **industries**. As a result the white South Africans have one of the highest standards of living in the world, and even most of the blacks are economically better off than those anywhere else in Africa. You might expect that this would make people more contented and ready to put up with apartheid, but in fact it is having the opposite effect. The new industries are nearly all in the white areas, but they depend on a skilled and educated black workforce living not too far from the job – the very opposite of apartheid. Many whites can see this, and since 1979 the Nationalist President Botha has tried to make some changes. For instance, blacks have been allowed to organize **trade unions** and to go on strike, and **black–white marriages** are now legal. But these are just tiny cracks in the system. Black people still have no say in how they are governed.

QUESTIONS

1 What defence would an Afrikaner put forward for the apartheid system?

2 Are historians likely to find Sources B and C useful?

3 Look back to pages 102–5. The changes in the rest of Africa were bound to affect South Africa.
   a What would these changes lead black South Africans to hope or fear?
   b What would these changes lead white South Africans to hope or fear?

4 Look back over pages 106–7.
   a What similarities are there between the way the racial problem has developed in the USA and in South Africa?
   b What differences are there?
   c What reasons can you suggest for the results being so different in the two countries?

SOURCE C

During the years 1985–7 violence of this sort became common in the black townships of South Africa.

9.4 SOUTH AFRICA, APARTHEID AND WORLD OPINION

South Africa leaves the Commonwealth

When the British colonies gained their independence they mostly decided to remain members of the **British Commonwealth** (see page 95) alongside the other self-governing dominions such as Canada and South Africa. So the Commonwealth became a worldwide organization of nations of many different races. It has no power to take action, but its members give friendly advice and help to each other, and its Prime Ministers meet regularly. Many Commonwealth nations keep the Queen as head of state, but others, like India, are republics.

In 1961 the South African government decided to make its country a republic. This meant that South Africa would have to apply again to be in the Commonwealth, and existing members would have a right to object. Obviously many of them would do this, for how could an organization of many races accept apartheid? The South Africans avoided such objections by not even applying to rejoin.

The United Nations and South Africa

The shootings at Sharpeville in 1960 (see page 110) horrified people all over the world, especially in countries which had recently gained their freedom. The General Assembly of the **United Nations** has again and again since 1960 passed resolutions condemning apartheid. It has asked members to break off relations with South Africa and to cut off trade, especially trade in weapons. But few have done so. Member nations of the UN need not obey resolutions of the Assembly unless they want to, and some leading members have had two strong reasons for not taking action against South Africa.

The first reason was connected with the **cold war**. Many of the new African governments were socialist. The USSR was keen to make friends among them and offered them weapons and other

▲ *Commonwealth Prime Ministers' meeting, 1986. Most of them wanted an agreement not to trade with South Africa or to invest in industry there. Margaret Thatcher, Prime Minister of Britain rejected this idea.*

QUESTIONS

1 Which countries of the British Commonwealth would be likely to object most strongly to apartheid? Explain your answer.

2 Look at Source A. What reasons might a British Prime Minister have for not wanting to cut off trade with South Africa or investment there?

3 Explain why the South African government supported rebellions in Angola and Mozambique.

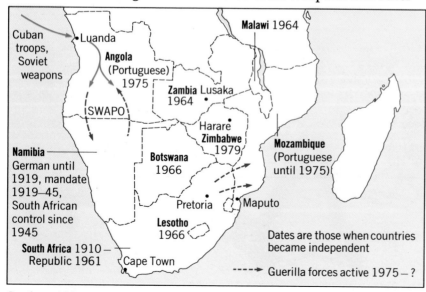

Southern Africa.

Map labels:
Cuban troops, Soviet weapons
Luanda
Angola (Portuguese) 1975
Malawi 1964
Zambia Lusaka 1964
SWAPO
Harare Zimbabwe 1979
Mozambique (Portuguese until 1975)
Namibia — German until 1919, mandate 1919–45, South African control since 1945
Botswana 1966
Pretoria
Maputo
South Africa 1910 – Republic 1961
Lesotho 1966
Cape Town
Dates are those when countries became independent
- - - - ► Guerilla forces active 1975 – ?

help. For instance, the Soviets helped the Angolans to overthrow Portuguese rule and the new Angolan government in 1975 was led by Communists. What would happen if white rule was overthrown in South Africa and the most powerful country in Africa then became friendly with the USSR? Tankers carrying oil supplies for the West in peace or war come round the Cape of Good Hope all the time. The USA and its allies therefore decided that they should not make an enemy of the white government of South Africa.

The other reason was the great success of South African mining and industry and its **trading links** with the West. With cheap labour and plenty of raw materials it was easier to make a profit by investing in South Africa than in most other countries. So many US, British and other European companies lent money or set up factories there. There was money to be made, too, by selling the South Africans machines for their factories or weapons for their army. The existing system in South Africa seemed to be good for business, so many people in the West did not want to disturb it.

Namibia

After the First World War, South Africa took charge of the former German colony of **South-West Africa** as a mandate under the League of Nations (see page 29). Then, when the UN was formed in 1945 this area became a **trusteeship territory**. The South African government refused to accept the UN's right to interfere and treated most of the territory as if it was part of South Africa itself, applying the apartheid policy there. So in 1966 the UN General Assembly passed a resolution that control of the area should be taken away from South Africa. It was easier to pass the resolution than to turn the South Africans out. **Namibia**, as the territory has become known, is still controlled by South Africa.

South Africa hits out

When **Angola** gained its independence from Portugal in 1975 the people of neighbouring Namibia hoped that they too might soon gain their freedom. They set up the **South-West Africa People's Organization (SWAPO)** and with Angolan help began a guerrilla war against the South Africans. But South Africa had a well-trained army with plenty of modern weapons, and it struck back with determination. One way to do this was to attack SWAPO's bases in Angola. Another was to encourage anti-communist Angolans to rebel and to give them help and weapons. The new Angolan government already had a good deal of help from the USSR. Now Fidel Castro agreed to send a **Cuban army** to help the Angolan government against the rebels whom South Africa was supporting. Fighting has been going on ever since.

On the other side of Africa, the people of **Mozambique**, like the Angolans, set up a socialist government when the Portuguese withdrew in 1975. Here too the South Africans encouraged a rebellion. Ever since, they have given money and weapons to guerrilla fighters attacking the Mozambique government.

Demonstrators against a British rugby team going to South Africa. In 1977 all British Commonwealth member countries agreed to try to stop all sporting links with South Africa.

4 Study Source B. What effort could playing games or refusing to play them have on Apartheid?

5 In 1986 the South African government brought in very strict laws to stop newspaper reporters and television teams telling the world about anti-apartheid demonstrations and riots and police action. Why do you think it did this?

10.1 HOW CHANGE CAME TO CHINA

In 1914 China was a sick giant. Europeans seemed to rule the world. Educated Chinese people in the past had looked down on the uncivilized 'foreign devils'. Now they were still proud of their past greatness, but many of them came to feel that, if they were to make China strong again, instead of despising foreigners they must copy some of their ideas. **Dr Sun Yatsen** led those who thought like this. He had been educated by European missionaries and he admired many Western ideas. In 1905 he founded a political party, the **Guomindang (GMD)**, which in 1911 overthrew the despotism of the Empress Tzu-Hsi. What modern form of government would the Chinese put in her place?

It took thirty-eight years to answer this question. The years from 1911 to 1949 were a time of disorder. Rival groups of Chinese struggled with each other and also with the Japanese. Out of this time of disorder was born a new, unified and determined China – the **Communist China** that we know today. Why did the Communists succeed? How did the events of this period shape the China of today?

Dr Sun's GMD put forward three main principles:

- **National independence:** freedom from foreign control.
- **Democracy:** China was to be governed by the consent of all its people through a proper system of elections.
- **'People's livelihood':** everybody should have a fair share of food and a reasonable standard of living.

Dr Sun and his friends were greatly encouraged by the Russian Revolution of 1917. Russia was their neighbour in the north, and the Communist attack on the class system and on inequality (see page 32) fitted in well with the GMD's third principle. So when in 1921 the **Chinese Communist Party (CCP)** was formed, it worked closely with the GMD.

But it was one thing to put forward principles; it was a different matter to persuade 500 million people to follow them, especially when 495 million of the people were illiterate peasants. When D. Sun died in 1925 his ideas were still dreams.

Chiang versus Mao

The new leader of the GMD was an able young general, **Chiang Kaisheck**. At first he worked with the CCP, as Dr Sun had done, and together they gained control of more and more of the country. But two serious disagreements developed.

First, most wealth in China came from the **land**. Most peasants were miserably poor, and in bad times they and their children starved. They paid up to 60 per cent of their crop in rent to the landowner. They longed to control the land themselves. The CCP was keen to overthrow the class system, so it encouraged the peasants to stand up to the landowners. But Chiang thought that the GMD government should co-operate with the landowning class, from which most educated Chinese came.

Second, modern **trade and industry** were beginning in China. Much of it was in towns like Shanghai which were controlled by the foreigners. Many factories, banks, railways and mines were

SOURCE A

'We have always been farmers. We didn't have our own land – we rented it. The landlord's name was Wang. Landlords didn't eat as we others did. They ate meat and vegetables every day. Wang was an incredibly mean person. If people couldn't pay, he punished them. People hated the landlords, but there was no way of getting round them. Everybody owed the landlord money. As long as you owed him money you couldn't get permission to leave the village to look for a better landlord. The landlords ate, and we worked.'

Memories of a Chinese peasant.

SOURCE B

'1 Speak politely.
2 Pay fairly for what you buy.
3 Return anything you borrow.
4 Pay for anything you damage.
5 Don't hit or swear at people.
6 Don't damage crops.
7 Don't take liberties with women.
8 Don't ill-treat captives.'

Summary of Mao's orders to the Communist Red Army. Why would Mao make rules like this?

SOURCE C

SOURCE D

American cartoon, 1896: the bear represents Russia; the eagle, Germany; and the vulture in the background, France.

Chinese communist cartoon, about 1940: a peasant family is being turned out for not paying its rent.

owned by foreign business people. Chiang was happy to work with these foreign capitalists to modernize China, and they were glad to support him. But to the CCP they were the enemies of the Chinese working class and were to be driven out.

In 1927 Chiang decided to destroy the CCP. Without warning he ordered his troops to slaughter as many Communists as they could catch. In the towns this was successful, and those members of the party who were not killed went into hiding or fled to the countryside. Here the CCP set up its own government in several areas. From now on the strength of the CCP was based firmly on the peasants. It was at this time that **Mao Zedong**, himself a peasant's son, began to emerge as leader. Meanwhile Chiang's government encouraged the growth of trade and industry. It also improved education and helped some of the peasants to own their own land. But these changes did not go very far.

For ten years, 1927–37, the GMD attempted to stamp out the Communists. It succeeded in much of the south and east, the richest part of the country, and in 1934 the CCP decided to withdraw to the north-west. This was the famous **Long March**, during which Mao was selected leader of the party. One hundred thousand men and women started on the 6,000-mile march to the remote mountain area of **Yanan**, beyond the reach of Chiang's armies. Only 20,000 got there. Perhaps it was a defeat, or perhaps it was a victory – only the future would tell. Mao and the CCP could safely organize and train in Yanan. From there they sent out their agents to encourage people in the rest of China to resist Chiang, to stand up to the landowners and to trust the CCP.

QUESTIONS

1 Study Source C.
   a What did the 1896 cartoonist think was likely to happen?
   b What was the cartoonist's opinion of this likely development – for or against? Explain your answer.
   c Why did this development seem likely at the time?

2 Study Source D. Explain the actions of the various people in the cartoon.

3 Which of Sources C and D would a historian find more useful in studying China?

4 Make a list of factors which made it difficult to carry out Dr Sun's 'three principles' in China. Which of these do you think was most important?

5 Why were Chinese peasants discontented? (Use Sources A and D.)

10.2 CHINA, 1937–49: WHY DID THE COMMUNISTS WIN?

CAUSATION

China was so weak in the 1930s that the Japanese were easily able to seize control of **Manchuria** in 1931 (see page 54). After that they gradually got control of most of the rest of north-east China. **Chiang** and the **GMD** worked hard to equip their army with all the latest weapons and to train it to use them. But Chiang was far more worried about the Communists than about the Japanese, and he did little to stop them. When he did try, in 1937, the Japanese marched south, won all the battles and within a year had control of south-east China. Chiang and his government had to flee to **Chongqing** in the remote south-west.

Mao and the **CCP** watched these events from their base in **Yanan**. Their **Red Army** had developed a different method of fighting: **guerrilla warfare**. They knew that the side with most modern weapons and ammunition was likely to win any conventional battles, and that both the GMD and the Japanese had far better supplies than they could hope for. So they relied instead on attacks at night, or on sudden raids on supply lines or small groups of the enemy. The Red Army could move easily almost anywhere in China among the peasants, who came to trust them. The Japanese controlled only the towns and main railways and roads. They could never stamp out the underground CCP resistance groups in the countryside.

What would happen when the Second World War ended and the Japanese withdrew? Who would get control: Chiang and the GMD, or Mao and the CCP? In 1946 fighting broke out to decide this.

SOURCE A

'When the enemy advances, we retreat. When the enemy halts, we harass. When the enemy retires, we attack. When the enemy retreats, we pursue.'

Mao Zedong, Red Army tactics.

SOURCE B

'It is absolutely necessary for the army to win the support of the peasant masses. If there is no movement of the armed peasantry, in fact there is no base, and the army cannot exist. Only by implanting itself deeply in the hearts of the people can it win.'

Pen Teh-huai, leading member of the CCP, 1935.

SOURCE C

'I have seen long lines of conscripts chained together on their way from their villages to training camps.'

'Sons of the rich never entered the army; sons of the poor could never escape.'

US reporters, writing about the GMD army in the 1940s.

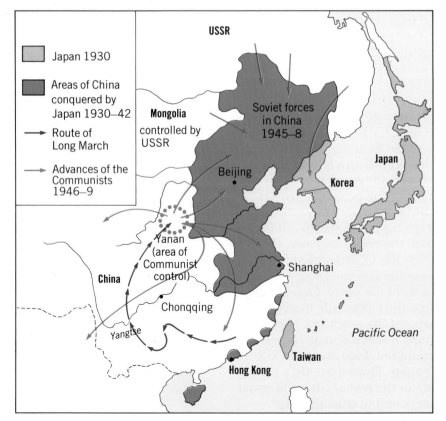

Civil war in China, 1937–49.

CAUSATION

SOURCE D

'The Reds had a very limited supply of armaments. For years they called the GMD troops their "ammunition carriers" as they claimed to capture more than 80 per cent of their guns and 70 per cent of their ammunition from enemy troops.'

Sheridan, 'China in Disintegration',
975.

SOURCE F

'We cannot afford, economically or militarily, to take over the continued failures of the present Chinese government.'

George Marshall, US Secretary of State,
1948.

SOURCE E

'The Communists (in September 1948) were now passing from guerrilla warfare to set battles. The battle of Huai Hai opened in November. Huai Hai is one of the major battles of the modern age. The forces were now about equal, 600,000 on each side. At first the Nationalists (GMD) fought well, but as their supply position deteriorated and the tactics of their generals were obviously at fault, morale collapsed. Several divisions surrendered, or even changed sides. The Nationalist army lost 600,000 men at the battle of Huai Hai. It was the end.'

C. P. Fitzgerald, 'China: Communist Victory', 1968.

Factors in favour of the GMD

The GMD had two main advantages. First, Chiang's government was accepted all over the world as the **rightful government of China**. As leader of the largest country in the world he had attended wartime meetings with Churchill, Stalin and Roosevelt. His representatives helped to found the new United Nations Organization, and sat in one of the permanent seats on its Security Council.

Second, since 1941 the British and the USA had sent Chiang **supplies**. When the Second World War ended, the USA sent him even more war material of all kinds including aircraft and military experts to give advice. You might expect that the USSR would have given help in the same way to Mao, but Stalin did not expect Mao to win and helped very little. In 1945 Soviet troops, by agreement with the other Allies, had occupied Manchuria. Stalin waited till 1948, when it was clear that Mao might win, to hand Manchuria over to the CCP.

In spite of Chiang's advantages, he lost. In 1949 he and his army fled to the island of **Taiwan**, leaving Mao and the CCP in complete control of the rest of China. Why did this happen?

EXERCISE

1 Historians have suggested that the following factors contributed to the victory of the CCP in 1949:
   - The peasants supported them.
   - The Long March put them in a good position (look at the map).
   - The Japanese attacks showed the GMD to be weak and the CCP to be effective in defending China.
   - Good political leadership by Mao.
   - Good military tactics of the Red Army.
   - The GMD made many mistakes.
   - The USSR supported the CCP.

   a Use the information on pages 114—5 and in the text and sources in this unit to find evidence for each of these possible reasons.
   b Which factor was most important?
   c Which was least important?
   d Was Mao's victory inevitable?

2 a Explain why the USA helped Chiang against the Communists.
   b Use Source F and your knowledge of events in Europe in 1945—9 to explain why the USA let the Communists win.

10.3 BIRTH OF THE PEOPLE'S REPUBLIC OF CHINA

The Communist Party takes control

In October 1949 **Chairman Mao** and the **CCP** set up the **People's Republic of China**. It was to be a 'democracy' like the USSR; everybody had a vote. But the CCP was the only important political party, so the real power lay in the hands of its leaders' **Politburo**. They still run China today.

The new government soon took a firm grip on its vast country. Most Chinese people longed for peace and were glad to be rid of Chiang's corrupt and brutal army. **'People's courts'** dealt with 'enemies of the revolution'. The number who were put to death is uncertain but is likely to have been well over half a million.

Land reform

In 1949, 80 per cent of Chinese people could not read and knew little about events outside their own village. They had learned to trust the CCP in the long struggle against the landowners, the GMD and the Japanese. How could the party keep their trust and support and get them to work together to modernize China and to make it strong? One essential was **land reform**. The CCP told the peasants to take over the land for themselves. It took a year or two to spread the change to every village, but by 1955 the landowner class had disappeared. The village lands were then organized into **collective farms**, as Soviet villages had been in the 1930s. By 1957, 93.5 per cent of Chinese peasants were organized into collective farms.

Control of press and education

An important way to hold the Chinese people together was to take over the **radio** and the **newspapers** and use them to spread Communist ideas. The new government also set up schools and universities to bring **education** to everybody for the first time. Since 1949 two generations of Chinese people have been brought up to accept communism.

Danger of attack

In June 1950, eight months after Mao's government came to power, the Korean War began. By November 1950 the Chinese **People's Liberation Army (PLA)**, as the Red Army was now called, was fighting against US troops in Korea (see page 88). It seemed possible that the USA might strike back by helping Chiang and the GMD to invade China from Taiwan, starting a new civil war in China to overthrow communism. So China needed a strong army with up-to-date weapons, and it needed them straight away.

SOURCE A

'The most violent revolts have happened where the local tyrants, gentry and lawless landlords perpetuated the worst outrages. The peasants are clear sighted. Who is bad and who is not, who is worst and who is not quite so vicious, who deserves severe punishment and who deserves to be let off lightly – the peasants keep clear accounts, and very seldom has the punishment exceeded the crime.'

Mao Zedong, 1951.

SOURCE B

'In a remarkably short time the new government had: suppressed banditry; restored the battered railroad system; replaced the graft-ridden bureaucratic system of local government with apparently incorruptible Communist "cadres"; introduced a stable currency and a nationwide tax system; begun an extensive program of public health and sanitation; provided a tolerably even distribution of available food and clothing.'

Report to a US Congressional Committee, 1967.

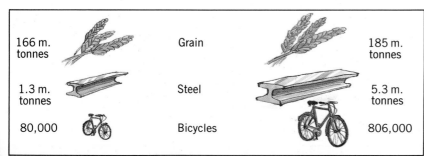

166 m. tonnes	Grain	185 m. tonnes
1.3 m. tonnes	Steel	5.3 m. tonnes
80,000	Bicycles	806,000

◀ *Agricultural and industrial production in China, 1952–7 (m.t. = millions of tonnes).*

SOURCE C

Soviet poster, 1949: it reads 'Glory to the great Chinese People who have gained freedom, independence and happiness.'

Industry – help from the USSR

In 1949 the Industrial Revolution had hardly begun in China. It now needed to **industrialize**, to be able to make modern machines of all kinds, if it was to be strong and independent. China needed power-stations, steel works and other basic industries. It needed bicycles and radio sets for the people. And the Korean War showed that it urgently needed tanks, planes and guns – perhaps even nuclear weapons.

The obvious source of help was the **USSR**. Mao went to Moscow and made a treaty with Stalin in February 1950. The Soviets promised to lend China money, and to send supplies, factory machines and experts to show it how to run a socialist economy.

SOURCE D

Huang Chin-chi, a landowner, is tried by a people's court…

QUESTIONS

1 **a** Look back at the cartoon, Source D, on page 115. What connection might there be between this and the events in Sources D and E? Explain your answer.

 b How does Mao (Source A) justify punishments like the one in Source E?

 c Do you accept his argument?

2 Source C shows warm friendship between the USSR and China. How can this be explained?

SOURCE E

…and executed, 1950.

10.4 CHINA GOES ITS OWN WAY

The Great Leap Forward, 1958

At the end of China's first **five-year plan** Mao was worried. The plan concentrated on industry and offered nothing much to the peasants except loss of their land to the collectives. In the USSR it was believed that communism could be built only on the support of the town workers, but Mao knew that in China the **peasants** had been the chief source of support for the CCP. China was very different from the USSR, and should travel along its own road to communism.

So in 1958 Mao launched the **Great Leap Forward**. The CCP now encouraged the peasants to make sweeping changes for themselves in the countryside. The collective farms were grouped together into **communes**, each with about 30,000 people. Each was to run its own schools, health care, farms and factories. They were to build dams, irrigation works, mines or anything else that they thought might work and be useful. And they were to do these things for themselves, though with guidance from the party. Communes set up cement works, small steel furnaces and back-yard factories of many kinds.

Some of their efforts, for instance the building of dams, laid the basis for future growth; but some of the things made in the back-yard factories were no use. Food production actually fell, and to avoid a famine the peasants were given private plots of land and encouraged to grow food to sell in the market. So, on the whole, the 'great leap' was a failure.

China and the USSR quarrel, 1959

The Soviet advisers were horrified at the Great Leap Forward, and at the independence it showed. The Soviet Communist Party expected those of other countries to work together under its lead. When in 1956 the Hungarians decided to go their own way they were forced back into line by Soviet tanks. China was far too big for that, but Khrushchev the Soviet leader could see no reason why he should go on supporting and helping China.

There were other reasons for the quarrel. Chiang and the GMD still ruled Taiwan, and the USA still accepted them as the rightful government of China. The USSR now had hydrogen bombs and missiles, and China hoped for Soviet help. Mao argued that the USA was only a 'paper tiger' – a threat by the USSR would be enough to stop US support for Chiang. But Khrushchev instead argued that nuclear weapons had made war unthinkable, and he travelled to the USA for a friendly meeting with President Eisenhower. He followed it with a visit to Beijing. There is no evidence about what was said, but it is clear the Mao and Khrushchev quarrelled bitterly. Soon afterwards the USSR withdrew all its advisers, including nuclear scientists, from China and stopped all economic aid. Each country accused the other of betraying the ideas of Marx and Lenin.

The Cultural Revolution, 1966–8.

Some leaders of the CCP had been worried about the Great Leap Forward. What China needed, they thought, was organization

Chinese poster showing a worker in the Tachai commune helping to build a dam.

'In Russia the revolution developed from the cities to the countryside, while in our country it developed from the country to the cities.'

Mao Zedong, 1950.

'The reason why the friendship between the great peoples of China and the Soviet Union is unbreakable is that it is built on the great principles of Marx, Lenin and Stalin.'

Mao Zedong, 1953.

'Our theory is made up of the universal truth of Marxism-Leninism combined with the practical reality of China. We must be able to think independently.'

Mao Zedong, 1959.

SOURCE **E**

SOURCE **F**

10.4

▲ *Red Guards spreading Mao's ideas.*

◀ *The cover of a copy of Mao's works. It shows a Red Guard waving his copy of the 'Little Red Book'. The 'Thoughts of Chairman Mao'.*

from above, with modern factories run by experts, not by enthusiastic peasants. They wanted strict control by the party, but also favoured the idea of a policy rather like Lenin's new economic policy in Russia. This had allowed peasants and small businesses to grow crops and make things to sell for profit.

Mao and his friends called this the **'capitalist road'**. They thought that giving power to experts in the towns, or giving some peasants a chance to make money, would squeeze the poor peasants out. They complained that the experts, the well-educated people and the party bosses were taking over China. These people should be forced to listen to criticism from below and to respect the point of view and the way of life of the peasants.

In 1966 Mao used his enormous prestige to get mass support for his ideas. He called on the students in schools and universities to form **Red Guards**. The army arranged for them to come to Peking from all over China. Mass rallies were held, and people were encouraged to criticize the party, the managers in factories, the teachers in schools, anybody in authority. This was called the **Cultural Revolution**. It caused chaos, but it gave Mao complete victory in the party.

Communes were now encouraged again. Team-work was to be the aim, not profitable sales. The slogan was 'Serve the people'. Experts from the towns were sent to peasant villages to learn from the peasants. To help young people from the villages to get into university, examinations were altered.

All this did not happen without a good deal of disorder. Many people were killed, and many more unfairly persecuted by the Red Guards. The education of scientists and other specialists was badly disorganized.

In 1969 Mao declared that the Cultural Revolution was over and he used the army to restore order and organization. But he continued with his other policies. Production of food and other goods remained low. No party leaders dared openly to disagree with Mao, but he was already 76 years old. What would happen when he died?

QUESTIONS

1 a Suggest dates for Sources A and E and F. Explain your reasons.
  b Choose either Source A or Source B and explain the purpose of the artist.

2 The Chinese and the Soviet Communists treated the peasants in very different ways.
  a Give examples of this.
  b Use Source B and your own knowledge to explain the reasons for this.

3 a What differences are there between Sources C and D?
  b How can these differences be explained?

4 What might the following people think about the Cultural Revolution?
  a a Red Guard.
  b a peasant.
  c the head of an important factory.
  Explain your answers.

10.5 CHINA SINCE MAO

In 1976 Mao died. Some of his friends, led by his widow, were keen to carry on with his policies. But most party leaders supported **Deng Xiaoping**, a practical politician rather than an idealist like Mao. Deng had been attacked as a bad Communist during the Cultural Revolution. Now he arrested Madame Mao and her friends. The trial of the **'Gang of Four'**, as they were called, was used to attack the Cultural Revolution and to show what harm it had done. Since 1977 Deng and his supporters have led the CCP and governed China.

Modernization

In China the Cultural Revolution had slowed down technological change by disrupting the education system. When Deng looked at Japan or even Taiwan he could see very rapid industrial and technological development. If China was to be strong and independent in the twenty-first century, he said, it must concentrate on the **'four modernizations'**: of agriculture, industry, science and technology.

To do this the Chinese leaders went back to the policies that had been used after the failure of the Great Leap Forward. Deng was convinced that people would work harder and better if they could see how their effort benefited themselves and their families. Many communes were allowed to break up. Collective farms could let individual peasants farm separately and sell for themselves everything they grew above a certain quota. People were encouraged to start small workshops and businesses, which provided jobs and useful goods as well as making a profit for the owners. Large-scale industry remained firmly in the hands of the government, but even in large factories managers were given more freedom to make decisions. If production went up and was of good quality they were allowed to pay better wages or spend more on new machines.

Friendship with capitalist countries

In the 1950s China and the USSR had seen the USA as their common enemy. But in the 1960s China's quarrel with the USSR grew more bitter. China even feared a Soviet attack, and in 1969 shots were exchanged at a disputed point on the frontier. By this time even the USA saw that there was no hope of Chiang and the GMD getting control of China again. So in 1971 the USA agreed that Communist China could take the Chinese seat on the UN **Security Council**. Then in 1978 China made a treaty of friendship with Japan, and Deng suggested that the USA, Japan and China should make a **defence agreement** against the USSR.

Japan, the USA and other capitalist countries such as Britain and France all saw the chance of profitable investment in the modernization of China. China needed industrial machinery of all kinds. Foreign banks were ready to lend China the money to buy it. Deng also agreed to set up **special economic zones**, where foreign capitalists could set up factories. This provided work and wages for Chinese people, as well as modern technology, and it helped to earn money for China.

SOURCE **A**

'Whatever system induces the peasants to produce more should be adopted, be it collective or individual. It does not matter whether the cat is black or white, so long as it catches mice.'

Deng Xiaoping, 1980.

SOURCE **B**

'One child is enough': Chinese poster.

QUESTIONS

1 Read Source A. Explain in your own words what Deng meant.

2 a Make a list of the main policies tried out in the 1980s inside China.

  b Choose the two most important and explain how each might be expected to work.

  c Explain why you think them the most important.

SOURCE C

Chinese students in Beijing, 1982.

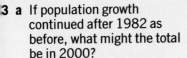

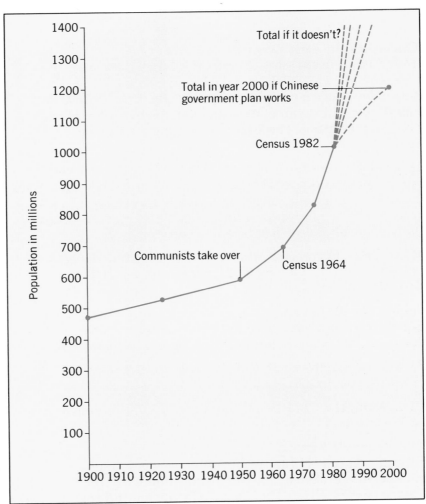

China's rising population, 1900–2000 (projected).

3 a If population growth
   continued after 1982 as
   before, what might the total
   be in 2000?
 b Does Source B show that
   Chinese people readily
   accept the 'one child' policy?

4 Deng was criticized as a bad
  Communist during the Cultural
  Revolution. Which parts of his
  policy since Mao's death might
  a strict Communist object to?

5 Look back at Sun Yatsen's
  three principles on page 114.
  Has the CCP fulfilled them?

Too many people?

Before the revolution China's population had been kept down by three killers: famine, war and disease. But since 1949 there have been few famines, no internal wars and far less disease. Medical services, including vaccinations, have been provided free, and a nationwide campaign has improved hygiene and water supply, so that far more babies survived. This was one of the big success stories of Communist China. But, as the graph shows, this success was leading to a massive new problem. All these new people needed food and jobs. What would happen if the population went on shooting up? In 1980 the government decide to slow it down by a campaign to encourage the **one-child family**. Contraceptives and abortion are easily available, and early marriage is discouraged – 25 is the recommended minimum age. Parents with more than two children now suffer reduced wages. Are these policies likely to work? By 2000 we should know the answer.

CHANGE

10.6 CHINA AND THE FOREIGNERS IN THE TWENTIETH CENTURY

Nineteenth and early twentieth centuries

Hong Kong   In 1841 Britain attacked China, and in 1842 the Chinese agreed to give Britain the island of Hong Kong. The British developed a prosperous trading city there. In 1898 Britain leased from China part of the mainland nearby so that Hong Kong could expand. The lease was for ninety-nine years, running out in 1997.

Treaty ports   Between 1858 and 1911 the Chinese agreed to allow foreign merchants special rights in certain ports. They could trade freely there and could have their own law courts. The Chinese government had little power there. The treaty ports were under British, French, German or Japanese control.

Manchuria   Occupied by Russia 1897–1905. Under Japanese influence 1905–31. Occupied by Japanese armies 1931–45 (see pages 54 and 71).

Peking   In 1900 an anti-foreigner rebellion broke out in China. Germany, Britain and France sent a joint army to Peking. It defeated the rebels and forced the Chinese to punish them.

Taiwan   Seized by Japan 1905. Returned to China in 1945. Controlled by the GMD since 1949.

Outer Mongolia   Independent of China 1912. Controlled by the USSR since 1924.

Late Twentieth Century

Taiwan   Since 1949 Taiwan and other smaller islands nearby have been controlled by the GMD, anti-communist followers of Chiang (see page 116). They claim to be the rightful government

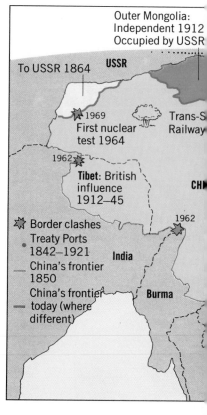

Outer Mongolia: Independent 1912 Occupied by USSR

To USSR 1864   USSR

1969 First nuclear test 1964

Trans-S Railway

1962

Tibet: British influence 1912–45

CH

1962

✳ Border clashes

• Treaty Ports 1842–1921

China's frontier 1850

China's frontier today (where different)

India

Burma

SOURCE A

HMS 'Nemesis' destroying a Chinese fleet in 1842. The 'Nemesis' was the first iron steamship ever seen in Chinese waters. From the 'Illustrated London News', 12 November 1842.

EXERCISE

1 a Make a list of the foreign countries which in 1914 controlled areas that were once part of China, or had special rights in China. Give brief details.

b Which parts that were once China are still controlled by foreigners today? Which are likely to be still under foreign control in the year 2000?

c How has China's relationship with foreign countries changed?

2 a What contrast between China in the nineteenth century and in the late twentieth century is shown by Sources A and B?

b Does this help to explain the contrast you noticed in question 1?

Occupied by Russia 1899–1905
Japanese influence after 1905
Occupied by Japan 1931–45

To USSR 1858

1969

Manchuria

jing •

1950 Vladivostok

Port Arthur

Korea

Shanghai

1954–62
Canton

Taiwan
Japan 1905–45
GMD rule 1949 onwards

Hong Kong (British)

Macao (Portuguese)

1am (formerly 1ch Indo-China)

of China. The Beijing government claims its own right to rule Taiwan. In 1954–62 the Beijing government began to attack the smaller islands near Taiwan. The USA helped the GMD to defeat these attacks.

Korea (see page 88) In 1950 the Chinese army drove the US-led United Nations forces out of Communist North Korea.

Frontier incidents The map shows places where there were frontier disputes with India and with the USSR. Troops were sent to these places and a few shots fired, but no important changes were made.

Hong Kong Hong Kong is a modern city of over 5 million people. It has flourishing modern industry, and its banks and businesses trade all over the world. Most of the people are Chinese, but they have no votes. The Governor and his staff are British. Much of the water supply comes from the mainland area leased from China in 1898. What will happen in 1997 when the lease runs out?

In 1984 the British and the Chinese governments came to an agreement. Britain agreed to withdraw in 1997 and hand the whole of Hong Kong back to China. In return China agreed to keep the British system of law in Hong Kong and to allow capitalist business and worldwide trade to carry on as before.

China's nuclear weapons In 1985 China had six intercontinental missiles with nuclear warheads, and two submarines firing twelve nuclear missiles each. It also had more than a hundred shorter-range nuclear missiles.

c What other factors might also explain the contrast shown in question 1?

3 In 1984 the British Foreign Secretary, Sir Geoffrey Howe, said: 'It would not be realistic to think of continued British administration of Hong Kong after 1997.' How can this be explained?

4 How might Chinese control of Hong Kong help Deng's policy of modernization?

5 What problems might Chinese control of Hong Kong cause for the Communist government of China?

6 What effects might Chinese control of Hong Kong have on the people of Hong Kong?

SOURCE **B**

China's first hydrogen bomb, 1967. The people waving in the foreground were added later by photo-montage. Why?

11.1 ISRAEL: A NEW STATE

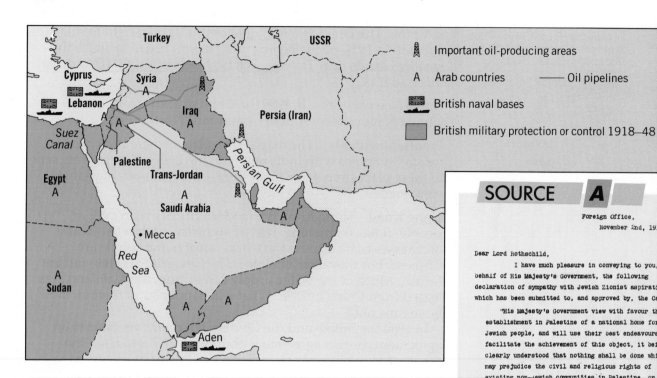

SOURCE **A**

Foreign Office,
November 2nd, 191

Dear Lord Rothschild,

I have much pleasure in conveying to you,
behalf of His Majesty's Government, the following
declaration of sympathy with Jewish Zionist aspirati
which has been submitted to, and approved by, the Ca

"His Majesty's Government view with favour th
establishment in Palestine of a national home for
Jewish people, and will use their best endeavours
facilitate the achievement of this object, it bei
clearly understood that nothing shall be done whi
may prejudice the civil and religious rights of
existing non-Jewish communities in Palestine, or
rights and political status enjoyed by Jews in an
other country".

I should be grateful if you would bring this
declaration to the knowledge of the Zionist Federati

▲ *The Balfour Declaration.*

In 1914 the **Middle East** was an Arab region. From North Africa to the Persian Gulf people shared a common religion, **Islam**, and a common language, **Arabic**. Jerusalem was a holy city for Christians and Jews as well as Muslims, so there were some Jews living nearby in Palestine, just as there were some Christians. But **Palestine** was an Arab land. There had not been a country called Israel since Roman times.

For some European Jews, however, **Israel** was also a dream for the future. The ancient Jewish name for Jerusalem was Zion, so they called themelves **Zionists**. In 1948 their dream came true – the state of Israel was set up and Jews flocked in. The local Palestinians and the other Arabs of the region objected bitterly, and fought hard against it. How was it that this new state was born in a hostile land?

The Balfour Declaration, 1917

One explanation is that in 1917 the British Foreign Secretary, **Arthur Balfour**, promised the Jews a 'national home' in Palestine. He was thinking not of what might happen in forty years time but of Britain's need for support against its enemies in 1917.

During the First World War Britain made a promise to the Arabs as well as to the Jews. Before 1914 Palestine and all the Arab lands from Egypt to the Persian Gulf were parts of the **Turkish Empire**. Turkey was on the German side, and the British promised the Arabs independence after the war in return for their support. In 1917–18 the British army, with Arab support, drove the Turks out of Palestine and the other Arab lands. When the war ended, Palestine was made a **mandate** under British control. Britain was now in an awkward position, with two promises to carry out.

SOURCE **B**

1 Read Source A.
  a Why did Balfour make this promise.
  b Was Balfour promising that the Jews could have a country of their own?
  c 'If it had not been for the Balfour Declaration, the State of Israel would not exist today.' Do you agree?

2 Look at the map.
  a List the Arab countries.
  b List the oil-producing countries.
  c In 1939 Britain agreed to limit Jewish immigration into Palestine. Why was this?

3 Look at Source B. What effect would pictures like this have had in Britain or in the USA at the time?

The British navy stops Jews landing in Palestine, 1947. The ship was ordered to return its 4,554 refugees to Europe. Haganah was the Jewish defence organization.▼

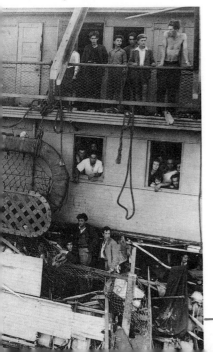

The British mandate and its problems, 1922–48

In 1922 only 11 per cent of the people in Palestine were Jews. Many Arabs were worried by Zionist talk of a Jewish state, but this did not seem very likely until the 1930s. Then Hitler took a hand. Jews fled in large numbers from **Nazi persecution**, and 30 per cent of the population of Palestine was Jewish by 1936. Jews had bought up whole villages and towns, and the Arabs felt that they were being squeezed out of their own land. They responded with riots, strikes and attacks on the Jewish settlers, who gave as good as they got. The British were not sure what to do. War with the Axis seemed likely, and if it broke out Britain would need Arab support. So in 1939 Britain set a **limit on Jewish immigration** into Palestine. This was intended to make sure that the Jews were never more than 30 per cent of the population.

For two years after the war Britain tried to carry on with this policy. But now the problem was far worse. The horrors suffered by the Jews in wartime Europe made thousands of them decide to settle in the 'Promised Land'. American Jews gave them money, and the US government demanded that Britain should let them in. Inside Palestine, Jews already settled there began a guerrilla campaign against the British. Britain was at this time exhausted by war and was starting to give up its worldwide empire (see page 94). It certainly could not afford a costly and unpopular struggle to keep the Jews out of Palestine, especially if the USA opposed it. So in 1947 Britain announced that the following year it would pull its troops out and hand over to the United Nations.

Israel is born, 1948

The UN suggested dividing Palestine into two separate states, one Jewish and one Arab. The Jews agreed, but the Arabs refused; so when the British troops withdrew the Jews announced in May 1948 that they were setting up the **State of Israel**. Egypt, Syria, Jordan and Iraq sent forces to help the Palestinians destroy the new state, and the first of Israel's many wars began. The Arabs outnumbered the Israelis many times over, but they were badly organized and disunited. The Israelis were unified, determined and ably led. By the time a cease-fire was agreed in 1949 they had captured far more of Palestine that the UN said they should have. Whole villages of Palestinians had fled or been driven out of what was now Israel.

A problem for the future

After 1949 the Israelis set about building a modern nation, with cities, farms and factories. About a million **immigrants** came to Israel in the next few years. They brought skill, knowledge and money which helped to make Israel strong and successful. Meanwhile 750,000 Palestinian Arabs who had fled from the fighting settled in **refugee camps** just over the new frontier – angry and determined to return one day to their homes. The neighbouring Arab countries were angry too. They refused to accept Israel and threatened that one day they would put right the wrong that had been done to the Arabs.

11.2 THE ARABS ATTACK ISRAEL

Arab nationalism

Until about 1950 most **Arab** lands were parts of another country's empire – the Turkish (or Ottoman) Empire, and later the British or the French. But in the twentieth century the Arabs, like the Indians and the Africans, demanded the right to run their own affairs. Ideas of self-determination, democracy and socialism spread among educated people. There were revolutions in many Arab countries in the 1950s and 1960s. For instance, in 1952 Colonel Nasser and a group of army officers seized power in **Egypt**, the largest of the Arab states. They promised to get rid of the British from Egypt, to modernize the economy and to make sure that the poor people shared the benefits. Nasser also reminded Egyptians and all Arabs of their past greatness. His radio station in Cairo suggested that people in all parts of the Arab world, from Aden in the south to Syria in the north, should work together to restore Arab prosperity and power.

This movement of **Arab nationalism** was a great danger to Israel. The Jewish state was hemmed in on three sides by Arab states, each of them with its refugee camps full of angry Palestinian Arabs. The refugees organized **guerrilla raids** into Israel. The Arab countries cut off Israeli **trade** through the **Suez Canal** and the Red Sea. The Arabs outnumbered the Israelis by twenty to one. If they combined their armies together effectively, Israel would be in deep trouble. The Israelis armed themselves in readiness.

There have been four Arab–Israeli wars – in 1948–9, 1956, 1967 and 1973 – and Israel has won them all. The maps show the extra territory it captured in three of them. The **1956** war, sometimes called the **Suez War**, was different because this time Israel was working with Britain and France. They wanted to regain control of the Suez Canal, and they failed because the USA opposed them (see page 102). Israeli troops won the battles they fought, but the British and French failure greatly encouraged Colonel Nasser and Arab nationalists everywhere, so it increased the danger to Israel.

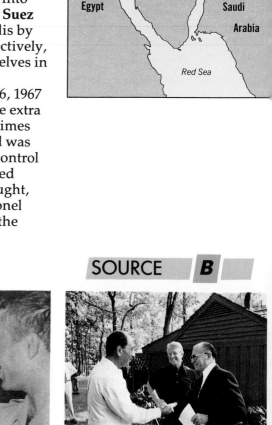

Boundary of British mandate of Palestine 1922–48

Israel as suggested by UN in 1947

Lands seized by Israel in 1948–9

Lebanon
Beirut
Syria
Mediterranean Sea
Tel Aviv
Amman
Jerusalem
Dead Sea
Port Said
Suez Canal
Jordan
Eilat Aqaba
Egypt
Saudi Arabia
Red Sea

SOURCE A

King Feisal of Saudi Arabia, Yasser Arafat, President Nasser of Egypt, King Hussein of Jordan, 1967.

SOURCE B

President Sadat of Egypt, President Carter of the USA and Prime Minister Begin of Israel, at Camp David, the US President's country home, 1978.

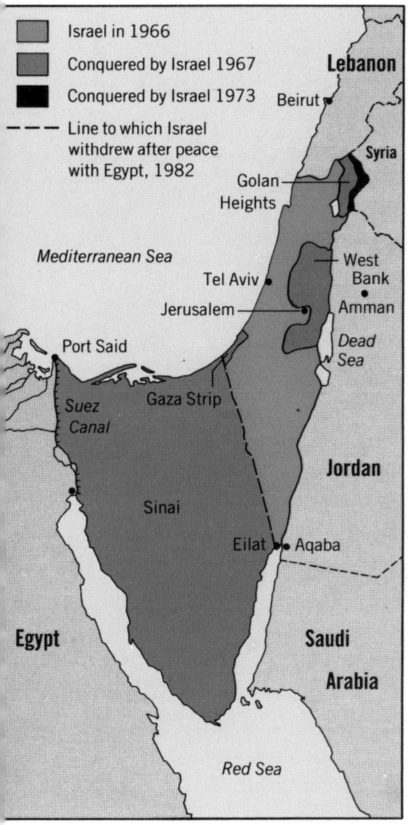
Israel in 1966
Conquered by Israel 1967
Conquered by Israel 1973
Line to which Israel withdrew after peace with Egypt, 1982
Lebanon
Beirut
Syria
Golan Heights
Mediterranean Sea
Tel Aviv
West Bank
Amman
Jerusalem
Dead Sea
Port Said
Gaza Strip
Suez Canal
Jordan
Sinai
Eilat
Aqaba
Egypt
Saudi Arabia
Red Sea

Your can see from the maps that the territory Israel gained made its frontiers easier to defend. For instance, after the **1967 Six-Day War** the Syrians could no longer shell Israel from the Golan Heights. The Palestinians could no longer use the West Bank of the river Jordan as a base for their guerrilla attacks.

The Palestinians

Israel's victories have added to the **Palestinian problem**. In 1967 another 300,000 refugees fled to the camps. Israel also found itself ruling over about a million unwilling Arabs in the **West Bank** area and in the refugee camps of the **Gaza Strip**. As the Arab countries failed in one war after another to overthrow Israel, the Palestinians turned more and more to guerrilla attacks. Some of them hijacked Israeli aircraft or made other terrorist attacks outside Israel. The **Palestine Liberation Organization (PLO)**, formed in 1964, tried to control these campaigns. Its leader, **Yasser Arafat**, gradually came to be accepted by the Arab countries as leader of the Palestinians.

A chance of peace?

Most of the weapons used in the Arab–Israeli wars came from Europe, the USA or the USSR. The USSR supplied Syria and from 1956 to 1974 Egypt. The USA supplied Israel and from 1974 on Egypt too. So the problems of the cold war became mixed up with the problems of the Middle East. People feared that a fifth Arab–Israeli war might bring the two superpowers into direct conflict.

In the 1970s this danger was linked to another. The USA and its allies now depended on a steady flow of **oil** from the Middle East. In 1973 the Arab oil-producing countries cut off oil to the USA because of its help to Israel. They might use this 'oil weapon' again. The USA would feel much safer if the Palestinian problem could be solved in a way that satisfied the Arabs.

In 1975–8 the USA tried hard to bring about a peaceful settlement. Nasser was dead now, and the US government persuaded **Anwar Sadat**, his successor as President of Egypt, to make peace. Israel agreed to withdraw from Egyptian soil, Egypt to let Israel use the Suez Canal. Would other Arab countries also agree at last to make peace with Israel?

No peace for the Palestinians

Any chance of peace spreading soon disappeared. All the Arab countries and the PLO denounced Egypt as a traitor to the Arab cause. The Israeli government encouraged Jews to settle on the occupied West Bank so as to make it into a permanent part of Israel, and this infuriated the Palestinians more than ever. The main PLO bases were in **Lebanon**. In 1976 and again in 1982 Israeli troops entered Lebanon to try to drive out the PLO. For a time Arafat did withdraw, but the fighting left Lebanon in chaos, with the Palestinians still using it as a base for guerrilla attacks. Israel was hated more than ever throughout the Arab world. There seemed to be no end to the problem, and no hope of peace.

11.3 ATTITUDES TO THE MIDDLE EAST PROBLEM

SOURCE

'The aim of Zionism is to create for the Jewish people a home in Palestine secured by public law.'

Declaration by a Zionist Congress, Switzerland, 1897.

SOURCE

'The League wants, before everything else, to form an Arab Empire stretching from the Tigris and the Euphrates to the Suez Isthmus, and from the Mediterranean to the Arabian Sea.'

Aims of the 'League of the Arab Fatherland', 1905.

SOURCE

'Subject to modifications, Great Britain is prepared to recognize and support the independence of the Arabs within the limits demanded. (*These included Palestine.*) I am convinced that this declaration will assure you beyond all possible doubt of the sympathy of Great Britain towards her friends, the Arabs.'

Letter from Sir Henry Mc Mahon, British Ambassador in Egypt to Sherif Hussein of Mecca, leader of the Arab rebellion against the Turks, 1916.

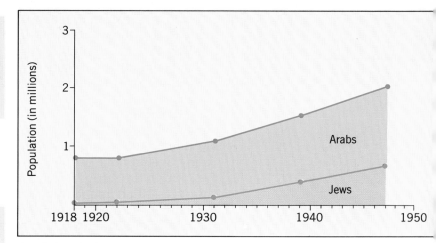

Population of Palestine 1918–47.

SOURCE

'The British government view with favour the establishment in Palestine of a national home for the Jewish people. I should be grateful if you would bring this declaration to the knowledge of the Zionist Federation.'

From the Balfour Declaration, issued by the British government, 1917.

SOURCE

'The Mandatory (Great Britain) shall secure the establishment of the Jewish national home and the development of self-governing institutions and also safeguard the civil and religious rights of all the inhabitants of Palestine, irrespective of race and religion.'

Instructions from the League of Nations to Britain, 1922.

SOURCE

'The land of Israel was the birthplace of the Jewish people. Here their religious and national identity was formed. Exiled from the land of Israel the Jewish people remained faithful to it in all the countries of their dispersion, never ceasing to hope and pray for their return. In recent decades they returned in their masses. They reclaimed the wilderness, built cities and villages… and brought the blessings of progress to all inhabitants of the country. On 29 November 1947 the General Assembly of the United Nations adopted a Resolution requiring the establishment of a Jewish State in Palestine.'

Proclamation of the State of Israel, May 1948.

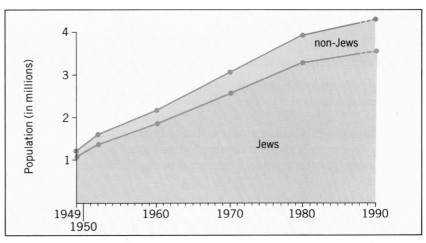

Population of Israel 1949–86.

SOURCE G

'Palestine is an Arab homeland bound by Arab National ties to the rest of the Arab Countries. The Palestinian Arab people has the legitimate right to its homeland and is an inseparable part of the Arab Nation. Jews of Palestinian origin are considered Palestinians if they are willing to live peacefully and loyally in Palestine.'

The Palestine National Covenant, May 1964.

SOURCE H

'I don't believe in the Jews' historical right to come back and take land from other people because we were here 2000 years ago. Instead we have the right because of the Holocaust. We have the right to part of this country and the Palestinians have a right to theirs.'

Israeli writer A.B. Yehoshua, speaking on TV, 1975.

QUESTIONS

1 Use the sources and your background knowledge:
   a to explain Arab hostility to the Jews in the Middle East.
   b to explain Jewish hostility to the Arabs.

2 What do you think was Britain's motive in making the promises in Sources C and D?

3 What effect might these promises have had on the situation in the Middle East? Give reasons for your answer.

4 What other factors in world history have influenced the conflict between Jews and Arabs?

5 Do you think that this conflict was inevitable? Give reasons for your answer.

11.4 PALESTINE AND ISRAEL: TWO POINTS OF VIEW

EVIDENCE

SOURCE A

(On 10 April 1948 Israeli forces attacked the Arab village of Deir Yassin near Jerusalem.)

'Most of the male inhabitants of the village fled. A small number of men and a large number of women and children remained. The irregular Jewish troops shot every one they saw in the houses, including women and children. In the meantime twenty-five men had been brought out of the houses. They were taken to a stone quarry and shot in cold blood.'

Sami Hadawi (a Jewish soldier in 1948), 'Bitter Harvest', 1979. 254 people were killed at Deir Yassin.

SOURCE B

'This refugee problem has been artificially maintained for political motives. Recent years have witnessed great expansion of economic potentialities in the Middle East. The revenues of the oil-bearing countries have opened up great opportunities of work and development into which the refugees could fit. But the Arab governments have so far sought to debar refugees from using them. Israel with her small territory has found homes and work in the past ten years for nearly a million newcomers. How much more easily could the vast Arab world find a home for a similar number of Arab refugees.'

Abba Eban, Israeli Ambassador to the UN, November 1958.

SOURCE C

'My parents live in the camp over the road. They lost their home in 1948 and then they had to get out again in 1967. Life is very hard in the tents. When it rains all the blankets get wet, and you have to huddle up together to keep warm. I want to join the *fedayeen* (guerrilla fighters) to liberate our country, and I think everybody ought to join, so as to change this terrible way of living.'

Fourteen-year-old Palestinian boy, speaking to G. Chaliland, a French journalist, in 1969.

SOURCE D

'In a refugee camp in Jordan, the mother of a freedom fighter who died in action says: "I am proud that he did not die in this camp. The foreign press come here and take our pictures standing in queues to obtain food, giving the impression that we are a nation of beggars. This is no life. I am proud to have sent my second son to replace my first, and I am preparing my eight-year-old boy for the day when he can fight for liberation too."'

PLO pamphlet, 1969.

SOURCE E

'Violent disturbances continued throughout the occupied West Bank and the Gaza Strip. Israeli troops shot dead a Palestinian youth during a riot in the West Bank town of Jenin and injured five others. Twenty people were arrested after Wednesday's lynching of a local man who reportedly worked as an informer for the Israelis. The dead man had earlier opened fire on a crowd of angry villagers, killing a four-year-old child and wounding thirteen others. Yesterday's death brings to at least sixty-eight the number of Palestinians who have been killed since the "uprising" began in early December. Disturbances and strikes were reported elsewhere in the occupied territories.'

The 'Guardian', 26 February 1988.

SOURCE F

Bomb-shelter in a Israeli village. Until the capture of the Golan Heights and the West Bank in 1967, Israeli villagers needed shelters against Palestinian attacks.

SOURCE G

Palestinian refugee camp in Gaza. The number of refugees has grown after each of the wars in the region.

EXERCISE

1 Read Source A. There has been much disagreement about the events at Deir Yassin.
   a How reliable do you think Source A is?
   b What effect would events like this, or even untrue rumours about them, have had on Arabs living in areas coming under Israeli control in 1948 or in 1967?

2 Read Source B.
   a What solution to the refugee problem did Abba Eban suggest?
   b Would the woman quoted in Source D be likely to agree with this suggestion? Explain your answer.

3 Read Sources C and D.
   a How reliable do you consider these sources to be?
   b Do these sources explain the long continuation of the Palestine/Israel problems?

4 Which of the sources on this page are biased? Does this mean they are of no use to historians?

12.1 DE-STALINIZATION

Joseph Stalin died in 1953. The Soviet leaders who took over from him breathed a sigh of relief that they themselves had survived the arrests and executions of Stalin's rule (see pages 36–9). They were determined to make sure that nobody else should build up the same sort of stranglehold on power in the Soviet Union. So they arrested and put to death Beria, the police chief who had organized arrests for Stalin. Then they announced that in future they would rule collectively. Since then several leaders have emerged, but they have based their power on the consent of the others and not on terror as Stalin did.

During Stalin's lifetime there could be no open criticism of the dictator. But in 1956 **Nikita Khrushchev**, then rising to power, made a speech to the Communist Party Congress openly attacking Stalin for the brutality which they all knew so well. The speech was made in secret, but news of it soon got out. It was the main event in a gradual process of **de-Stalinization** in which the party blamed Stalin and attacked his methods. The new Soviet leaders also released many, but not all, of the people Stalin had imprisoned, and allowed writers more freedom to criticize the government. At the same time they switched more production to consumer goods, food and housing, and promised that this new post-Stalin USSR would be as rich as the USA in twenty years or so. This dream never came true, but life was a great deal better for the average Soviet citizen. Just at this time Soviet scientists sent up the first man-made satellite, and it looked as if in rocket technology and nuclear weapons the USSR was at least level with the USA. The Soviet system seemed successful and secure at last.

Peaceful co-existence

Stalin had believed that war between communism and capitalism was inevitable sooner or later. The Soviet Union had been attacked twice, in 1919 and in 1941, and it should be prepared for a third attack. But Khrushchev now argued that nuclear weapons made war too risky even for the capitalists. There was bound to

Leaders of the USSR since Stalin

1956–64 Khrushchev
1965–82 Brezhnev
1982–84 Andropov
1984–85 Chernenko
1985–   Gorbachev

SOURCE B

'It is against the spirit of Marxism-Leninism to transform one person into a superman possessing supernatural characteristics akin to those of a god. Such a belief about Stalin was cultivated among us for many years. Stalin discarded Lenin's method of convincing and education . . . for that of violence, mass repressions and terror. After the war Stalin became even more capricious and brutal. Everything was decided by him alone without any consideration for anyone or anything.'

Khrushchev's 'secret' speech to the Soviet Communist Party, 1956.

SOURCE A

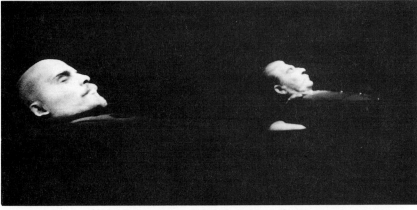

Stalin's body on show beside Lenin's in the Soviet 'shrine' in Red Square, Moscow, 1953. In 1956 it was removed and given ordinary burial.

Valentina Tereshkova, the world's first woman in space, 1963.

QUESTIONS

1 Look at Source A. Why was Stalin's body moved?

2 How might Soviet successes in space and with nuclear weapons have helped to change the policy of the USSR?

3 a Make a list of the changes inside the USSR carried out after Stalin's death.

   b What effect might news of these changes have had in the 'satellite' countries of Eastern Europe?

4 a What criticisms does Khrushchev make of Stalin in Source B?

   b Why was he so outspoken?

   c The US government soon got a copy of this speech and published it widely. Explain why.

   d What effect would this speech have had on the Communist leaders of Eastern Europe?

be a long period in which the two rival systems continued side by side. In 1955 he and his colleagues began discussions with the USA, Britain and France about withdrawing troops and making a real peace in Europe. The USSR did withdraw Soviet troops from Finland and Austria. Perhaps the cold war was coming to an end.

Different roads to communism

Stalin had insisted in the 1940s that the governments of the new Communist countries of Eastern Europe should keep in step with the USSR, which had led the way towards communism for so long. He encouraged these 'satellites' to follow the USSR's example of the 1930's – to industrialize themselves, to turn peasants into collective farmers or town workers and to build up their armies. The sooner they did this, the sooner they would be ready to help the USSR to defend socialism against the next attack by the capitalists. Stalin refused to allow countries such as Poland, East Germany and Hungary to accept Marshall Aid and he forced them to trade with the USSR instead of with Western Europe. The result was low wages and hard work throughout the region. Stalin's policies were highly upopular, and several Communist leaders in the 'satellites' objected. But, like others who disagreed with Stalin, they ended up either in prison or dead.

The one exception to this was **Yugoslavia**. The Yugoslavs, led by **Marshal Tito**, had set up their own Communist system without Soviet help. In 1948 Tito defied Stalin's orders, and it looked as if the Red Army might be sent into action again. But the USA and Britain gave Tito economic help and promised military support, and no Soviet attack was made. Yugoslavia has retained its own special brand of communism ever since.

In 1956 Khrushchev and his colleagues abolished the **Cominform**, the Moscow organization for keeping the other Communist parties in line. They announced that there were many different roads to communism which the different national parties must choose for themselves. Khrushchev also visited Tito and reopened friendly relations with Yugoslavia.

What De-Stalinization did not mean

Khrushchev and his friends had not stopped believing in communism. They still said that the Communist Party must play the leading part in each country, and must retain power in its own hands. Criticism, discussion and even disagreement among Communists might be useful, but it had its limits. Criticism which attacked the party was considered **counter-revolutionary** and should be stamped out.

In the same way, **peaceful coexistence** did not mean that the Soviet Union would lower its guard. Stalin's successors believed that the capitalists would do all they could to weaken Soviet defences. In 1954 the Eastern European Communist countries (except Yugoslavia) all signed the **Warsaw Pact**. This was an agreement to keep up a joint system of defence centred on the Red Army.

12.2 PROBLEMS IN EASTERN EUROPE

East Germany and the Berlin Wall, 1949–61

The **German Democratic Republic** (GDR) had been set up by the Soviets, not by the people of East Germany. Its leaders were trying hard to strengthen communism by building up industry and improving education and social services. First, however, they needed to gain acceptance among their own people. For instance, there were serious riots in 1953.

One of the main problems was the city of **Berlin**. The Western Allies controlled the western part of Berlin, and the **Federal Republic** (West Germany) used it as a shop window to show the attractions of life in the West. In West Germany the standard of living was going up fast – people called it an **'economic miracle'**. Good jobs were available there for skilled workers and professional people, and there was freedom to say what you liked or go where you liked. All an East German had to do to go there was to walk into the western part of Berlin. In the years 1949–61 more than 2.6 million people, about 15 per cent of the population of the GDR, fled to the West. No country could stand a loss like that for ever. In 1961 the GDR and the USSR agreed to stop the flood of refugees by building the **Berlin Wall**. It divided the city into two halves, with check-points to control movement between them. It was brutal, but it worked. The flood of refugees stopped, and by 1970 people were beginning to talk about an East German 'economic miracle' too. The Berlin Wall is still there.

Poland, 1956

In 1956 there was a wave of strikes in **Poland** because of low wages and high prices. The Polish Communist Party leader resigned, and the party chose a new leader, **Wladyslaw Gomulka**, who had been imprisoned by Stalin. The government also promised that it would allow more open discussion and criticism in future. This worried the Soviets – they knew that many Poles were bitterly anti-Soviet and anti-communist. But Gomulka promised Khrushchev that he had no intention of weakening the power of the Communist Party in Poland or of leaving the Warsaw Pact. Khrushchev decided to take a chance and leave Gomulka in power. He made this clear in October 1956.

SOURCE A

SOURCE B

A man throwing a stone at a Soviet tank in Berlin, 1953. In June of that year there were serious riots against the Soviets.

QUESTIONS

1 Study Source B.
   a What criticism of Soviet power in Eastern Europe might be based on this source?
   b How might a Soviet Communist defend his or her country against these criticisms?
   c This picture is from Western news media. How might this affect its value as evidence?

2 a Make a list of the countries discussed in this unit. Against each write the date and briefly the causes of conflict with the USSR.

◀ *Angry Hungarians break up Stalin's statue in Budapest in 1956.*

Hungary, 1956

Also in 1956 there were widespread student riots and strikes in **Hungary**. There too there was a Communist leader who had been imprisoned by Stalin, **Imre Nagy**, and the Hungarian party now appointed him as leader. The Soviets hoped that this might end the trouble as in Poland. Nagy knew, however, that the Soviets were very unpopular in Hungary, and he knew how Khrushchev had denounced Stalin's bullying behaviour. So he boldly announced that his government would allow free elections and he would leave the Warsaw Pact. He ordered the Red Army to leave Hungary. Instead, on 4 November the USSR sent in its tanks to take control of **Budapest**, Hungary's capital. About 200,000 Hungarians fled from the country and many thousands were killed. The Soviets arrested Nagy, shot him and handed power to less independent-minded Hungarian Communists.

Czechoslovakia, 1968

Czechoslovakia was the only Eastern European country which had been a genuine democracy before the war, with real freedom of speech. From 1948 until 1968 Communists of a Stalinist type ran its government. Then in 1968 the Czech Communist Party picked a new leader, **Alexander Dubcek**. He promised Czechoslovakia what he called 'socialism with a human face' (see page 138). But knowing what had happened in Hungary he promised to keep the party in sole control and to keep Czechoslovakia in the Warsaw Pact. The Soviet leader of the time, **Leonid Brezhnev**, distrusted Dubcek and considered his ideas dangerous. So did the governments of East Germany, Poland, Bulgaria and Hungary. In August 1968 they jointly invaded Czechoslovakia. Seeing that it was useless to resist, Dubcek resigned, and his reforms were withdrawn.

Poland again, 1970–81

After 1956 the state-controlled economy of **Poland** did well. Trade expanded with both West and East, and standards of living went up. Then in the 1970s the bad times came back. Poland owed money, and the government tried to solve the problem by cutting wages and raising prices. There were many strikes. In the late 1970s the workers organized their own trade union, **Solidarity**, and elected a shipyard worker, **Lech Walesa**, as its leader. He was careful not to criticize the Warsaw Pact, but he demanded that the government should accept the right to strike and allow more freedom of speech and opinion. The government accepted. By 1981 Solidarity had about 8 million members, many of them also members of the Communist Party.

The leaders of the party were now very worried that they might lose control of this 'monster' which they had allowed to grow. So in December 1981, after anxious discussions with the Soviet leaders, they banned Solidarity and declared **martial law**. This meant that they took power to ban all meetings and to imprison people without trial. Such steps, however, did nothing to solve Poland's economic problems or the government's problem of getting the confidence and support of the people.

b (i) 'These conflicts were mainly caused by de-Stalinization.' (ii) 'These conflicts were mainly caused by the cold war.' (iii) 'These conflicts were mainly caused by economic discontent in Eastern Europe.' Choose one of these explanations and give reasons for your choice.

3 The Eastern European countries have been called 'Soviet satellites'. Is this a fair description? Use the information in this unit to support your answer.

12.3 THE 'PRAGUE SPRING' OF 1968

EMPATHY

In 1967 people in **Czechoslovakia** were very discontented. Trade and industry were doing badly, and the standard of living was falling. Writers who disagreed with the government had been imprisoned; student demonstrators were arrested and beaten up by the police. Many Communists felt that the leaders of the party were out of touch with the people's problem. In January 1968 the Communists elected **Alexander Dubcek** as Party Secretary, and in April he put forward the following **reforms**.

- The tight control of industry by party high-ups and planners was to end. As much freedom as possible was to be left to managers and workers.
- Censorship of the press was to end.
- People were to be allowed to hold meetings and discuss politics freely.
- There was to be genuine discussion between Communists and non-communists in a reorganized parliament.
- People were to be free to travel abroad.

These reforms were very popular, and the news media and ordinary people made full use of their freedom. Prague was full of excitement and hope that spring.

From April until 21 August the main question on everybody's lips was, 'What will the USSR do?' Strong Warsaw Pact armies held exercises in Czechoslovakia that summer. They might easily be used to overthrow Dubcek. During the spring and summer the Czech Party Secretary held several meetings with Brezhnev and other Communist leaders. He promised them:

- that he would keep the Communist Party in firm control of Czechoslavakia;
- that he would keep Czechoslovakia firmly in the Warsaw Pact;
- that he would stop the Czech press criticizing the USSR.

SOURCE A

'We cannot consent to hostile forces forcing your country from the socialist path, and creating the threat of tearing Czechoslovakia away from the socialist commonwealth.'

Statement by the Communist parties of the USSR, Bulgaria, Hungary, East Germany and Poland, July 1968.

SOURCE B

'When forces that are hostile to socialism try to turn the development of some socialist country towards capitalism the suppression of these counter-revolutionary forces becomes not only a problem of the country concerned, but a common problem and concern of all socialist countries.'

Statement by Leonid Brezhnev, Soviet leader, August 1968.

SOURCE C

'Change would threaten the tenure of office (of Communist Party leaders in Eastern Europe) and there would possibly be reprisals for the purges of the past. For the ordinary Communist official much was at stake. For them the material gains of government jobs were perhaps the main consideration. They enjoyed higher salaries than the average working person. They had advantages of many kinds (such as access to better housing and shops which stocked a wider variety of goods). Most importantly they were able to obtain the best educational opportunities for their offspring.'

T. E. Vadney, 'The World since 1945', 1987.

SOURCE D

'I personally witnessed a scene in Opletalova Street in which a tank crew refused to obey an officer's order to disperse a crowd of people.

'However, let us not think, because of such episodes, that the occupation soldiers would hesitate if they were ordered to start firing at us with all their weapons. Let us show them again that they are unwelcome guests here, that they are our enemies today.'

Czechoslovak radio broadcast, 24 August 1968.

SOURCE **E**

Prague, 1968: a Czech stands on a Soviet tank and waves the Czech flag.

SOURCE **F**

A Czech argues with a Soviet soldier outside the Prague radio building, 1968.

SOURCE **G**

Prague poster, 1968. The tank is labelled 'USSR' in Russian script. The weeping figure is Lenin.

EXERCISE

1 Dubcek promised Brezhnev that he would keep Czechoslovakia under the control of the Communist Party and in the Warsaw Pact. Brezhnev ordered the invasion of Czechoslovakia anyway.

  Does this mean Brezhnev simply did not believe Dubcek? Explain your answer.

Look again at the material on Poland on pages 136–7.

2 How do you think a Polish shipyard worker would react to:
  a news of Dubcek's reforms?
  b news of the invasion of Czechoslovakia?

3 How do you think a Polish Communist Party leader would react to:
  a news of Dubcek's reforms?
  b news of the invasion of Czechoslovakia?

A congress of the Czech Communist Party was due to be held in September. There was little doubt that it would give Dubcek enthusiastic support. Perhaps this explains why on 21 August 500,000 Warsaw Pact troops marched in and seized control of Prague and other Czech cities. There was little bloodshed, because Dubcek told people not to resist. He himself was taken to Moscow, where he was forced to cancel the reforms. After his return to Prague he was forced out of power. Dubcek's attempt to lead his country towards a new sort of socialism had failed.

13.1 WAR IN VIETNAM

In 1945–54 **France** tried and failed to regain control of its pre-war colony in **Vietnam**. By 1954 the Viet Minh, the Communist nationalists led by **Ho Chi Minh**, had won control of the northern part of the country. They then agreed to stop fighting and to hold an election. Everybody expected that they would win and would soon be in control of the whole country. But the South Vietnamese government refused to hold an election. A bitter struggle then began which killed at least 2 million people. It spread destruction to the neighbouring countries as well as throughout Vietnam. In the end, after twenty-one years of bloodshed, the Communists finished up in control of both halves of Vietnam and of two neighbouring countries as well. Why did this struggle take place, and why did the Communists win?

The domino theory

The main cause of the **Vietnam War** was the US determination to stop the spread of communism and to win the cold war. Mao's success in China seemed to the US government to threaten the whole of South-East Asia. Most of the countries in it were newly independent colonies (see map, page 100), and their governments were still shaky. In all of them Communists would be encouraged by the successes first of Mao and then of Ho Chi Minh. The USA feared that, with a small push from outside, Communists could topple all these governments one after another, like a row of dominoes. The US government believed that for its own defence it needed to keep the US navy in control

(see map, page 100)

SOURCE B

In 1963 Diem banned a Buddhist celebration and used troops to crush a protest march. This Buddhist monk burned himself to death.

Vietnam and its neighbours.

Map key:
- Ho Chi Minh Trail
- US navy and airforce bases (also in Taiwan & Philippines)

China
North Vietnam
Hanoi
Burma
Laos
Hong Kong
Thailand
US navy
South Vietnam
Saigon (now Ho Chi Minh City)
Cambodia (now Kampuchea)
Malaysia

SOURCE A

'Let every nation know, whether it wishes us well or ill, that we shall pay any price, bear any burden, meet any hardship, support any friend, oppose any foe, to assure the survival and success of liberty. To those new states which we welcome to the ranks of the free we pledge our word that one form of colonial control shall not have passed away merely to be replaced by a far worse tyranny.'

US President J. F. Kennedy, January 1960.

SOURCE C

'Most of the nations of Asia cannot by themselves and alone resist the growing might and grasping ambition of Asian communism. Our power, therefore, is a vital shield. And an Asia so threatened by Communist domination would imperil the security of the US itself. Moreover we are in Vietnam to fulfil one of the most solemn pledges of the American nation. Three Presidents over eleven years have promised to help defend this small and valiant nation. We cannot now dishonour our word.'

US President L. B. Johnson, 1965.

'The inhabitants of the southern part of Vietnam have not been able to enjoy freedom, and have not had the chance to be masters of their own destiny, precisely because the Americans in the name of the protectors of freedom have in fact been protecting regimes which stamp out that freedom.

Ly Chanh Trung, a South Vietnamese professor, 1968.

QUESTIONS

1 Answer the following to decide why the USA intervened in Vietnam in 1954.
  a Use the map in this unit and the maps on page 88 to make a list of the 'dominoes' in the domino theory, starting with China.
  b Why did the US government think in 1954 that these countries might become Communist?
  c Why did the US government decide to act to stop this happening?

2 Use Sources A and C and your own knowledge to explain why the USA turned to open war in Vietnam in 1964.

3 Read Source D.
  a What support can you suggest for Ly Chanh Trung's complaint that South Vietnamese governments were 'stamping out freedom'?
  b How might a US general or politician have answered Ly Chanh Trung?

of the Western Pacific. So in 1954 it decided to stop the area going Communist by propping up the next domino in the row: South Vietnam.

All help short of war, 1954–64

For ten years the USA tried to keep South Vietnam non-communist by doing everything except sending US troops into action. It gave money, weapons and advice to an anti-communist politician, Ngo Dinh Diem, and helped him to form a government. But Diem represented only his own rich friends and relations, and he kept himself in power by brutality and corruption. The Vietnamese Communists, or **Vietcong**, could meanwhile move safely among the peasants in the countryside, and made guerrilla attacks on Diem's forces. Diem tried to stop this by forcing the peasants to move into fortified villages, but this caused more and more of the peasants to support the Vietcong.

In 1963 the USA encouraged the Vietnamese army to overthrow Diem, and army generals took over the government. Elections were held in 1966, but most of the power remained in the hands of the generals.

Open war, 1964–8

In 1963 **President Kennedy** of the USA needed a success. Cuba, only ninety miles from the USA, had recently turned to communism under Fidel Castro, and an attempt to overthrow Castro had failed. Kennedy wanted to show US power and determination to defend the world against communism. So he promised the new South Vietnamese President greatly increased support.

Up to now the North Vietnam government had not sent its own troops to help the Vietcong in the south, but in 1964 it began to do this. It sent them through the neighbouring countries Laos and Cambodia along paths that came to be known as the **Ho Chi Minh Trail**.

In 1963 US President Kennedy was assassinated. The next year **Lyndon Johnson**, who had taken over as President, had to fight an election. He knew that a tough policy in Vietnam would be popular in the USA. US generals told him that the surest way to defeat the Communists there was to attack North Vietnam, to bomb factories and supply routes and thus cut off the lifeline of the Vietcong in the south. Johnson accepted this advice and sent in US bombers against the north. He also sent US troops to fight openly in the south. He was certain that his modern forces with their high-technology weapons would soon crush the Vietcong and the forces of tiny North Vietnam. Johnson's action was highly popular – 85 per cent of the US population supported it.

Four years later there was a US army of over half a million men in action. Yet North Vietnam, though badly battered, was still there. Men and supplies were still moving down the Ho Chi Minh Trail, and in the south the Vietcong were still fighting strongly. By 1968, 36,000 US soldiers had been killed in Vietnam. Nothing much had been gained. Johnson had failed.

13.2 HOW THE VIETNAM WAR WAS FOUGHT AND LOST

SOURCE **A**

Vietnamese children fleeing after a napalm attack. Napalm was a burning chemical which was sprayed from the air on to the Vietcong and their hide-outs.

Vietnamization and defeat, 1968–75

In 1968 **Richard Nixon** was elected President of the USA. His plan was to bring US troops home by encouraging the South Vietnamese to take over the fighting themselves. They greatly increased the size of their army, and Nixon gave them modern weapons of all kinds. The policy was called **Vietnamization**. Nixon also bombed the Ho Chi Min Trail and helped the South Vietnamese to invade both **Cambodia** and **Laos** to try to cut off supplies to the Vietcong. In reply the North Vietnamese also invaded Cambodia and Laos and set up Communist governments there. But however heavily the USA bombed these countries and Vietnam, the Vietcong were as active as ever.

By now the war was bitterly unpopular in the USA, and Congress refused to vote the money needed to carry on. In 1973 the US government withdrew its last troops. It continued to send supplies to the South Vietnamese for another two years, but South Vietnamese armies were no more successful than they had ever been. Many soldiers deserted, taking their weapons with them. At last, in 1975 the North Vietnamese armies and the Vietcong captured Saigon and took over in the south. Vietnam became a single country again, with a Communist government.

SOURCE **B**

US plane spraying chemicals to destroy the tropical vegetation which gave cover to the Vietcong. This killed trees and poisoned animals and people.

People in North Vietnam rescuing their possessions after an air raid.

SOURCE C

SOURCE D

Cartoon from the 'Guardian', 3 May 1972. A US citizen is asking Nixon: 'If this boy of yours is real, how come we gotta wind him up all the time?'

SOURCE E

'You never knew who was the enemy and who was the friend. They all looked alike. They all dressed alike. They were all Vietnamese. Some of them were Vietcong. Here's a woman of 22 or 23. She is pregnant and she says her husband isn't a Vietcong. But she watches your men walk down a trail and get killed or wounded by a booby-trap. Maybe she planted it herself. The enemy was all around you.'

US Marine Captain E. J. Banks.

SOURCE F

'When the ten helicopters landed this morning in the middle of these huts, six men jumped out of each chopper. We were firing the moment we hit the ground. We fired into the huts all we could. Then we burned the huts. Everyone is crying and begging that we don't separate them. Then they watch in terror as we burn their homes. Yes, we burn all rice and shoot all livestock.'

US soldier's letter home, 1968.

QUESTIONS

1 Read Sources E and F. How does Source E help to explain the behaviour of the soldiers in Source F?

2 a Make a list of the methods used by the US forces and the South Vietnamese shown in the sources in this unit.

b US leaders often said that the real battle was for the 'hearts and minds' of the people of Vietnam. What effect would these methods of fighting have on this battle?

3 What is the message of the cartoon, Source D?

13.3 WHY DID THE USA LOSE IN VIETNAM?

SOURCE A

US student shot. Soldiers shot dead four students who were part of a protest against the Vietnam War at a US University in 1970. Four hundred universities and colleges were closed by student strikes.

SOURCE B

THERE IS NO HONOR IN AN UNHONORABLE WAR! 40,000 DEAD DON'T MAKE WRONG : RIGHT

Demonstration in Washington D.C., November 1969.

SOURCE C

US helicopter over a supply dump set on fire by Vietcong guerrillas.

SOURCE D

◀ *Americans and South Vietnamese struggling to get away from Saigon as the North Vietnamese closed in, 1975.*

SOURCE E

'The North Vietnamese victory was a triumph for Russian military hardware as well as for Vietnamese courage and determination. The final offensive was made possible by Russian long-range artillery, and the skies above it cleared by Russian-built anti-aircraft missiles.

'Sunday Times', 4 May 1975.

SOURCE F

'The North Vietnamese needed no more than fifteen tonnes of supplies a day in order to maintain their effort in the South. And since the Soviet Union and China were furnishing North Vietnam with nearly six thousand tonnes of aid daily, only a tiny fraction had to trickle down the Ho Chi Minh trial for the Communists to wage war.'

S. Karnow, 'Vietnam', 1983.

SOURCE G

'President Ford expressed his frustration at the refusal of Congress to grant his request for assistance to South Vietnam and angrily regretted the limitations placed upon his power over the last two years. He said: "I believe that there is a great deal of credibility in the domino theory. I hope it doesn't happen. I hope other countries in South-East Asia – Thailand, the Philippines – don't misread the will of the American people into believing that we're going to abandon our position in South-East Asia. We're not."'

Account of a press conference held by US President Ford, April 1975.

QUESTIONS

The USA was in the 1960s and 1970s the most powerful country in the world. Why did it lose the Vietnam War? Historians have suggested the following possible answers:

- Soviet support for North Vietnam.
- Many Vietnamese supported communism.
- Many Vietnamese disliked having their country controlled by foreigners.
- The Vietnamese were horrified at the damage done by the US army.
- The Vietnam War was fully covered by the world news media, including television.
- People in the USA turned against the war.

1 Which of these six possible factors do you consider most important? Give your reasons.

2 Do you think that a historian needs all these factors to explain why the USA lost?

14.1 EUROPE UNITED?

World history from 1914 to 1939 is mainly about the actions of European nations such as Britain, Germany and the USSR. Since 1945 things have been different. The USA and the USSR have become superpowers, and Europe has been divided into two halves. Most of **Western Europe** has been linked together with the USA in NATO, and most of **Eastern Europe** with the USSR in the Warsaw Pact.

This dividing and weakening of Europe led West Europeans to combine together in the **European Community** or **Common Market**. When this was first discussed in the 1940s some people thought that it would quickly develop into a 'United States of Europe' – a new superpower. Forty years later is is still not clear whether this might happen, but the European Community has become one of the world's giant economic organizations – the biggest apart from China. In Eastern Europe a rather different organization, **Comecon**, has been set up.

Comecon

In 1949 **Stalin** refused to allow the East European countries to accept Marshall Aid from the USA (see page 85). Instead he formed them into the **Council for Mutual Economic Assistance (Comecon)**. Comecon has played an important part in arranging and financing economic development in the Communist world. The USSR is by far the largest member and has always controlled Comecon. As well as the European members shown on the map, Cuba and Vietnam are members. Comecon remains completely dependent on the Soviet Union.

The European Community and Comecon.

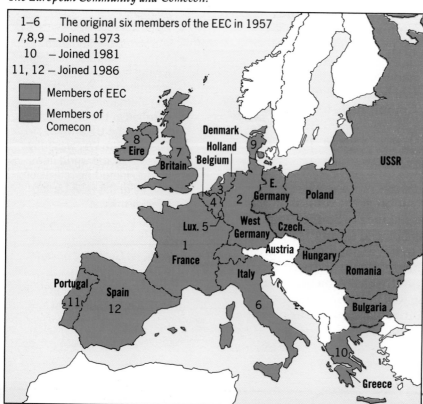

1–6   The original six members of the EEC in 1957
7,8,9 – Joined 1973
10   – Joined 1981
11, 12 – Joined 1986

▪ Members of EEC

▪ Members of Comecon

SOURCE A

'Only a unified Europe allied to the USA and other free peoples will be able to meet the danger which threatens Europe and the whole free world. They are determined to develop their political co-operation. The will for political unification is already contained in the treaties for the foundation of the EEC.'

Statement by the governments of the six founder members of the EEC, 1961.

SOURCE B

'Whether we join or not, this Community will grow stronger; and if we are outside, our freedom will be less, not more. As members of the Community we shall be in a position to safeguard the future of Britain in years to come.'

Sir Alec Douglas-Home, British Foreign Secretary, 1970.

SOURCE C

Cartoon, 1967. The car driver is British Prime Minister Harold Wilson. The policeman is France's General de Gaulle.

The Common Market is founded, 1957

After the war, Western Europe's most serious problem was how to start up trade and industry again. The coal and steel industries on both sides of the river Rhine were close enough to work together easily. So in 1950, at the suggestion of the French, the **European Coal and Steel Community (ECSC)** was set up. There were six members: France, West Germany, Belgium, Holland, Luxemburg and Italy. They agreed to put all coal and steel production under a joint authority on which all six governments would be represented.

There were other arguments too for unifying Western Europe. One of these was the cold war. Most West European countries joined NATO in 1949 to defend themselves against any Soviet threats. Then in 1954 West Germany was permitted to start to rebuild an army as part of the NATO forces. This greatly worried many people in Europe. Germany had invaded its neighbours twice this century. Once Germany recovered its strength, how could they be sure that it would not do so again? Putting West German coal and steel under an international authority helped, by giving West Germany's neighbours some control over the factories from which the steel for armaments would come.

The successful setting up of the ECSC led to discussions about further co-operation. The result, in 1957, was the **European Economic Community (EEC)**. The EEC had the same six members as the ECSC. They agreed to bring about completely free trade between their countries in gradual stages, but to have a common customs duty on trade with outsiders. There were 180 million people in the six countries, so manufacturers there would have a huge market to sell in – bigger even than the USA. They agreed also to set up a **Council of Ministers** to control the new system, and a **Commission** of officials to run it. There was also a **European Court** to settle disputes.

Should Britain join?

The six countries wanted **Britain** to become a member, but the British refused. They still looked on themselves as a world power, rather than a European one, and wanted to go on buying foodstuffs cheaply from Canada, Australia and New Zealand instead of paying high European prices. This would help to keep the Commonwealth together.

The British government had thought that without Britain the EEC would not be very successful. Yet by 1961 they could see that they had been wrong. The EEC was doing very well, and Britain's economy was doing badly. Britain's failure at Suez showed how little world power it really had. So in 1961 and again in 1967 Britain applied to join the EEC. This time it was the Europeans who refused. The main obstacle was **General de Gaulle**, President of France, who distrusted the British and thought that they were far too much under the influence of the USA. Then in 1969 de Gaulle fell from power: and when Britain applied for a third time, it was admitted. Together with Denmark and Ireland, Britain joined the EEC in 1973.

SOURCE D

'The first reason for being in the Common Market is peace and security. Another main reason is to provide a world role for Britain. As a nation of 55 million people Britain has some voice but not enough. Traditionally Britain has always been part of a larger grouping, the Commonwealth. Most of the Commonwealth countries have become independent. The Community opens windows on the whole world for Britain which since the war have been closing.'

Margaret Thatcher, a government minister, speaking in the debate about joining the Common Market, House of Commons, April 1973.

QUESTIONS

1 **a** Make a list of the members of the EEC, with their dates of joining.
  b Make a list of the reasons for the setting up of the Common Market.
  c Choose the reason which you consider to be the most important and explain why you think so.

2 **a** Explain why Britain did not join the EEC at first.
  b Explain the meaning of the cartoon, Source C.

3 What arguments does Source D make about Britain's membership? Why were the arguments for this stronger in 1973 than in 1957?

14.2 THE EUROPEAN COMMUNITY SINCE 1973

Four hundred million people   Since 1973 three other countries have joined the EEC: Greece in 1981 and Spain and Portugal in 1986. So there are twelve member states now with a total population of 400 million. This makes the Community much larger than the USA and nearly as rich.

Completing the Common Market   As well as getting rid of customs duties inside the Community, members have agreed to allow complete freedom of transport and freedom of movement for people to work or set up businesses in all member countries. They have also agreed to bring together their taxation systems. For instance, they agreed all to use a Value Added Tax (VAT). They have not yet been able to agree on a common currency, but in most other matters of trade and industry the Community acts more and more like one huge country. It has a chance to bargain with the USA, the USSR and Japan on at least equal terms.

Political control   One criticism of the Community is that it is not controlled democratically. There is a **European Parliament**, and since 1979 its MPs have been elected by the people of each member country. But the Parliament has no real power to control the actions of the Council of Ministers of the Commission which runs the day-to-day business of the Community. The ministers are appointed by the different governments, and for important decisions they all have to agree; so one member government can block an action which it dislikes.

Aid to poor regions of Europe   Some parts of the Community are poor and others rich. Portugal has a GNP per head of only $1,970 a year compared with Denmark's $11,200. In Britain the north is poorer than the south. The Community helps the poorer areas by making grants to encourage new industry or other developments.

The European Court   This court makes decisions that apply in all member countries. Most cases are about trade, but some are about human rights. For instance, decisions of this court forced Belgium to allow the same rights to women workers as to men.

Aid to and trade with poor countries outside Europe   European countries like Britain and France still trade a good deal with the Third World countries that were once in their empires. In 1975 the EEC agreed with a group of sixty-six Third World countries to help them by buying their farm produce and any manufactured goods. They also agreed to pay for hospitals, roads and other development projects in these countries. This helped, but the amounts of aid were small, and changes in prices and rates of interest they had to pay on borrowed money has made the poor countries on the whole worse off today than they were in 1975.

EEC 'barley mountain' in Lincolnshire.

SOURCE **B**

'The real aim of the Market is, of course, to become a single country in which Britain would be reduced to a mere province. Unless you want to be ruled more and more by a continental Parliament in which Britain would be a small minority, you should vote 'No'.

'The Common Market authorities buy up home-produced food purely to keep the prices up. This they store in warehouses, thus creating mountains of beef, butter, grain, etc. Some of this food is deliberately made unfit for human consumption and some is sold to countries like Russia at prices well below what the housewife in the Common Market has to pay.'

Pamphlet issued during the referendum held in 1975 to decide whether Britain should stay in the EEC.

Common Agricultural Policy (CAP) When the EEC was first formed its farms were backward and inefficient, but the French and German governments needed the votes of the farmers. So the CAP was brought in to keep farm prices high. It did this by fixing prices and buying up any produce which farmers could not sell at those prices. This encouraged them to grow more and more, and the EEC has built up huge stores of unwanted produce – butter 'mountains' and wine 'lakes'. The EEC spends far more on this than on anything else, thirty times as much as on helping the developing countries.

Rich and poor in Europe

Country	Average wealth produced (GNP) per person (US $)	Total population (millions)
Portugal	1,970	10.2
Greece	3,550	9.9
Spain	4,290	38.6
Ireland	4,850	3.6
Italy	6,520	57.1
Belgium	8,280	9.9
UK	8,460	56.5
Netherlands	9,290	14.5
France	9,540	55.2
West Germany	10,940	61.0
Denmark	11,200	5.1

(For comparison: average in the world's 37 poorest countries, $270; average in the world's 19 richest countries, $11,810.)

QUESTIONS

1 a Make a list of the things the EEC does.
  b Which of these do you consider most important? Explain your answer.

2 Source B was published in 1975 for the referendum to decide if Britain should stay in the EEC. Two-thirds of those who voted said we should. How would you have voted? Explain why.

3 Read the following opinions about the Common Market:
  ● 'A club of rich nations aiming to get richer.'
  ● 'The beginnings of the United States of Europe.'
  ● 'An organization to unify Western Europe against the USSR.'
  ● 'The European Community will be able to hold the balance between the USA and the USSR.'
Choose one and use evidence from this unit to explain why you agree or disagree with it.

The EEC budget for 1987. The total amount spent is 36,795 million 'European Currency Units' (ECUs) – about £25 billion.

14.3 JAPAN'S POST-WAR RECOVERY

In 1945 **Japan** was in ruins. The damage caused by the atomic bombs at Hiroshima and Nagasaki was only a tiny part of the total. A quarter of all homes had been destroyed. Most Japanese factories were smashed, and most Japanese ships were at the bottom of the sea. Millions of people were unemployed. Hundreds of thousands were starving.

Japan becomes a democracy

The US **General MacArthur** was in command of the armies of occupation, and until he was dismissed by President Truman in 1951 (see page 89) he was the effective ruler of Japan. In 1947 MacArthur set up a new Japanese government system. Japan had had a parliament, called the **Diet**, since 1889, but the real power had been held by groups of nobles and generals. Since 1947 the Diet has been elected by all adults and controls the government. The Japanese had immense respect for their Emperor, **Hirohito**, so MacArthur kept him as figurehead. In this way the new system gained the respect of the people.

For centuries the Japanese tradition has been to work together by agreement and discussion (Source A). Perhaps this explains why the democratic system has worked very smoothly. The same party has been in power for the last thirty years.

Getting people back to work

The first concern of the new Japanese government was to get people to work again. The USA helped with money. Between 1945 and 1951 it gave $2,000 million to Japan. Many people argued that the large business firms like Mitsubishi had been partly to blame for the war, and so they should be broken up, but little of this was done. In the countryside, however, there was a sweeping reform. With MacArthur's support, the government took the land from the landowners and gave it to the peasants. This helped to solve the immediate food supply problem, but it also had an important long-term effect. Since the 1950s the Japanese countryside has been full of contented and hard-working people. As they got richer they had more money to spend on industrial products, so industry prospered too.

Japan gives up the right to go to war

There was no doubt that Japan's attacks on its neighbours and on the USA at Pearl Harbor had caused the war in the Far East. The Allies, specially the USA, wanted to be sure that Japanese power would never again threaten to take control of the region. The Japanese people were ready to agree – they had seen enough of the horrors of war and wanted no more. So in the new constitution of 1947 Japan agreed to give up the right to have an army and to go to war. The Japanese have not kept entirely to this, since they now have a **'Self-Defence Force'** of about 250,000 men. But they have spent far less on defence than most other countries. This has been an important reason for Japan's industrial growth. When other countries were investing their capital in nuclear weapons and tanks, Japan was investing money in factories to make television sets and video recorders.

SOURCE

SOURCE **A**

'In order to achieve harmony, individual judgements and actions should be forbidden, and discussion at all levels should be respected.'

Laws of Prince Shotoku, Japan, seventh century AD.

SOURCE **B**

Devastation in Tokyo, 1945.

SOURCE **C**

Macarthur and Hirohito, 1945.

Spending on defence, 1979	
Country	Percentage of total Income (GNP)
USA	4.6%
UK	5.4%
Japan	1.0%

(Japan has spent about the same percentage ever since the 1940s. But since then its GNP has gone up about a thousand times.)

Japan and the US become allies

Japan's impressive recovery began with the Korean War, which took place almost on Japan's doorstep. The UN (mainly US) forces needed a local base and a constant flow of supplies of all kinds for a war. In the war years 1950–3 the USA spent $4,000 million in Japan. This helped Japanese industry back on to its feet.

By 1951 the USA was treating Japan like a useful friend, not an enemy. In that year the USA and all its wartime allies except the USSR signed a peace treaty with Japan. (The USSR and Japan have still not officially made peace.) On the same day the USA and Japan signed a defence treaty in which the USA agreed to defend Japan if it was attacked, and Japan asked the USA to keep armed forces in Japan. They are still there.

SOURCE E

The Japanese 'Self-Defence Force' on parade.

Rice growing on terraces in the Japanese countryside. In 1946 the peasants were given control of the land. They have been rich and contented ever since.

SOURCE F

'Land, sea and air forces will never be maintained. The Japanese people for ever renounce war as a sovereign right of the nation, and the threat or use of force as a means of settling international disputes.'

Japanese constitution, article IX, 1947.

QUESTIONS

1 Some people suggested in 1945 that the Emperor Hirohito should be tried as a war criminal. Explain why General MacArthur did not put him on trial.

2 Explain how the following helped Japan's industrial recovery:
 a The land reform.
 b Renouncing war.
 c The Korean War.

3 No other warlike nation has ever agreed to a law like Source F.
 a Why did Japan agree to it?
 b Has Japan kept to it?
 c Why did the USA agree in 1951 to defend Japan?

14.4 JAPAN BECOMES AN INDUSTRIAL SUPERPOWER

You do not need to read a history book to know how successful **Japan's industry** has been in the last forty years. You can see the Japanese products for yourself in car-parks and television shops all over Britain. During the 1950s and 1960s many countries became richer, including Britain, but Japan's economy grew about twice as fast as most others. Then in the 1970s came the oil crisis (see page 166), which slowed down economic growth; but Japan recovered more quickly than other countries and went on growing richer fastest. Today Japan produces 50 per cent of the world's ships, 25 per cent of its cars and 90 per cent of its video machines. You can see from the graph that by 1985 the average Japanese was far richer than the average Briton. Only the USA, Switzerland, Norway, Canada and Sweden produced more wealth per head than Japan.

Japan increased its wealth like this in spite of a serious drawback: the Japanese islands provided hardly any of the essential raw materials for its industry. For instance, all Japan's oil and nearly all its coal and iron had to be imported.

Japan had some well-established industries before the war, like textiles and shipbuilding, and these were quickly rebuilt. By 1956 Japan was the world's leading shipbuilder. But its main success since then has been in new industries like **cars, electronics** and **plastics** which use the new technologies of the post-war period.

Why has Japan been so successful?

Ever since 1868 the Japanese government has encouraged its people to study **new technologies** and to bring them to Japan. Since the war Japan's Ministry of International Trade and Industry has continued to do this, and has helped new industries to get started.

Japanese firms are keen to invest in **new techniques**. As they began to make money at the time of the Korean War they invested it in long-term improvements instead of taking a quick profit. The banks and the government also helped to make sure that capital was available for promising new ideas.

Perhaps the most important reason for Japan's success has been the Japanese tradition of **harmonious co-operation** (see page 150, Source A). It applies in industry just as in politics. About 30 per cent of the workforce are 'lifetime employees', who are very unlikely ever to be sacked. All employees of big companies belong to a trade union that is part of the company organization. Strikes are rare. Wages rise with the prosperity of the company, and employees look on themselves as members of the company and not as members of a working class struggling for its rights. The other 70 per cent of people work for small employers or for themselves, and they have much less security and worse wages. But since the 1950s their standard of living has improved steadily, and there have been few serious conflicts.

Shopping street in Tokyo, 1986.

The Japanese Nissan motor-car factory in Sunderland, 1985.

US President Nixon in Beijing, 1972. ▶

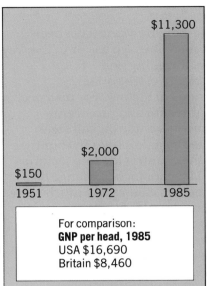

$11,300

$2,000

$150

1951   1972   1985

For comparison:
GNP per head, 1985
USA $16,690
Britain $8,460

The Japanese get richer: wealth produced per head of population (GNP), 1951–85.

Japanese goods in a British shop.

Japan's relations with China

Ever since 1949 the USA had refused to recognize Mao's government, and had insisted that Chiang's GMD government in Taiwan was the rightful government of China (see pages 116–19). Japan loyally supported the USA in this. In 1971 **President Nixon** without warning swung round and made friends with Mao. In 1971 Communist China took up the Chinese seat in the UN, and in 1972 Nixon visited China in person. He hoped to use China to counterbalance the USSR. From the Japanese point of view the fact that Japan could now open up its own contacts with China was of great long-term importance.

China is a giant nation, and throughout history Japan has lived in China's shadow. From 1949 until 1971 the two were on opposite sides of the cold war, and links were few. Since 1971 relations have been far easier – even more since 1977 when China began on Deng's policy of rapid modernization (see page 122). China has a quarter of the world's population, badly needs technology and capital in large amounts and is determined to get them. Japan, its closest neighbour, needs both markets for its products and raw materials for its industry. Japan has the most modern technology in the world and also a ready supply of capital to invest. So it seems likely that contacts between Japan and China may be very important for the twenty-first century.

QUESTIONS

1 a Make a list of the Japanese-manufactured items owned by your household.

b Since about 1972 several countries including Britain and the USA have attempted to cut down imports from Japan. Why do you think they have tried to do this?

c Japanese car firms have in the 1980s built factories in Britain and in the USA. Why have they done this?

2 What difficulties stood in the way of Japanese industrial development in the post-war period?

3 Make a list from this unit and from pages 150–1 of the reasons why Japan has been so successful.

4 a Look back at page 54 and then explain briefly why Japan attacked China in the 1930s.

b Look at pages 88 and 116 and explain briefly how Japan and China came to be on opposite sides of the Cold War.

c Are any of these reasons for conflict between Japan and China still important today?

15.1 SCIENTIFIC AND TECHNOLOGICAL CHANGE

The rate of change speeds up

Many of the major changes of the last eighty years have been technological ones: changes in the machines we use or in the way we do practical things like cooking, travelling and communicating. There have been plenty of important **technological changes** in other periods of history. For instance, the Industrial Revolution of the eighteenth and nineteenth centuries produced railways, steamships and iron and steel machinery of many kinds. It changed people's lives in countries like Britain by moving them from the countryside into factories and industrial towns. But since 1914 technological change has affected much more of the world and has taken place much more rapidly than before. It took about two hundred years from 1711 when the first steam engine was made until abut 1900 when railways and steamships were in use in most parts of the world. Compare this with the thirty years or less that it took for electronic computers to spread across the world after the first one was made in 1946.

One reason for this speeding up is the **success of the earlier technologies**. The people who developed the aircraft, cars and computers of the twentieth century were able to use the older machines such as steam engines. They could use railways and steamships to bring the materials they needed from anywhere in the world. Cars and aircraft need oil. Electrical machines need metals like copper and aluminium. In the years since 1914 the rich countries where the new inventions were being developed have been able to obtain essential materials like these from all over the world.

A second reason why technology has changed so much since 1914 is that before then people had made important **scientific advances** which pointed the way to new possibilities. For instance, in the nineteenth century Louis Pasteur and Robert Koch proved that germs cause some diseases. Then in the twentieth century scientists like Fleming and Florey went on to find penicillin and other substances which could kill the germs and cure the diseases.

A third reason for rapid technological change is that since 1914 Europe and North America (and more recently Japan) have been rich enough to be able to invest large sums of money in developing new machines like aircraft and computers. The capitalist system of competition in the market (see page 40) encouraged business people to look round for **money-making ideas**, such as drilling oil wells or building factories in other regions of the world.

Electricity

One of the key technologies of the twentieth century has been **electricity**. The basic scientific discoveries were made by **Michael Faraday** and others in the 1820s and 1830s, and the first power-stations were built in 1881. The main problem was how to transmit electricity over long distances, and this was not solved until about 1900. By 1910 a large and efficient power-station could

SOURCE A

Triumphant explorer, 1911: Roald Amundsen at the South Pole.

SOURCE B

Triumphant explorer, 1971. James B. Irwin on the Moon.

be built near a coalfield or a hydroelectric dam, and cables could carry its power for many miles. The graph shows how production increased in Britain after that. Electricity can take the power of a steam engine or a water turbine – perhaps several million horsepower – and send it along cables to a machine in a factory, to a locomotive on a railway or to a food-mixer in a kitchen.

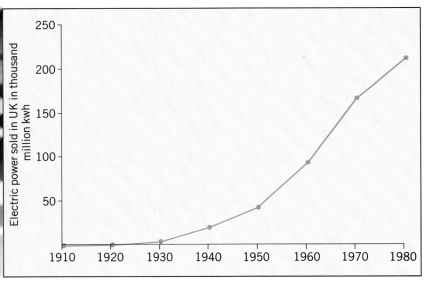

Electricity used in Britain, 1910–80.

SOURCE C

Electricity pylons. The cables carry high voltage current over many miles.

QUESTIONS

1 a What technology is being used in Source A? Include technology not seen in the photograph, but needed to make it possible.

b What technology is being used in Source B? Include technology not seen in the photograph, but needed to make it possible.

c What technology used in Source B was not available in 1911?

d Going back in time another sixty years from 1911 would take you to 1850. Is there technology in use in Source A which was not available in 1850?

2 a Make a list of ten electrically powered devices which you often use.

b Find out from relatives or other older people when they first used or owned each of them.

c Work out the average dates for the whole class.

d How well do these dates fit in with the information in the graph?

3 Choose one of the developments or inventions mentioned in this unit which you consider to have been especially useful. Explain your choice.

4 a Make a list of the reasons given in this unit why the period since 1914 has been one of very fast technological change.

b What other reasons for this can you suggest?

c Are these reasons likely in the future to continue to encourage rapid technological change?

15.2 COMMUNICATIONS IN THE GLOBAL VILLAGE

In 1985 about a third of the world's population watched the Live Aid concert organized by Bob Geldof to help famine relief in Africa. So many people had seen the dreadful scenes of distress that the appeal fund raised $120 million.

The global system of **telecommunications** that made this possible was beginning to develop in 1914. There was already a worldwide **telegraph** system. Scientists were beginning to understand the electromagnetic waves that make **radio** and television possible, and some ships already used radio. The First World War encouraged improvements for naval and army signals. Then in the 1920s broadcasting systems were set up in most countries. By 1939 most homes in rich countries like Britain had a 'wireless set'.

Scientists had suggested before 1914 how **television** might work. In the 1920s the radio and electrical firms could see that there would be a big market, and the inventors got busy. Public television broadcasts began in the 1930s (Britain was first in 1936), and in the 1940s and 1950s television began to spread rapidly, first in the USA and then in Europe. During the Second World War there were many developments such as radar (see below) which led to better and more reliable television sets after the war. By 1960 there were about 10 million sets in Britain, one in almost every home. By 1986 there were about 500 million in the world.

Radio waves can be used as **radar** to scan the sky or the sea for distant planes or ships. As Europe got ready for the air war of 1939–45, most countries developed radar systems. During the war **radio signals** were also used to enable pilots to navigate accurately. After the war these new techniques were put to peaceful use. Radar and radio navigation systems were the basis for the development of a worldwide network of **air traffic control**. Radio and radar also made possible the **rocket weapons** and the **space rockets** of the post-war period. Space rockets must be in constant radio contact with mission control, and a radar early warning system is needed by any country which hopes to fight with guided missiles.

The successful rocket technology of the 1950s and 1960s has had two results for global communications. One was military: the **'spy in the sky'**. By the end of the 1960s both superpowers had satellites with television cameras scanning each other's country all the time in minute detail. The second result was the establishment of **communications satellites**. These could be placed in orbit and used to transmit television, radio or telephone messages to all parts of the world. The first of these satellites, Telstar, was sent up in 1962. Satellites of this type made possible the vast audience for the Live Aid concert. Viewers all over the world could still see only what their TV stations chose to show them. But they could see with their own eyes what was happening on the other side of the world.

The Live Aid concert, 1985.

'All Germany hears the Führer with the People's Radio.' Nazi German advertisement, 1930s. ▶

SOURCE C

Vietnamese child, 1972. Television helped public opinion turn against the war, and the USA withdrew its armies from Vietnam in 1975.

SOURCE D

US satellite photograph of a Soviet warship under construction, 1984.

QUESTIONS

1 The population of the world in 1985 was about 4,800 million.
   a How many people watched the Live Aid concert?
   b How many were there for each television set in the world, on average?

2 ● 'Radio and television have greatly increased the power of governments to control people.'
   ● 'Radio and television have greatly increased the power of ordinary people to know what is happening and to think for themselves.'
   a Which sources support the first statement?
   b Which support the second statement?
   c What other historical examples of either statement can you think of?

3 a How did war or preparation for war help to bring about communications developments?
   b Would other factors have caused these developments even without the wars?
   c 'Up to now the warlike results of the coming of radio and television have been much more important than the peaceful ones.' Do you agree?

4 In 1983, 125 million Americans watched an episode of M*A*S*H*. The 1984 Olympic Games were broadcast to countries with a total of 2,500 million viewers. The television shows with the most viewers are entertainment and sport. Does all this mean that the coming of television is not really of much historical importance?

15.3 CARS, AIRCRAFT AND OIL

A new engine and its effects

Engines using petrol or other types of oil were invented in the later nineteenth century. These **internal combustion engines** were much lighter than steam engines of the same power. They were just right for the new 'horseless carriage' which by 1914 had developed into the motor car. Since then very similar engines have come into use to drive buses and lorries, boats, farm tractors and anything else that needs a light and portable source of power. The nineteenth century has been called the 'age of steam'. We could call the twentieth century the 'age of oil'.

The effects of the new engine were of great importance. Towns spread further into the countryside. Horses disappeared from farms as tractors took over. Buses and cars changed the everyday life of ordinary people in countries like Britain. By the 1930s most families in the USA had a private car of their own, and the age of mass motoring had arrived. In Britain and other European countries mass motoring with its motorways did not arrive until the 1960s.

The other new machine made possible by the new engines was the **aeroplane**. The first powered flight was in 1903, but until after the Second World War aircraft were not of much commercial importance. For war, however, they were vital, as Britain was to find in 1940. They have dominated battlefields on land and sea ever since. The Second World War encouraged many improvements – for instance, jet engines which made planes much faster. Since the 1950s the aeroplane has made travel around the global village far quicker for those who can afford it.

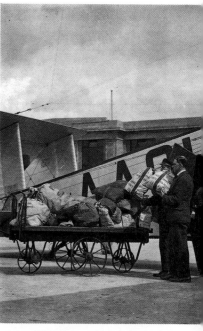

Air mail being loaded, London, 1919. Planes like this DH16 were developed for use in the First World War.

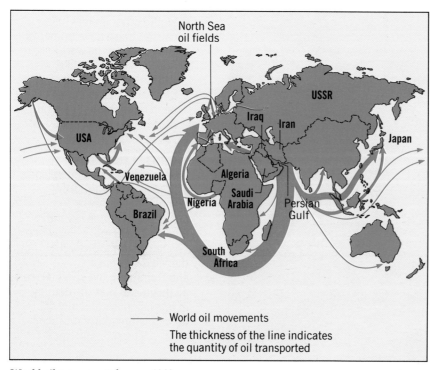

North Sea oil fields

USSR

Iraq

Iran

Japan

USA

Venezuela

Algeria

Nigeria Saudi Arabia

Persian Gulf

Brazil

South Africa

→ World oil movements
The thickness of the line indicates the quantity of oil transported

World oil movements by sea, 1982.

QUESTIONS

1 **a** Make a list of machines using internal combustion engines which you often use directly or indirectly.

b Ask somebody over 60 years old when they first used or owned motor vehicles, aircraft or other machines using internal combustion engines.

c Make a list of the ways such machines have affected everyday life and work. Choose the most important of these and explain your choice.

2 Use your answer to question 1b together with the graph to choose a date when the 'age of oil' might be said to have begun. Explain your choice.

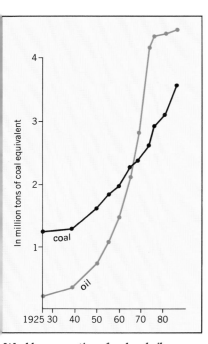

World consumption of coal and oil, 1925–87.

Oil, a worldwide industry

The steam-powered factories of the nineteenth century needed **coal**. So in 1914 the rich countries were on the whole those with plenty of coal, like Britain. The USA also had good supplies of the new fuel, **oil**, and that is one reason why the motor car developed fastest there. But most industrialized countries have little or no oil of their own. Even the USA has since about 1970 used more than it produces. The world's main oil reserves, on the other hand, are in countries where there is little industry. About half of them are in the semi-desert lands of the Middle East. So the rich countries which need the oil for their cars and aircraft have set up a worldwide **oil industry**. Oil companies such as BP and ESSO run oilwells in many lands and have fleets of tankers to carry the oil across the world.

3 Look back at pages 52, 56 and 74.
  a What effect has the internal combustion engine had on war since 1914?
  b What effect have wars had on the development of cars and aircraft?

4 Use the map and your background knowledge to answer the following:
  a Make a list of the countries which imported a great deal of oil in 1982.
  b Make a list of countries which exported a great deal.
  c What major country does not need imports of oil?
  d Explain why the USA, Britain and their allies might think it important to be able to control or influence (i) the Middle East, (ii) the Persian Gulf and (iii) South Africa.

Boeing 707, 1958. This plane halved the flying time across the Atlantic and made cheap air travel possible.

15.4 SPACESHIPS AND SATELLITES

CAUSATION

In 1957 the first man-made satellite was launched. Since then hundreds of others have been sent up into earth orbit. Why did the **exploration of space** begin at this time? How important has it been? What consequences has it had up to now?

Why did it happen then?

To send a **satellite** into orbit you need a rocket which can lift it off the ground and accelerate it up to at least 18,000 mph. You also need guidance and communication systems to steer it in the right direction and to get back information from it. Such systems were made possible by the improvements in radio of the 1930s and 1940s. At the same time rockets made of the light metals developed by the aircraft industry, and fuelled by a mixture of paraffin and liquid oxygen, were developed in the USSR, Germany and the USA. The German V2 which Hitler used to bomb London in 1944 showed how important rockets might be in war. As the cold war developed after 1948 both the USA and the USSR could see that rockets which could carry nuclear warheads would be almost unstoppable. They set out to make them as soon as possible. The rockets which began to place satellites in orbit in 1957 were a by-product of this military technology.

The competition between the USA and the USSR was not simply a matter of weapons. Each superpower was keen to show the world how successful it was. In the 1950s the USA was clearly the world's leading industrial power, so Americans were horrified in 1957 when **Sputnik**, the first satellite, showed publicly to all the world that the USSR was ahead in space. By 1961 **Yuri Gagarin**, the first cosmonaut, was orbiting the Earth while the USA had little to show but a string of failures. In 1962 the Americans began a crash programme to put the **first man on the Moon**. By 1969, at a cost of $25,000 million, they had succeeded. The Soviets concentrated on developing **manned space stations**; they have kept a series of them in Earth orbit since 1974. Meanwhile the USA has worked on a re-usable space vehicle, the **Space Shuttle**, to take a satellite up into Earth orbit and then land again like an aeroplane. Both superpowers have sent space probes to other planets of the solar system.

Are spaceships important?

Satellites have had a very important effect on world communication and on military spying, as you can see on page 156. They have also enormously increased our **scientific knowledge** in two main ways. The first of these is knowledge of our own Earth and of the region of space near it, through which so many satellites travel all the time. For instance, satellites can photograph weather systems, and they have also discovered and measured radiation in space and the atmospheric layers which protect us against it. The second increase is of our astronomical knowledge. Until 1957 this was based on what telescopes could see through the thick blanket of the Earth's atmosphere. Since then satellites have brought back or sent back a flood of new information about the Moon, the planets and the Sun.

SOURCE A

'The Earth is the cradle of humanity, but mankind will not stay in the cradle for ever.'

K. E. Tsiokolvsky, who in 1933 designed a Soviet rocket which rose to a height of three miles.

SOURCE B

'I believe that this nation should commit itself to achieving the goal, before this decade is out, of landing a man on the Moon and returning him safely to Earth. No single space project in this period will be more exciting, or more impressive to mankind, or more important for the long-range exploration of space; and none will be so difficult or expensive to accomplish.'

US President Kennedy, May 1961.

SOURCE C

'A small step for me, but a giant leap for mankind . . .'

Neil Armstrong, as he stepped out on to the surface of the Moon, 21 July 1969.

SOURCE D

'This is the greatest week in the history of the world since the Creation.'

US President Richard Nixon, greeting Armstrong on his return to Earth, July 1969.

CAUSATION

SOURCE E

'Total weight of spacecraft in orbit in 1968: scientific spacecraft – 10 tonnes; military spacecraft – 200 tonnes.'

D. King-Hele, 'Space in the Sixties', 1970.

SOURCE F

▶ *A satellite seen above the Earth. This satellite was taken into Earth orbit by a space shuttle and will be retrieved some months later.*

EXERCISE

1 a Make as complete a list as you can of the technological advances in other fields which helped to make space travel possible, with the approximate date of each.

   b 'Until . . . . . space travel was impossible. It was just a dream.' Suggest a date to fill the blank, and explain your choice.

2 The politicians who decided on space research and the engineers and astronauts who carried it out were motivated by:
   ● Desire for better weapons.
   ● Desire for national prestige.
   ● Desire for exploration and adventure.
   ● Desire for scientific knowledge.

   a From the sources in this unit, select those which provide evidence for any of these motives. Write down the letter of the source, and the letter of the motive for which it is evidence.

   b Choose the motive which you think was most important and explain your choice.

3 Look back at your answers to questions 1 and 2. They both help to explain why space exploration began when it did. Were any of the technological or human causes *essential factors*? Were any of them *minor factors* which just hurried up something that was bound to happen in any case?

4 a Make a list of the consequences of space research.

   b Which of them has been most important up to now?

   c Which of them is likely to be most important in the long run?

   d Were these consequences intended or accidental?

   e Do you agree with the assessments of the importance of the lunar landing made in Sources C and D?

SOURCE G

Werner von Braun, the rocket designer, stands in front of a US 'Saturn' rocket of the type used in the successful lunar landing. Von Braun had designed the wartime German rockets but since 1945 he and many of his team had worked in the USA.

15.5 MEDICINE SINCE 1914

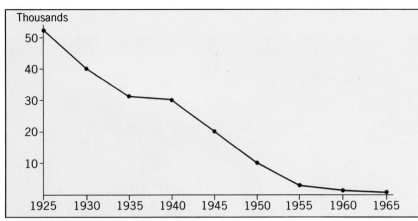

Graph 1: deaths of people aged 0–44 from infectious diseases, 1925–65 in Britain.

SOURCE **A**

'For most of the infectious diseases there was nothing to be done beyond bed rest and good nursing care. Then came the start of the real revolution in medicine (the coming of the new drugs such as penicillin). It was almost beyond belief. Here were patients who surely would have died, improving within a few hours of being given the medicine and feeling extremely well within the next day or so.'

Dr Lewis Thomas, writing in 1985 about his experience as a young doctor.

High-technology medicine

Twentieth-century developments in science and technology have strongly influenced **medicine**. In 1914 scientists had identified the **germs** that cause some diseases, but almost all the **drugs** doctors used were ancient remedies. No one knew how they worked or was sure if they worked at all. But the scientists were already looking for drugs that could kill germs inside the body. In the 1920s and 1930s they began to find them, and since then have found many others which can deal with most infectious diseases. **Penicillin** is probably the most important of these, since it can kill a wide range of germs. It came into use in 1943 after a crash wartime programme of development in Britain and the USA.

The new drugs like penicillin greatly helped the surgeon by making operations safer. So did the **blood transfusion system**, developed before and during the First World War. At about the same time, **X-rays** came into use. Like the more recent ultrasound scanners, they enable doctors to see what is wrong inside the body. Other machines such as **heart–lung machines** can take over for a time the work of human organs. By the 1960s surgeons using such high-technology methods could replace a damaged organ with a healthy one taken from an accident victim.

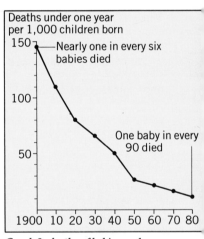

Graph 2: deaths of babies under one year in Britain, 1900–80.

Health in rich and poor countries, 1980		
	In 18 rich countries (including Britain)	In 30 poor countries
Deaths of infants under 1 year old per 1,000 born	11	130
Expectation of life	74 years	48 years
Number of people to each doctor	620	19,400

Source: World Bank, 1980.

SOURCE B

Health for all by the year 2000 – essential needs if this aim is to be reached.

- Education about health problems.
- Promotion of food supply and proper nutrition.
- Safe water and basic sanitation.
- Maternal and child health care, including family planning.
- Immunization against the major infectious diseases.
- Prevention and control of the main local diseases.
- Treatment of common diseases and injuries.
- Provision of essential drugs.

World Health Organization, 1981.

QUESTIONS

1 If your class had all been born about 1910, how many of you would have died before your first birthday? (Use graph 2.)

2 Use Source A to explain graph 1.

3 Make a list of the infectious diseases you have been vaccinated against. Use this to explain graph 1.

4 'The development of electricity made high-technology medicine possible.' Do you agree?

5 How have the wars of the twentieth century influenced the development of medicine?

6 Look at Source B.
  a How many of the eight essentials are connected with high-tech medicine?
  b Choose one of the essentials which you consider most important and explain your choice.

Health care for everyone?

New medical techniques become fully effective only when everybody can make use of them when they need to. **Vaccination** to stop people getting diseases is a good example. The technique has been known since 1798, first for smallpox and then for several other diseases. Since 1914 many new vaccines have been developed. What has made them important is the fact that governments in many countries have made them freely available and have persuaded most people to be vaccinated. This policy began with smallpox vaccination in the nineteenth century. By 1914 deaths from smallpox were rare in countries such as Britain, but were still common in poorer countries. In 1948 the **World Health Organization** was set up to help the the governments of these countries with money and expert advice, including help against smallpox. Since 1980 there have been no cases of smallpox anywhere in the world.

In 1914 no government provided a complete health service for all its citizens as many do today. You paid to see a doctor or to go to hospital if you could afford to. Otherwise you probably did without. The first government to bring all doctors and hospitals into a free government system was the USSR after the revolution of 1917. The other Communist countries, such as China, later did the same. In Britain a great deal of free medical care was introduced during the Second World War to deal with air-raid casualties and to keep a nation at war healthy enough to fight. In 1948 the **National Health Service** was set up to provide medical care of all kinds for everybody when they needed it. Many other countries followed this British lead, though their systems all differed in detail.

Most countries in the world, however, are still too poor to provide modern medical care for everybody. You can see this from the table.

SOURCE C

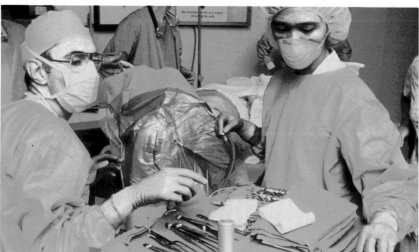

An operation today at Edinburgh Royal Infirmary.

15.6 THE POPULATION EXPLOSION

The **population** of the world has been increasing faster and faster for several hundred years. During the last eighty years the increase has been called an 'explosion'. You can see from the graph that, starting 400 years ago, world population took 250 years to double, then only 100 and in the years 1925–75 only 50. How long do you think it will take to double again?

We do not know exactly why this happened. One factor must be the **medical changes** discussed on pages 162–3. Of course high-technology medicine and national health services have been important mainly in the the richer countries of the world. But since 1945 governments in poorer countries, where most of the world's people live, have made many improvements. Helped by the World Health Organization, they have wiped out smallpox and greatly cut down the death rate from other diseases like malaria. So they have kept more children alive long enough for them to grow up and have families of their own.

All these extra people have to eat, and **improved food** must be another explanation for the spurt in the world's population. Tractors and other machines powered by internal combustion engines have helped farmers grow the extra food needed. So have the chemists who have found new ways to make fertilizer and the botanists who have developed new and more productive strains of wheat or rice. Using these techniques, India, for instance, increased its wheat production from 12 million to 33 million tonnes between 1966 and 1980. People called it the **green revolution**.

A third factor which has helped to make the increase in population possible is **better transport and communications**. Unless we could carry the extra food around the global village how could it keep more and more people alive?

SOURCE **A**

A family planning poster in Turkey. It reads: 'Family planning does not mean preventing births! The Holy Koran says "Have as many children as you can look after."'

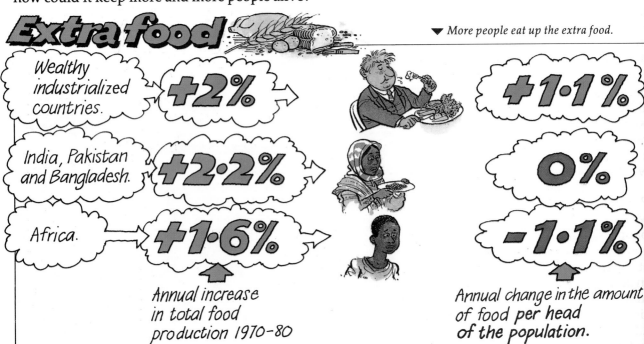

Extra food

Wealthy industrialized countries. → **+2%**

India, Pakistan and Bangladesh. → **+2·2%**

Africa. → **+1·6%**

Annual increase in total food production 1970–80

▼ *More people eat up the extra food.*

+1·1%

0%

–1·1%

Annual change in the amount of food per head of the population.

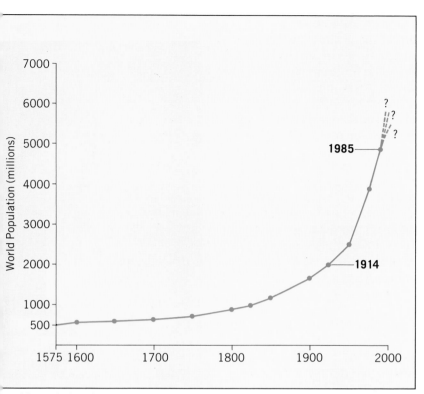

World population since 1575.

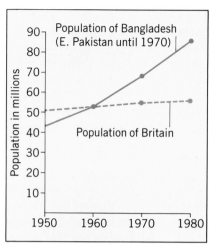

Population of Bangladesh and Britain, 1950–80.

Problem for poorer countries

In the richer countries, as better standards of living and medical care brought down the death rate, parents had fewer children. This process began in the 1920s and 1930s. So although the population still went on rising in countries such as Britain, it did not rise fast enough to cause any difficulties. Matters were very different in the poorer countries of **Africa**, **Asia** and **Latin America**. In Africa and Asia especially young people have always been needed to work on family plots of land, and to support their parents in old age, because there was no old-age pension. So, although the death rate began to fall in the 1950s, people still went on having as many children as before. This meant that the population rose as fast as the food supply, and people stayed just as poor as before, with famines from time to time when things went wrong.

Population control

Many countries have tried to solve this problem by encouraging people to have **smaller families**. They spread knowledge about contraceptives and other methods of **birth control** such as sterilization. It is difficult to change people's attitudes and habits in something so personal, but there is some evidence that this may be happening. In the 1960s the world's population was rising by two per cent every year. In 1988 it was only rising by 1.7 per cent, and if this continues it could stop rising altogether in the next century.

QUESTIONS

1 a How many more people were there in 1985 than in 1914?

b Make a list of the reasons for this rapid increase.

c What is the main difference between the population changes in Britain and in Bangladesh, as shown in the graph?

d Explain the reasons for this difference.

2 Look at Source A.

a What message is it trying to give?

b What can you tell from the poster about the difficulties in spreading ideas about family planning?

3 'The world population increase was caused by scientific and technological improvements.' Do you agree? Explain your answer.

4 'In the past fifty years the world has doubled the number of people and doubled the amount of food grown. This proves that we can do it, so we need not worry about the rise in population.' Do you agree?

15.7 A WORLD ENERGY PROBLEM?

The new machines of the twentieth century need **energy** in amounts unheard of in earlier periods. Power-stations, cars, aircraft, central-heating systems and machines of all kinds in farm and factory use far more fuel than did the simpler machines of the past. And these simpler machines, such as windmills, watermills and horse-drawn carts, used energy that could never run out as long as the wind blew, rain fell and grass grew. It was **renewable energy**. But the new machines use mainly oil and coal and gas – **fossil fuels**, formed millions of years ago. These are not being renewed. Could we ever use them all up?

Until the Second World War this did not seem at all likely. New oilfields and coal-mines could easily be opened up if needed. But since 1950 two things have happened. First, world energy use has risen about four times. Between 1945 and 1970 we used up as much fossil fuel as we had used in the whole of history before 1945. The richer countries used most of it. If the people of the poorer countries were to have the same sort of advanced machinery, world energy supply would have to go up another four times. But the second development is that geologists have found it harder and harder to locate new supplies of coal and oil, so it looks as if we are already starting to run out. Counting all the reserves known to exist in 1982, if we went on just using energy at the 1982 rate, without any increase, the oil would last 32 years, the gas 50 years and the coal 250 years. The world has been guzzling fossil fuels at a rate that it cannot keep up for long.

The oil crisis of the 1970s

When things that people need are scarce, the price goes up. In the 1970s the world had a foretaste of what will happen when oil gets really scarce. In 1960 the main oil-producing countries set up the **Organization of Petroleum-Exporting Countries (OPEC)** so that they could negotiate better prices with the oil companies. Then in 1973 war broke out between Israel and its Arab neighbours (see pages 128–9). Much of the world's oil comes from the Arab countries of the Middle East, and in 1973 they refused to sell oil to any country which supported Israel. The 1973 war did not last long, but in 1980 another war began in the Middle East, this time between Iraq and Iran, both oil producers. These wars put OPEC in a strong bargaining position.

In 1973 the price of oil was $3 a barrel. By 1980 it had gone up to $30. Prices of many other things went up as a result, and this was a cause of unemployment and distress all over the world. After 1980 the prices fell again, because there was still really enough oil being produced to satisfy the world's need. The oil crisis of the 1970s was only an early warning of what will happen when fossil fuels begin to run out unless alternatives are found.

Solving the energy problem

Several solutions have been suggested:

Nuclear energy   Even before the atomic bomb was made, scientists could see that the heat from nuclear energy might be used to drive the steam engines in a power-station. During the

New York street scene, 1980s.

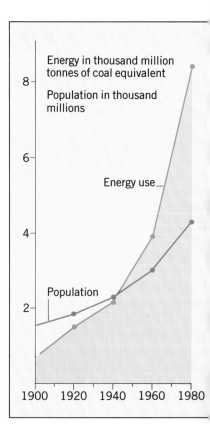

Energy in thousand million tonnes of coal equivalent

Population in thousand millions

Energy use

Population

World energy use and world population.

SOURCE B

The world's worst nuclear accident was in 1986 at the Chernobyl power-station in the USSR. The wreckage had to be buried in concrete. A radioactive cloud spread across northern Europe. Thousands may die of cancer as a result.

1950s they successfully tried this out. It looked as if the world was lucky – just as fossil fuels were beginning to be used up, a completely new source of energy was becoming available. Since then, nuclear power-stations have been built in many countries. France, for instance, which has no coal or oil, now generates about sixty per cent of its electricity from nuclear energy.

But nuclear energy has two serious problems. First, up to now it can be made only from a rare type of **uranium**, and it wastes most of the energy in the process. World uranium reserves would last for only a few years after the oil has run out. The second problem is **pollution**. Nuclear reactors and the waste from them give off poisonous **radiation** which can kill people or cause cancer. Some of the waste will remain dangerous for over 1,000 years. The engineers in the nuclear industry claim that both these problems can be solved. Many other people are less confident, and at the end of the 1980s the future of nuclear energy is uncertain.

Developing renewable sources   Hydroelectric power-stations use a renewable source of energy, rainfall, but they are possible only in wet and mountainous regions. A few power-stations are also driven by the wind or the tides. In Iceland they use the heat from the Earth's interior. Other methods have tried to use the Sun's rays directly. Just 0.02 per cent of the energy which reaches the Earth from the Sun would provide the whole world with as much energy as the richest countries use now. Perhaps when fossil fuels become more scarce, one or more of these methods will solve the problem.

Conservation   When there seemed to be plenty of energy, people wasted a great deal. Since about 1970 governments have encouraged them to save it. Engines can be designed to use less fuel. **Insulation** can stop heat leaking away. Waste heat from power-stations can be used to heat buildings. The world energy problem may partly be solved by methods like these.

QUESTIONS

1 In the 1980s there were many debates about whether or not to build new nuclear power stations.
   a What effect would an event like the one shown in Source B have on this debate?
   b In spite of such events new nuclear power stations are still being built. How can this be explained?

2 Many poor people in Africa and Asia cook using wood-burning fires or stoves using paraffin oil.
   a What effect might the rise in population (page 164) have on their wood supplies?
   b What effect would the oil price rise of the 1970s have on their oil supplies?

3 Study Source A.
   a Explain how a city like this needs a great deal of energy.
   b Use this source, together with your historical knowledge, to explain the changes shown in the graph.

4 'The world energy problem is a problem of the global village – it affects everybody, rich and poor alike.' Do you agree?

15.8 POLLUTION FILLS THE GLOBAL DUSTBIN

SOURCE **A**

'The present emissions of pollution are causing widespread damage in parts of Europe and North America to material resources of vital economic importance such as forests, soil and water.'

UN Committee on Long-Range Trans-Boundary Air Pollution, 1983.

SOURCE **B**

'10,000 million tonnes of industrial and domestic waste are dumped in the Mediterranean Sea each year. The concentration of lead in the Mediterranean is ten times that in the oceans.'

UN Environment Programme report, 1984.

SOURCE **C**

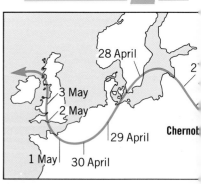

Path of the radioactive plume which originated from Chernobyl at 12.00 GMT, April 26, 1986.

The new machines of the twentieth century have caused a very serious problem. Human beings have always used the air, the sea and the earth as a natural waste-disposal system. Wind, water and bacterial action took waste matter away and rotted it down. The sewage systems of industrial cities were simply a way of helping water and bacteria to get on with this job. It seemed as if nature had provided the human race with a self-emptying dustbin. But in the years 1945–75 two new problems arose.

New sorts of waste were produced which would rot down only slowly if at all. The best example is the **radioactive waste** from nuclear power-stations. Others are man-made chemicals like **DDT**. This was used all over the world in the 1940s and 1950s to kill pests such as the mosquitoes which carry malaria. In the 1960s scientists showed that it was also killing many harmless animals, and might harm human beings too.

Much more waste of a familar sort was being produced. For instance, in 1975 the world used about four times as much energy as in 1945. Most of it came from burning coal or oil, which produces **sulphur dioxide** gas. So four times as much sulphur dioxide was being sent into the atmosphere, turning four times as much of the rain into very dilute sulphuric acid. By the 1980s the effects of **acid rain** could be clearly seen. Most of the forests in southern Norway were badly affected, and half its lakes had no fish.

At the same time as the problem of **pollution** was increasing, scientists were learning more about planet Earth. They showed how its amosphere, its oceans and its living creatures fitted together into a balanced system. Pollution might upset this balance. Space research brought knowledge of a layer of **ozone** high in the atmosphere which protects living matter from harmful radiation. In the 1980s scientists began to find holes in this layer. They were able to show that this was probably caused by a man-made gas, **CFC**, which is used in aerosol sprays and in foam plastics such as fast-food containers. The holes, they argued, were letting extra radiation through and causing an increase in skin cancer.

Controlling pollution

Most countries have passed **laws** to control pollution. The use of DDT has been tightly restricted in Europe and North America. Of course it takes time for scientists to prove the harmful effects, and for people to persuade their governments to act. CFC gas had been damaging the ozone layer for more than twenty years before 1987 when governments began to limit its use. Another difficulty is that much pollution is **international** – Norway's acid rain is caused mainly by power-stations in Britain. So action against pollution must be international too. The United Nations has set up committees to study pollution problems, but has no way of forcing all countries to accept the same rules.

SOURCE D

'Peking has become one of the world's most polluted capitals, with air 35 times dirtier than London's. Soot from the burning of coal, and sulphur dioxide emissions from heavy industry, send air pollution above state limits in Peking and fifty other cities. The country has 168,000 "polluting factories" despite an environmental protection law. The factories surveyed annually produced 3,790 tonnes of heavy metals, including mercury and lead. Most of it was dumped into rivers and seas, polluting 30,000 miles of waterways.'

The 'Guardian', 20 April 1988.

SOURCE E

Volunteers of the organization Greenpeace trying to stop nuclear waste being dumped at sea. In 1983 thirty nations agreed to prohibit sea dumping. Britain and Japan refused.

QUESTIONS

1 **a** Make a list of the main sources of pollution in the later twentieth century. Use pages 154–68, your own knowledge and the press and television news.

   b Against each source of pollution, write symbols from the following list:
   N – new substance since 1945.
   P – persistent; decays only slowly or not at all.
   E – connected with the use of energy.
   I – international; effects spread over several countries.
   G – global; affects the whole world.

   c Look at the population graph on page 165. How might the world population 'explosion' affect the pollution problem?

   d Explain why pollution is a more serious problem in the later twentieth century than it was earlier.

2 Study Source D.
   a Where is the *Guardian* reporter likely to have got his or her information?
   b How can we tell from this source that the Chinese government is worried about pollution?
   c If the government is so worried, why do they let pollution continue?

3 Decisions about the control of pollution might be made by:
   • Factory owners or managers.
   • Scientists.
   • National governments.
   • Ordinary people and voters.
   • The UN and other world organizations.

   Which one of these is best able to make the right decisions and which one is least able? Explain your choice.

16.1 POOR COUNTRIES IN A RICH WORLD

You read in pages 94–105 how many countries of Asia, Africa and the Caribbean gained **independence** from European empires in the 1940s, 1950s and 1960s. These newly-independent countries were all poor by European standards. So were the South American countries which had gained independence from the Spanish and Portuguese empires in the nineteenth century. These countries are often lumped together as **'developing countries'** or the 'developing world' in contrast to the 'developed world' of Europe and North America. Sometimes they are called the **Third World**. (The capitalist world led by the USA and the Communist world led by the USSR are the other two 'worlds'.)

The word 'developing' gives the impression that these poorer countries are like children growing up, hoping to 'catch up' with countries such as Britain. Is this what is really happening? What obstacles make the development of the poor countries difficult? What have the nations of the world done since the 1950s to deal with the problems of development?

After the Third World countries gained their freedom they complained that, although they were no longer ruled by foreign empires, they were still controlled by the **worldwide trading system** run by the developed world. Much Third World income came from producing raw materials for industry in the developed world; but Third World mines and plantations were often owned by business corporations based in Europe or North America. Even when they were not, American and European business people controlled world trade and could influence the prices paid for Third World goods or the rate of interest paid by poor countries for borrowing money. In 1945 Britain and the USA, as part of their plans for recovery from the war, set up the **International Monetary Fund (IMF)** and the **World Bank**. The IMF lends money to countries that get into difficulties with their currency, and the World Bank lends money to help with development. The rich countries, like the USA and Britain, pay the money and make the rules. The Third World countries argued that this meant that the IMF and World Bank always worked in favour of the rich countries of the developed world.

In 1962 the United Nations set up a new organization: the **UN Conference on Trade and Development (UNCTAD)**. This was controlled by Third World countries, so they used it as an opportunity to complain bitterly about the working of the world trading system. What they wanted was a guaranteed sale of their products in the developed countries at a good price. But the richer countries would not agree. They argued that the system was working well. They were investing money in the Third World wherever they saw a chance to make a profit. They were also giving a certain amount of money or lending it on specially easy terms to poor countries. They gave this **aid** directly, or through the World Bank, or through UN bodies such as the World Health Organization. People all over the world were becoming steadily better off in the 1950s and 1960s, even some of those in the Third World.

1st

3rd

☐ Developed industrial countries wi a capitalist economy

☐ Developed industrial countries wi a communist economy

First, Second and Third Worlds.

SOURCE A

Flood victims in Khartoum.

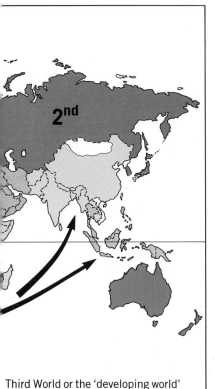

Third World or the 'developing world'

Third World countries with less than $400 GNP per head in 1980

Measuring poverty and wealth

The figures used in this unit come from World Bank reports. They are worked out by estimating for each country the total wealth produced by all its people in a year. This is called its **gross national product (GNP)**. Then, to see how much there is for each person, the GNP is divided by the total population. The result is **GNP per head**. Of course some people get much more than this average figure, and others much less. Also the GNP takes no account of things that have no cash price – the quality of life. It is a crude measure, but the best we have.

SOURCE B

'Many hundreds of millions of people in the poorer countries can think only of survival and elementary needs. For them work is often not available, or, when it is, pay is very low and conditions barely tolerable. Homes are constructed of impermanent materials and have neither piped water nor sanitation. Electricity is a luxury. Health services are thinly spread and in rural areas only rarely within walking distance. Primary schools, where they exist, may be free and not too far away, but children are needed for work and cannot easily be spared for schooling. Permanent insecurity is the condition of the poor. There are no systems of social security in the event of unemployment, sickness or death of a wage-earner in the family. Flood, drought or disease affecting people or livestock can destroy livelihoods without hope of compensation.'

'North–South: A Programme for Survival' (the Brandt Report), 1980.

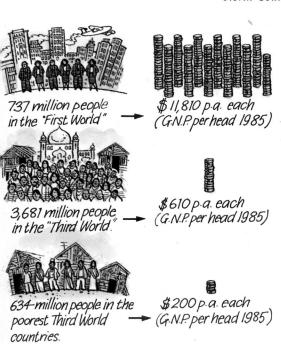

Rich countries and poor countries, 1965–85.

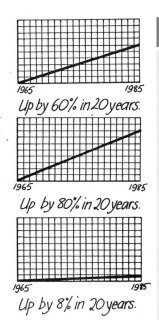

QUESTIONS

1 a From Source B make a list of the main ways in which people in the poorer countries are worse off than people in Britain.

b Which of these would they themselves think most serious? Explain your choice.

2 There are homeless people even in rich countries such as Britain. Which problems in Source B apply to them too?

3 a What criticisms have Third World leaders made of the world trading and financial system?

b Use the figures in the diagram to support or oppose their point of view.

16.2 WORSENING POVERTY SINCE THE 1970s

Oil and debt crises

In the 1970s a serious new problem arose for the whole world. **Oil prices** went up by about ten times (pages 166–7). This helped one group of developing countries – the oil producers such as Saudi Arabia, which became very rich. But the others were badly hit by the rising price of fuel. As they developed, they needed oil for motor transport and for farm and factory machinery. Now they could not afford it. The oil crisis also caused **unemployment** in the developed world, so factories there needed less raw materials, and the price of Third World products fell.

Some of the richer developing countries, such as Brazil, were able to solve the problem for a time by borrowing heavily from banks in the USA and in Europe. But in the 1980s the lending banks' **rate of interest** rose sharply, and Third World borrowers found themselves in a hopeless position. This has become known as the **debt crisis**. Even to pay the interest on what they owed took more money than they could earn by exporting goods. The poor countries had to send large sums in cash to the rich ones, instead of the other way round. They demanded that something should be done to reorganize the debts, but nothing could be agreed.

First World mother and family at home, Britain.

Food shortages

By 1980 it was also becoming clear that, even apart from the oil crisis, the poorest Third World countries were not escaping from their poverty. This was partly because in these countries the **population** was rising fastest. As the graph on page 165 shows, it was rising faster than the farmers could increase the supply of food. If they tried to earn money for development by growing 'cash crops' like cotton, this meant growing **less food**. It often caused **soil erosion** too, and so did the cutting down of trees and bushes for firewood. Sometimes there were serious **famines**.

In Africa just south of the Sahara Desert, 10 million people fled from their homes in 1984–5 to escape famine. That was just one of many instances – people are going hungry all the time. According to World Bank figures, there were 730 million people who did not have enough to eat in 1980. In 1970 there had been only 600 million. It looked as if 'development' was going in the wrong direction for about one in five of the human race.

So far no answer to these problems has been found. In 1980 an unofficial group of politicians led by Willy Brandt, formerly Chancellor of West Germany, studied the problem. The **Brandt Report** argued that what was needed was a carefully co-ordinated programme of aid to the poorest Third World countries, paid for by each developed country giving at least 0.7 per cent of its GNP. In 1987 a UN commission led by Gro Harlem Brundtland, Prime Minister of Norway, produced the **Brundtland Report**, making detailed suggestions as to how this could work and solve the problems. The 1990s and early twenty-first century will show whether humanity has the will to attempt these methods, and whether they can work.

SOURCE **B**

Third World mother and family at 'home', Calcutta, India.

Droughts and floods		
People affected each year by:		
	Drought	*Flood*
1960s	18.5 million	5.2 million
1970s	24.4 million	15.4 million
1980s	(no figures yet, but 30 million affected by the drought of 1984–5 in Africa alone)	

How much aid?

- Aid given to the developing countries by all First World countries put together:

1965	*1985*
$20,680 million	$28,800 million
(0.48% of GNP)	(0.35% of GNP)

- Aid given in 1986:

  Britain gave $1,796 million (0.33% of GNP)
  The USA gave $9,784 million (0.23% of GNP)
  Norway gave $797 million (1.2% of GNP)

- In 1948–52 the USA gave about 2% of its GNP in Marshall Aid to Europe (see page 84).

- In 1980 the USA spent 4.6% of its GNP on defence. Britain spent 5.4%.

ACTIVITY

Find out how much money it takes to keep a cat or dog for a year in Britain today. Multiply by 1.8 to turn it into US dollars. Then use the diagram on page 171 to compare this with the GNP per head of Third World countries.

QUESTIONS

1 Study Sources A and B.
 a What differences are there between the living conditions of the families?
 b What conclusions, if any, can be drawn from this contrast?

2 Explain how each of the following has helped to cause problems for people in the Third World.
 a rising population
 b rising rates of interest.

3 **a** The droughts and floods shown in the table may be due to climatic changes. Explain how human activities may have helped to cause them.
 b These disasters have taken place mainly in Third World countries. Could they have any effect on the 'Developed World'?

4 Use Source B on page 171 to suggest how Third World countries might spend money they receive as aid from the richer countries.

5 Study the table 'How much aid?'
 a Would you say that aid to the Third World went up or down in the years 1965–85?
 b Do the figures in this table show that the problem of world poverty could easily be solved?

16.3 IRAN – AN ISLAMIC REVOLUTION

Iran had once been the great and powerful Persian Empire, but in 1914 it was controlled by the Russians in the north and the British in the south. The rich **oilfields** of the south were just becoming important as the age of the motor car and the aeroplane dawned. The Anglo-Iranian Oil Company, which later became BP (British Petroleum), was developing the oil. By 1950 its oil refinery at Abadan was the biggest in the world.

The Shah modernizes Iran

Many Iranians wanted to modernize their country and to control it themselves. In 1925 an army officer, **Rheza Khan**, made himself Shah, or Emperor, and began to modernize the army, with help from the Germans. The British did not trust him, so in 1942 they agreed with Stalin to force him to resign in favour of his young son **Muhammad Reza**. Then in 1951 a nationalist leader, **Dr Mossadeq**, gained power as Prime Minister. Mossadeq **nationalized** the Iranian oil industry. This step was very popular in Iran, and there was nothing the British could do to stop it. The US government was glad to see Britain losing sole control of Iranian oil, because US companies wanted a share of it. But the USA did not trust Mossadeq – perhaps he might lead Iran on to the Soviet side in the cold war that was just beginning (see page 80). So in 1953 the USA encouraged the Shah to use his army to overthrow Mossadeq.

The Shah now set up a strongly anti-communist government and kept firm control of it himself for the next twenty-six years. These years, 1953–79, saw an enormous expansion of oil output, and the Iranian government became rich. The Shah used some of the money to equip the Iranian forces with all the latest weapons, mainly bought from the USA. As British military power disappeared from the region, it looked as if Iranian power was taking its place. The Shah also encouraged the growth of industry and the modernization of education. European and American ideas spread among richer people. Western dress came into use. Women were allowed to vote.

▼ *Iran and its neighbours in the Middle East.*

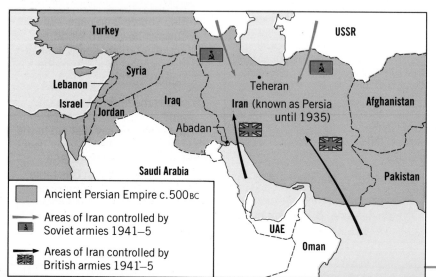

Ancient Persian Empire c.500 BC

Areas of Iran controlled by Soviet armies 1941–5

Areas of Iran controlled by British armies 1941–5

SOURCE A

Empress Soraya.

SOURCE B

Khomeini stopped the Shah's westernizing policies and said that women should only appear in public with their heads and bodies fully covered.

SOURCE C

'In southern Tehran working-class residents set up barricades and threw petrol bombs at army trucks. Helicopter gun-ships were used to dislodge the rebels. In Jaleh Square tanks surrounded the demonstrators and, unable to persuade them to disperse, shot to kill. That night the military authorities announced that the day's casualties totalled 87 dead. But the opposition declared that the dead numbered more than 4,000. September 8th became known as "Black Friday". It placed a sea of blood between the Shah and his people.'

The 'Guardian', 17 September 1978.

Opposition to the Shah

These changes suited the small class of rich Iranians, army officers and business people who surrounded the Shah. But for many ordinary Iranians they meant moving into a city to work for low wages and living in an overcrowded slum. To the Islamic religious leaders of the country's **Muslims**, the changes looked like the work of the Devil. The Shah's programme of modernization weakened the power of the Islamic clergy and led people away from the traditions of Islam, towards American ideas.

The Shah crushed both types of opposition ruthlessly. His police force, **Savak**, arrested people without trial, beat them and tortured them. Many opponents of the Shah fled into exile.

The revolution of 1979

One of the exiles was a Muslim leader, the **Ayatollah Khomeini**. From his exile in Paris he denounced the Shah's wicked ways, laying much of the blame on the USA. He used television, radio and taped speeches to spread his ideas inside Iran. In 1978–9 this led to marches and strikes by the discontented poor, which the Shah's police could not control. The Shah was a sick man, dying of cancer. In January 1979 he fled from the country, and Khomeini returned in triumph. He announced that Iran was now an **Islamic republic**, and set about restoring the old ideas of morality.

The change was wildly popular with most ordinary Iranians. Groups of students and others formed committees to round up people who still supported the Shah or who opposed the Ayatollah's ideas. Many opponents of the new regime were put to death.

A defeat for the USA

One of the revolutionary groups arrested fifty-three Americans at the US Embassy and held them hostage for more than a year, demanding that the Shah should be sent back to be tried. The world's press and television gave this full coverage, and the US people demanded action to rescue the hostages. But when an attempt was made, it failed miserably, and the hostages were released only after the Shah had died. Iran had successfully humiliated the greatest power on earth. Khomeini was more popular than ever.

QUESTIONS

1 a Which of Iran's neighbours gained independence in 1948?
  b How might this have influenced Dr Mossadeq?
  c Why could Britain do little to stop Dr Mossadeq nationalizing Iranian oil? (Clue: page 94.)

2 Use Source C and the other information in this unit to explain why the Shah was so unpopular in 1978.

3 Look at Source D.
  a What explanation would the revolutionary guard give for his actions?
  b Why was it difficult or impossible for the USA to rescue the hostages? (Use the map.)

4 a In Source C the authorities say 87 were killed, and the opposition say 4,000. How can this be explained?
  b In Source D why is the banner in English?
  c 'Modern news media play an important part in world politics.' What part did they play in the events in Iran?

SOURCE **D**

Iranian revolutionary guard holding Americans hostage at the US Embassy, Tehran, 1979. The pictures are of the Ayatollah Khomeini.

16.4 IRAQ ATTACKS IRAN: THE GULF WAR

Two branches of Islam

The Islamic religion has two main branches: the **Sunni** and the **Shi'ite** Muslims. Iran is the main Shi'ite nation, but there are many Shi'ites in other countries, as you can see on the map. The Shi'ites outside Iran are usually poor people, often discontented with their life under Sunni rule. So when they heard of the success of the Ayatollah's revolt against the Shah in Iran they were full of excitement and hope. The Sunni rulers of Iraq, Kuwait, Saudi Arabia and other Gulf states were worried. Perhaps there would be revolts in their countries too, inspired by Khomeini's example.

Iraq takes a chance – and fails

The Arab states along the Persian Gulf had also been worried about the great increase in Iran's power under the Shah. **Iraq** and Iran had quarrelled over their frontier, and Iraq had come off worst. So in 1980, when the Ayatollah's revolution had badly disorganized the Iranian forces, the ruler of Iraq, **Saddam Hussein**, saw his chance. He sent his army into southern Iran, hoping to seize **Abadan**, the source of Iran's oil wealth, and so cut Iran down to size. But the attack failed, and instead a bitter war began which lasted eight years. The other Gulf states gave support to Iraq, because a victory for Iran might spread the Ayatollah's revolution throughout the region.

The effect of the Iraqi attack was to unify Iran under Khomeini even more than before. The Ayatollah told young Iranians that if they died fighting in this holy war they died as martyrs and would be rewarded in the afterlife. 'Human waves' of attack were used against the modern weapons Iraq had bought from the USSR and France. But Iran also had modern weapons, and was able to buy more on the world market. In 1986 Iran even made a secret deal for the USA to supply it with arms. In exchange it would get the Shi'ite Muslims in Lebanon to release American hostages they had captured.

Oil supplies in danger?

It seemed likely that the Gulf War would stop supplies of oil flowing through the Gulf. As you can see from the map on page 158, Europe and Japan were dependent on Gulf oil, and even the USA could not easily manage without it. So this danger worried the USA and its allies greatly. But both Iran and Iraq needed to sell oil to pay for the weapons they imported. Both made attacks on oil tankers in the Gulf, but neither was able to stop the other exporting oil. The flow of oil continued, and so did the flow of money to pay for the war.

A truce is called

With both sides well supplied with arms, the war was a stalemate. Then in 1988 the UN was able to persuade them both to stop fighting. Neither side had gained anything from a war which had killed about half a million people.

SOURCE A

'The Ayatollah announced that as a special favour schoolboys aged between 12 and 19 would be allowed to join troops to fight for their country. The admission papers of these volunteers were known as "passports to paradise", as they offered a high chance of martyrdom. The enthusiasm of these boys was very strong – many of them seemed eager to clear minefields by walking or riding bicycles straight into them. They often had military training of no more than a week's duration, and many seemed uncertain as to how to handle their firearms.'

British newspaper report, 1982.

SOURCE B

A 12-year-old Iranian guards Iraqi prisoners, July 1988.

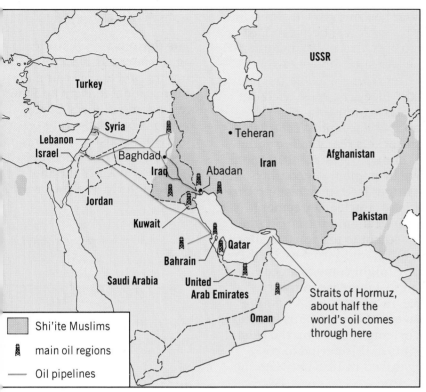

Shi'ite Muslims

 main oil regions

Oil pipelines

Straits of Hormuz, about half the world's oil comes through here

ran and its neighbours.

QUESTIONS

1 a Suggest two reasons why Iraq wanted to attack Iran.
 b Why did 1979 seem a good time to do this?

2 Study Sources A and B.
 a How can the behaviour of the Iranian boys be explained?
 b Do you think that these sources are likely to be reliable? Explain your answer.

3 Look at the map.
 a Which countries could easily stop any ships going through the Straits of Hormuz?
 b What worldwide effect would this have?
 c Why do you think it has not been done during the Gulf War?

4 Iraq's main supply of arms has come from the USSR.
 a Why should the USSR supply these:
 (i) when the Shah ruled in Iran before 1979, and
 (ii) when the Ayatollah ruled in Iran after 1979?
 b Many of the people of the southern part of the USSR are Muslims. How might this affect Soviet policy towards Iran?

SOURCE   C

A Danish oil tanker, carrying oil from Saudi Arabia to Holland, on fire after an attack by Iranian gunboats in the Gulf, March 1988.

16.5 A THAW IN THE COLD WAR

In the 1960s both sides in the **cold war** had nuclear weapons and intercontinental missiles to deliver them. A war between East and West would do so much harm to both that only a madman would start one. This meant that the two superpowers would have to learn to live peacefully together. The Soviet leader Khrushchev talked of **peaceful coexistence**. The West used the French word *détente*, which means relaxing tension.

Peaceful coexistence did not mean that East and West trusted each other. Each side had its nuclear rockets ready to fire at the other at a moment's notice, and this shows how little trust there was. Since the 1960s, also, there have been plenty of conflicts. But there have been some changes that might lead to increasing trust. The most important of these is a series of **nuclear agreements** (see below). Then in 1975 at a conference in **Helsinki** the USSR, the USA and all European countries agreed not to use force to alter existing frontiers in Europe. If both sides could trust each other to stick to this, the cold war in Europe might come to an end.

During the 1970s there was also a great increase in **trade** between East and West. For instance, in 1972 the USA and the USSR agreed to treble the trade between them. Perhaps friendly co-operation in trade, travel and sport might build up the trust that was needed. One of the highlights of this period of co-operation was the **space link-up** organized in 1975 between the Soviet *Soyuz* and the US *Apollo* spaceships.

Nuclear agreements, 1963–88
1963 The 'hot line'   This is a telephone line that puts the leaders of the USA and the USSR into immediate contact with each other. At the height of the Cuba crises of 1962 Kennedy and Khrushchev had found communication difficult, and they knew that misunderstandings could have plunged the world into nuclear war. The 'hot line' might make this less likely.

SOURCE A

▼ *All together in space. Soviet and US astronauts meet in the 'Soyuz' space station, 1975.*

Americans hugged in Russia after joint space triumph

SOURCE B

'The flight was of historic significance as a symbol of the present process of easing the international tension and the improvement of US–Soviet relations on the basis of peaceful coexistence. It was a practical contribution between the USA and the USSR in the interests of world peace.'

Leonid Brezhnev, Soviet Prime Minister, July 1975.

SOURCE C

'The truth of the nuclear age is that the United States and the Soviet Union must live in peace or we may not live at all. The pattern of war must be broken for ever.'

Jimmy Carter, US President, on signing the SALT 2 treaty, June 1979.

QUESTIONS

1 Study the list of nuclear agreements. Choose the one that you think most important. Explain your choice.

2 Brezhnev in Source B suggests that the *Soyuz/Apollo* link will help world peace.
   a How did he think it would do this?
   b In what other way might space rockets help world peace?

3 Study Source C. Why did Carter think that 'we must live in peace or we may not live at all' and that 'the pattern of war must be broken for ever'?

SOURCE D

Soviet and US leaders kiss and make friends? Carter and Brezhnev in 1979.

4 Look at Sources A, D and E.
  a Why do you think these photographs were taken?
  b Does this affect their value as evidence?

5 In 1972, 32 per cent of US government spending was on defence. The USSR probably spent a higher percentage. How might this help to explain the nuclear agreements to limit the building of nuclear weapons?

6 a What objections might a Soviet or a US general have to arms control agreements?
  b How might such objections be overcome by (i) 'spy-in-the-sky' satellites or (ii) allowing inspectors as in the INF treaty?

1963 Test ban treaty   The testing of nuclear bombs had caused an increase in radioactive substances in the atmosphere. These were known to cause cancer. The treaty banned tests in the atmosphere, in outer space and under water. The USA, the USSR and Britain signed.

1968 Non-proliferation treaty   This was an agreement by the USA, the USSR and Britain not to spread nuclear weapons to other countries by letting them have materials or advice. Since then 114 other countries have agreed never to develop nuclear weapons. France has had its own bombs since 1960 and China since 1964. Six other countries are believed to be making nuclear weapons in secret. These are Israel, India, Pakistan, South Africa, Brazil and Argentina. Neither France, China nor any of these six have signed the treaty.

1972 and 1979 SALT 1 and **SALT 2 (Strategic Arms Limitation Treaties)**   The USA and the USSR agreed a limit on how many long-range missiles or heavy bombers carrying nuclear weapons each could have: 2,400 each. Each already had about this number – enough to destroy the other many times over. They agreed that 'spy-in-the-sky' satellites could check whether they were sticking to the limit agreed. The USA Senate refused to accept SALT 2, but in practice both sides have stayed within the limits agreed in it.

1987 INF (Intermediate Nuclear Force) treaty   The USA and the USSR agreed to dismantle all nuclear missiles with a range between 300 and 3,400 miles and not to build any more. They agreed also to let inspectors into their countries to check that this agreement was being carried out.

1980s START   The SALT treaties only placed a limit on the number of long-range weapons. **Strategic Arms Limitation Talks (START)** aim gradually to get rid of those that exist. These talks have been going on since 1980.

SOURCE E

Ronald Reagan and Mikhail Gorbachev sign the INF treaty in 1987.

16.6 NEW WEAPONS AND NEW PROTESTS

The arms build-up continues

In both the USA and the USSR there were teams of defence experts, soldiers, scientists and engineers whose job it was to think up new weapons systems and bring them into use. 'Peaceful coexistence' made very little difference to them. They went on steadily making new weapons or improving the old ones, as the following list shows.

Improved guidance systems   The earlier missiles could hit only a big target like a city. By the 1970s the improvements meant that they could hit an enemy's missile bases and perhaps knock them out before enemy missiles could be fired.

Missiles in submarines   Nuclear-powered submarines can hide safely on the sea-bed. Even if their home country is reduced to a radioactive desert, they can strike back with deadly effect. By 1985 the USA had 568 submarine missiles and the USSR 980.

Multiple targeting   During the 1970s the Americans found ways of putting eight warheads on one missile. During its flight they could send each of the eight to a separate target. Each of the eight could do several times as much damage as the Hiroshima bomb.

Cruise missiles   These can travel several thousand miles, closely hugging the ground, so that the enemy cannot see them coming on its radar. Cruise missiles are quite small and can be moved around on lorries, ships or planes. They came into use in the 1980s.

Anti-missile systems   These are designed to destroy enemy missiles in space while they are on their way. In 1974 the USA and the USSR agreed that they would set these up to protect only one or two sites in each country. In 1983 President Reagan announced that the USA was working on a complete system to protect the whole of the USA – the 'strategic defence initiative' or *Star Wars*. To do this it must be sure to destroy every single attacking missile. It could cost $1,000 billion. Most defence experts thought that this was impossible, but in 1985 Britain and other Western European countries agreed to join in the research. They wanted a share of the money.

Public opinion and nuclear weapons

The damage done by the atomic bombs of 1945 was horrifying. Then in the 1950s hydrogen bombs a thousand times worse were made. By 1980 there were in existence about 50,000 nuclear weapons, large and small, with in total about a million times as much explosive power as the bomb that destroyed Hiroshima. What would a nuclear war be like?

One answer to this question that became clear to scientists in the 1970s was that it would fill the upper atmosphere with clouds of radioactive dust, blotting out the sunlight and causing a **'nuclear winter'**. Radiation would kill animals and plants and perhaps destroy the environment that makes human life possible. It would be a global catastrophe.

SOURCE A

'Professor Zagladin claimed yesterday that the introduction of the SS20 missile (by the USSR) was a modernization measure and served only to establish equality with the West.'

'The Times', 14 October 1981.

SOURCE B

'There is no question that the Soviet momentum has brought them from a position of clear inferiority to their present status of at least strategic equality with the USA. It is essential to proceed with our modernization programme.'

General D. Jones, 'US Military Posture', 1981.

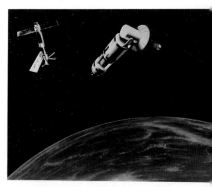

Star Wars: artist's idea of a 'killer' satellite in space using a laser beam to knock out an enemy missile.

SOURCE C

Demonstration against nuclear weapons, US cruise missile base at Greenham Common, England.

SOURCE D

THE FALKLANS WERE 'DISARMED'
LOOK WHAT HAPPENED TO THEM !!!
'STOP C.N.D. NOW'
IF YOU THINK THE SOVIET THREAT IS A MYTH
POLAND
CCCP
KGB APPROVED
JUST ASK A POLE

Demonstration in favour of nuclear weapons, 1982.

This nightmare possibility encouraged movements against nuclear weapons in several countries.

In Britain the Campaign for Nuclear Disarmament was founded in 1957, but it grew greatly in the 1970s and 1980s. It proposed that Britain should give up its nuclear weapons 'unilaterally' – that is, without first making a bargain that others would do the same. In 1982 the Labour Party accepted this as part of its policy. In 1985 a public opinion poll showed that only 35 per cent of British people agreed with this.

In the **USA** demonstrations against nuclear weapons have taken place since the 1960s. In the 1980s polls have shown that most people favour a 'freeze' on new nuclear weapons by agreement with the USSR. But the same polls showed that 78 per cent of Americans think that the Soviets wanted agreements only when they gain an advantage.

Public opinion in France supports having nuclear weapons, and there has not been much argument about it.

In the **USSR** and **China** the news media are carefully controlled by the government and the Communist Party. There is no evidence of disagreement on nuclear weapons.

West Germany, Holland and **Belgium**, which are all members of NATO, have no nuclear weapons of their own. In 1980 NATO decided to install the new US cruise missiles in these countries and in Britain. All four governments agreed to this. They said the missiles were needed to balance new Soviet SS20 intermediate range missiles. There were violent demonstrations against the cruise missiles, especially in Britain and West Germany. In 1987, soon after the new system was set up, the USA and the USSR signed the INF treaty (see page 179) and agreed to withdraw both the cruise missiles and the SS20s.

QUESTIONS

1 Professor Zagladin and General Jones (Sources A and B) are defence experts.
   a What do they agree about?
   b Choose one of the weapon developments described. What arguments might they use to persuade their governments to spend money on it?
   c If an expert has been working for years on a new weapon, what advice is he or she likely to give if someone suggests scrapping it?

2 **a** How reliable are pictures like Sources C and D as evidence of public opinion?
   b Explain why public protest movements against nuclear weapons developed strongly in the 1970s and 1980s.

3 Use the sources and your background knowledge to explain why nuclear weapons have continued to be developed despite public protests.

16.7 CONFLICT IN AFGHANISTAN

Afghanistan is an isolated and poor country. Until 1979 it had not been influenced very much by events in the outside world. Then it suddenly became the centre of a conflict between the USSR and the USA. From 1979 to 1988 it was occupied by a Soviet army of 135,000 men, while Afghan guerrilla fighters were given arms and money by the USA. In nine years of fighting 13,000 Red Army soldiers, and uncounted numbers of Afghans, were killed. Towns and villages were destroyed. About half of Afghanistan's 16 million people fled from their homes as refugees. By 1988 it was clear that the Red Army could not prevent the guerrilla attacks, and the Soviet government decided to withdraw and leave the Afgans to settle their own affairs.

The Red Army moves in

The people of Afganistan are mainly poor peasants and hill tribesmen. During the 1960s and 1970s their country was developing slowly with aid from various countries but mainly from their giant neighbour the USSR. There were two groups of Afghan Communists: a moderate group who thought that change towards a socialist system should be slow, and an extreme group who wanted to move fast. In 1978 the extreme group seized control of the government.

This caused a widespread rebellion and much disorder. In December 1979 Brezhnev announced that the Afghan government had asked for Soviet help and he sent in the Red Army. For the first time since 1945 it had occupied a new country. Its first action was to overthrow and execute the extreme Communist Prime Minister, and put a moderate Communist in his place.

The US reaction

President Carter's response was to send large-scale military help to **Pakistan**, another bordering country. He also told US athletes not to attend the 1980 Olympic Games in Moscow. The 'thaw' in the cold war (see pages 178–9) seemed to be at an end, and in 1980 the US Senate refused to accept the SALT 2 treaty on nuclear weapons to which the USA and the USSR had recently agreed. Meanwhile in Pakistan the Afghan revels set up camps and supply depots for the US weapons, and the nine long years of guerilla warfare began.

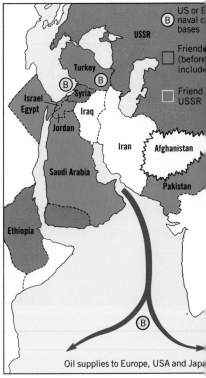

Afghanistan, and US and Soviet allies in the region.

SOURCE **A**

'The invasion of the small nation of Afghanistan threatens Iran and Pakistan and might lead to Soviet control of much of the world's oil supplies. Along with other countries we will provide military equipment, food and other assistance to help Pakistan to defend its independence against the seriously increased threat from the north. History teaches perhaps few clear lessons. But one such lesson learned by the world at great cost is that aggression unopposed becomes a contagious disease.'

 US President Carter, 4 January 1980.

SOURCE **B**

Foreign help for the rebels in Afghanistan in 1978 'created a real threat that Afghanistan would lose its independence and be turned into a military bridgehead on our country's southern border. (So we sent in our troops.) To have acted otherwise would have meant leaving Afghanistan a prey to imperialism. It would have meant watching passively the organization on our southern border of a centre of serious danger to the security of the Soviet Union.'

Leonid Brezhnev, 12 January 1980.

Leonid Brezhnev, Soviet leader 1964–82. Brezhnev had been a loyal member of the Communist Party since 1923. In 1968 he had used the Red Army to overthrow the government in Czechoslovakia (see pages 138–9). He had claimed then that one socialist country had the right to interfere inside another to prevent capitalism being restored.

Jimmy Carter, US President 1977–1981. Carter believed strongly in democracy and disliked communism. He also wanted friendly relations with the USSR and had agreed to the SALT 2 arms control treaty in 1979 (see pages 178–9). In 1979 fifty-three US citizens were taken hostage in Iran. At first Carter said that they could not be rescued. Then he sent helicopters which tried and failed. In 1980 he had to stand for re-election as President. His opponent, Ronald Reagan, accused him of weakness and promised a much tougher stand against communism.

What they both knew

- In 1975 the US attempt to support the South Vietnamese government against the Vietcong had failed. One important reason was the help the USSR gave to North Vietnam (see pages 140–5).
- There was a world oil crisis (see pages 166–7). The US and its allies in Europe and Japan got about half their oil from the Persian Gulf.
- In 1979 the Shah of Iran, a close ally of the USA, was overthrown by the Ayatollah Khomeini. Khomeini looked on the USA as 'the Great Satan' (see pages 174–5).
- The Ayatollah stood for a worldwide movement to restore the purity of the religion of Islam. Islam is the main religion in Afghanistan and also in the Soviet republics in the south of the USSR. The Soviet government is officially atheist and discourages all religions.
- Pakistan was a firm friend of the USA and relied on the USA for supplies of arms and military training.

SOURCE **C**

Cartoon from the 'Sunday Times', 29 November 1981.

SOURCE   **D**

In 1988 there were about 8 million Afghan refugees, 3 million of them in Pakistan, like those in the picture.

QUESTIONS

1 Look at the cartoon.
  a What explanation does the cartoonist suggest for US fears of the USSR?
  b What explanation does the cartoonist suggest for Soviet fears of the USA?

2 Read the captions to the pictures of Carter and Brezhnev. In each case, how does the information help to explain their actions in 1979?

7 Read each of the five items 'What they both knew'. Decide how each item might influence Carter or Brezhnev or both of them.

4 Write two explanations of the conflict over Afghanistan in 1979, one from Carter's point of view and one from Brezhnev's.

5 Write a balanced explanation of the conflict from an impartial point of view.

HISTORY AND THE FUTURE

History can never tell you what is certainly going to happen. What it can do is point out trends and changes in the past that seem likely to continue into the future. For instance, in 1914 the USA had been growing richer and more powerful for a long time, so at that time plenty of people were saying that it would get much more important as the twentieth century went on. They were right. But sometimes history takes an unexpected twist. For instance, in 1914 the European nations had been building up larger and more powerful overseas empires for a long time, and they controlled much of the world. Hardly anybody in 1914 imagined that within fifty years all these mighty empires would have disappeared from the map. You can probably think of other examples – both of changes that began before 1914 and continued as expected in the years that followed, and also of important new developments in the years since 1914 that could not have been expected (see question 1, page 187).

If you now think about the present time, and look at the changes and trends that you have read about in this book, you can see some that seem almost certain to continue into the 1990s and the twenty-first century. A clear example is the rise in the world's population. The young mothers of the early twenty-first century have already been born, and there are so many of them that the population is bound to go on rising. You can probably think of other examples of trends likely to continue (see question 2, page 187). Of course, unlikely and unexpected developments are bound to occur too. Your knowledge of the history of the world since 1914 should help you to make sense of the trends that continue into the twenty-first century. It cannot tell you much about the unexpected developments in which you will find yourself taking part. But if you have gained from your study some practice in using evidence, thinking about changes in human affairs and looking for their causes, you should be better able to deal even with the unexpected changes as they arise.

SOURCE 2

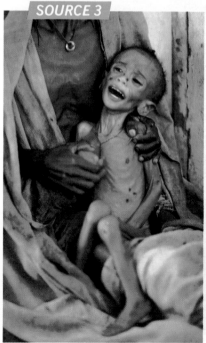

SOURCE 3

SOURCE 1

SOURCE 5

SOURCE 6

SOURCE 7

SOURCE 4

SOURCE 8

World is declared to be free of smallpox

A formal declaration that smallpox had been eradicated was made yesterday at the thirty-third World Health Assembly in Geneva.

Announcements that smallpox was on the point of eradication have been made several times in the last four years as the World Health Organization thought that its intensified eradication programme was coming to an end. But the announcements have always been followed by renewed outbreaks, most notably in the Horn of Africa during the war between Somalia and Ethiopia.

A total of 3,229 cases were notified in Somalia in 1977 but since October 26 of that year no further cases, other than a laboratory-associated outbreak in the United Kingdom, have come to light.

SOURCE 9

SOURCE 10

SOURCE 11

SOURCE 12

SOURCE 13

SOURCE 14

EXERCISE

1 a Make a list of the sources with their approximate dates. For instance, for Source 1 you might put: 'First World War tank'.

b Each source reperesents a long-term development. Add a brief description of this to your list. For Source 1 you might put: 'Technology makes new weapons', or 'Development of the internal combustion engine'.

c Think of other long-term developments and add these to your list.

d Choose the development which you consider most important and explain your choice.

e Against each item in your list write 'E' if a well-informed person in 1914 might have expected it to happen and 'U' (for unexpected) if this is unlikely.

f Choose one 'E' and one 'U' item and explain your choices of symbol.

2 Use the same list as for question 1.

a Add the letter 'F' (for future) against any items which you think are likely to continue as important developments into the twenty-first century.

b Choose one 'F' item and one with no 'F' and explain these choices.

3 The late twentieth-century world has often been called the 'global village'.

a Make a list of the changes since 1914 that could be said to have helped to bring this about.

b 'The Earth is of limited size. In the late twentieth century it has looked likely that this might place a limit on the growth of . . .' Make a list of possible endings to this sentence.

4 Look at the cartoon (Source 16). The board on the front of the bus shows the problems into which the cartoonist thought the world was moving. If you were drawing a similar cartoon for a world moving from the 1980s into the 1990s or from the twentieth century into the twenty-first, what would you put on the board?

'Good luck Kid – and by the way, there don't seem to be any brakes!' Cartoon, New Year's Day, 1980. The people in the bus are the political leaders of 1980.

INDEX

Details of Written Sources

In some sources the wording or sentence structure has been simplified to make sure that the source is accessible.

Jean M. Auel, *The Clan of the Cave Bear*, Hodder and Stoughton 1980: 1.3A
Lucinda MacCray Beier, *Sufferers and Healers*, Routledge and Kegan Paul 1987: 1.4A
R. Binding, *A Fatalist at War*, Allen and Unwin 1916: 3.3E
R. W. Breach, *Documents and Descriptions*, Oxford University Press 1966: 3.1A and D, 6.4H, 7.4B, 7.4C, 6.11G
Weldon Brown, *The Last Chopper*, Kennikat Press Washington 1976: 13.3G
Alan Bullock, *Hitler, A Study in Tyranny*, Penguin 1962: 3.3C, 5.6B, 5.6C, 6.5A, 6.5D
G. M. Carter, *Which Way is South Africa Going?*, Bloomington Industry 1980: 16.5C
W. S. Churchill, *The Second World War*, Cassell 1948–53: 6.10A, 6.10B, 6.10C. 6.11B
M. Clark and P. Teed, *Portraits and Documents of the Twentieth Century*, Hutchinson 1972: 7.4A
Kenneth S. Davis, *The American Experience of War*, London 1967: 6.11F
Issac Deutscher, *Stalin*, Oxford University Press 1949: 4.5F
J. Ehrman, *Grand Strategy: October 1944–August 1945*, HMSO 1956: 6.11A
Peter Fisher, *The Great Power Conflict after 1945*, Blackwell 1985: 16.5B
C. P. Fitzgerald, *China: Communist Victory* London 1968: 10.2E
The Guardian 26.2.88, 11.4E; 20.4.88, 15.8D; 17.9.78, 16.3C
John Hamer, *The Twentieth Century*, Macmillan 1980: 3.4A, 6.4E, 6.4F
S. M. Harrison, *World Conflict in the Twentieth Century*, Macmillan 1987: 6.5C, 8.2A, 10.2C, 10.4C, 11.4A, 13.1C, 13.2E
Tom Harrison and Charles Madge, *Britain by Mass Observation*, Century Hutchinson 1986: 6.4I
Derek Heater, *Our World Today*, Oxford University Press 1985: 16.1B
H. Johnson, *The Socialist Sixth of the World*, Gollancz 1939: 4.5D
Hugh Higginson, *Vietnam*, Heinemann 1975: 13.1D
Hitler, Mein Kampf, (1924 trans. R Mannheim) Sentry Paperbacks 1943: 5.6A
David Horowitz, *Containment and Revolution*, Blond 1967: 7.4D, 10.2F
Tony Howarth, *Twentieth Century History*, Longman 1979: 6.4B, 7.5A, 10.4B and D
H. A. Jacobsen and A. L. Smith, *World War II Policy and Strategy*, Santa Barbara 1979: 6.10D
General D. Jones, *US Military Posture*, 1981: 16.6B
D. King-Hele, *Space in the Sixties*, 1970: 15.4E
Keesing's Contemporary Archives, Longman Group UK Ltd, 14.1A and D, 14.2B, 15.8A and B, 16.4A
W. D. Leahy, *I Was There*, New York 1950: 6.11E
Harold Macmillan, *Pointing the Way*, Macmillan 1973: 8.6B
Roy Medevev, *Let History Judge*, Macmillan 1971: 4.5A
Harry Mills, *Twentieth Century World History in Focus*, Macmillan 1984: 9.2F, 10.2C

Jan Myrdal, *Report from a Chinese Village*, Penguin 1967: 10.10A
Bryn O'Callaghan, *A History of the Twentieth Century*, Longman 1987: 4.5B, 5.4B, 9.1B, 9.2C, 9.2E, 10.5A, 11.4C, 13.2F
Houston Peterson, *Great Speeches*, Simon and Schuster 1954, 3.3B, 3.4B
Purnell *History of the Twentieth Century*, BPC Publishing Ltd 1969: 3.4F, 3.6A, 3.6B, 5.3B, 5.3C, 8.1A, 8.2B and E, 9.1A, 14.3F, 15.4A, 15.4B, 15.4D
John Ray and James Hagerty, *The Twentieth Century World*, Hutchinson 1986: 8.3A, 8.6A, 14.1B
Maud Pember Reeves, *Round About a Pound a Week*, G. Bell and Sons 1913 (reprinted by Virago 1979): 1.2A
T. H. Rigby, *The Stalin Dictatorship*, Methuen 1968, 12.1B
A. Roberts and P. Windsor, *Czechoslovakia 1968*, Chatto 1969: 12.3A, 12.3B
Schools Council History 13–16 Project: *The Rise of Communist China*, Holmes Macdougal 1976: 10.2A and B, 10.3A
Schools Council History 13–16 Project: *Arab-Israeli Conflict*, Holmes Macdougal 1977: 11.4B and D
John Scott, *Beyond the Urals*, Indiana University Press 1973: 4.5C
J. Sheridan, 'China in Disintegration', from Purnell *History of the Twentieth Century*, BPC Publishing 1969: 10.2D
William L. Shirer, *The Rise and Fall of Adolf Hitler*, Secker and Warburg 1960: 6.2B, 6.2E, 6.4A, 6.4G, 6.5G, 6.5H, 6.5I, 6.9B, 6.9C, 6.9D
Alexander Solzhenitzyn, *Gulag Archipelago*, Fontana 1974: 4.5E
T. C. Sorenson, *Kennedy*, Hodder and Stoughton 1965: 13.1B
The Suffragette, 7 August 1914: 3.3D
Peter Tasker, *Inside Japan*, Sidgwick and Jackson 1987: 14.3A
A. J. P. Taylor, *English History 1914–45*, Oxford University Press 1965: 6.2D
Thomas Lewis, *The Youngest Science: Notes of a Medicine Watcher*, Oxford University Press 1985: 15.5A
Harry S. Truman, *Memoirs*, Doubleday 1955: 6.11D
T. E. Vadney, *The World Since 1945*, Pelican 1987: 12.3C
Harriet Ward, *World Powers in the Twentieth Century*, Heinemann 1985: 10.1B, 10.3B
John Williams, 'The French Army Mutinies' from Purnell *The History of the Twentieth Century*, BPC Publishing 1969, 3.3F
Institute of History of the Czech Academy of Science, *The Czechoslovak Black Book*, London 1969: 12.3D

The author and publisher would like to thank the following for permission to reproduce extracts from copyright material:

Bev. Gilligan for extracts from an article in *Woman* magazine 8/2/86; Annabel Ferriman for extracts from an article © Times Newspapers Ltd 1980, 9/5/80; Frederick Bonnart for extracts from an article © Times Newspapers Ltd 1981, 14/10/81; *The Guardian* for extracts from the 17/9/78, 26/2/88 and 20/4/89 editions; George Sassoon for permission to reproduce one verse from 'The General' by Siegfried Sassoon.